# PATTERNS OF SUSTAINING PEACE

The Complex Impact of Peacebuilding Institutions in Post-Conflict Societies

Julia Leib

First published in Great Britain in 2024 by

Bristol University Press
University of Bristol
1–9 Old Park Hill
Bristol
BS2 8BB
UK
t: +44 (0)117 374 6645
e: bup-info@bristol.ac.uk

Details of international sales and distribution partners are available at bristoluniversitypress.co.uk

© Bristol University Press 2024

British Library Cataloguing in Publication Data
A catalogue record for this book is available from the British Library

ISBN 978-1-5292-3487-9 hardcover
ISBN 978-1-5292-3488-6 ePub
ISBN 978-1-5292-3489-3 ePdf

The right of Julia Leib to be identified as author of this work has been asserted by her in
accordance with the Copyright, Designs and Patents Act 1988.

All rights reserved: no part of this publication may be reproduced, stored in a retrieval system, or
transmitted in any form or by any means, electronic, mechanical, photocopying, recording, or
otherwise without the prior permission of Bristol University Press.

Every reasonable effort has been made to obtain permission to reproduce copyrighted material.
If, however, anyone knows of an oversight, please contact the publisher.

The statements and opinions contained within this publication are solely those of the author and
not of the University of Bristol or Bristol University Press. The University of Bristol and Bristol
University Press disclaim responsibility for any injury to persons or property
resulting from any material published in this publication.

Bristol University Press works to counter discrimination on grounds of gender,
race, disability, age and sexuality.

Cover design: Lyn Davies
Front cover image: Getty/Chris Griffiths
Bristol University Press uses environmentally responsible print partners.
Printed and bound in Great Britain by CPI Group (UK) Ltd, Croydon, CR0 4YY

FSC
www.fsc.org
MIX
Paper | Supporting
responsible forestry
FSC® C013604

For Sebastian and Juna

# Contents

| | | |
|---|---|---|
| List of Figures and Tables | | vi |
| Preface | | ix |
| 1 | Introduction: The Challenges of Institutional Peacebuilding | 1 |
| 2 | How to Assess Peacebuilding Success: Conceptualizing the Sustaining Peace Scale | 20 |
| 3 | Liberal Peacebuilding, Path Dependence and Commitment Problems | 51 |
| 4 | A Set-Theoretic, Multi-Method Approach to Peacebuilding | 77 |
| 5 | Institutional Patterns of Peacebuilding Success | 102 |
| 6 | Assisted Accountability in Sierra Leone | 135 |
| 7 | The Spoils-of-Peace Approach in South Africa | 169 |
| 8 | Conclusion: How a Focus on Configurations Provides New Insights for Peacebuilding Research | 195 |
| Notes | | 204 |
| References | | 210 |
| Index | | 240 |

# List of Figures and Tables

## Figures

| | | |
|---|---|---|
| 1.1 | State-based armed conflicts by type, 1946–2020 | 4 |
| 1.2 | Type of conflict termination, 1946–2019 | 7 |
| 1.3 | Conflict recurrence rate by type of termination, 1989–2019 | 8 |
| 1.4 | The holistic institutional framework for the study of peacebuilding processes | 14 |
| 2.1 | The sustaining peace continuum | 36 |
| 2.2 | The three-level concept structure of sustaining peace | 36 |
| 2.3 | Comparison of different measures for peacebuilding success according to the selected data | 45 |
| 2.4 | Patterns of peacebuilding success across regions, 1989–2016 | 46 |
| 2.5 | Average distribution of peacebuilding success over time (according to the year of conflict termination) | 48 |
| 3.1 | The selection process of relevant peacebuilding institutions | 66 |
| 4.1 | Analytical level of the SMMR design | 78 |
| 4.2 | Ideal types for within-case studies after fsQCA | 87 |
| 5.1 | Scatterplot for the enhanced intermediate solution for sustaining peace (SP) | 110 |
| 5.2 | Scatterplots for the two terms of the enhanced intermediate solution for sustaining peace (SP) | 112 |
| 5.3 | Scatterplot for the enhanced intermediate solution for the absence of sustaining peace (~SP) | 115 |
| 5.4 | Configurational model of peacebuilding institutions and sustaining peace (SP), 1989–2016 | 117 |
| 5.5 | Venn diagrams showing peacebuilding patterns for sustaining peace (SP) across types of conflict | 121 |
| 5.6 | Scatterplots for enhanced intermediate solutions for sustaining peace (SP) according to type of conflict | 125 |
| 5.7 | Venn diagrams showing peacebuilding patterns for sustaining peace (SP) across conflict regions | 127 |
| 5.8 | Scatterplots for enhanced intermediate/conservative solutions for sustaining peace (SP) across regions | 131 |

| 6.1 | Political map of Sierra Leone | 137 |
|-----|-------------------------------|-----|
| 6.2 | Timeline of conflict events and fatalities in Sierra Leone, 1991–2001 | 139 |
| 6.3 | Possible mechanistic constellations compatible with conjunction INT★TJ | 144 |
| 6.4 | Timeline of the assisted accountability approach in Sierra Leone, 2002–2013 | 146 |
| 6.5 | Constellation of the assisted accountability approach | 149 |
| 6.6 | Application of the credible commitment mechanism in Sierra Leone | 150 |
| 6.7 | UNAMSIL uniformed personnel, 1999–2005 | 152 |
| 6.8 | Application of the accountability mechanism in Sierra Leone | 159 |
| 7.1 | Political map of South Africa | 171 |
| 7.2 | Timeline of the spoils-of-peace approach in South Africa, 1991–1999 | 177 |
| 7.3 | Constellation of the spoils-of-peace approach | 178 |
| 7.4 | Application of the spoils-of-peace mechanism in South Africa | 181 |
| 8.1 | Cross-case and within-case level results for the outcome set sustaining peace | 197 |

## Tables

| 1.1 | Alternative theoretical assumptions and their expected causal direction | 11 |
|-----|-------------------------------------------------------------------------|-----|
| 1.2 | Summary of the multi-method research design | 16 |
| 2.1 | Czempiel's matrix for the 'development' of peace within the framework of the international system | 23 |
| 2.2 | Conceptualization of the sustaining peace scale | 39 |
| 3.1 | Explanatory peacebuilding conditions and their expected impact on sustaining peace | 74 |
| 4.1 | Calibration and fuzzy values for the outcome set sustaining peace (SP) | 90 |
| 4.2 | Calibration and fuzzy values for the condition extensive international commitment (INT) | 94 |
| 4.3 | Calibration and fuzzy values for the condition inclusive power sharing (SHARE) | 96 |
| 4.4 | Calibration and fuzzy values for the condition comprehensive security sector reform (SSR) | 97 |
| 4.5 | Calibration and fuzzy values for the condition holistic transitional justice approach (TJ) | 99 |
| 4.6 | Measurement and calibration of peacebuilding conditions | 100 |
| 5.1 | Necessary conditions for the presence (SP) and absence (~SP) of sustaining peace | 104 |

| | | |
|---|---|---|
| 5.2 | Enhanced truth table for the analysis of sustaining peace (SP) and its absence (~SP) | 105 |
| 5.3 | Enhanced intermediate solutions for the analysis of sustaining peace (SP) based on three consistency thresholds | 107 |
| 5.4 | Configurations of peacebuilding institutions sufficient for sustaining peace (SP) | 108 |
| 5.5 | Enhanced intermediate solutions for the analysis of the absence of sustaining peace (~SP) | 114 |
| 5.6 | Results for the cluster analysis of the enhanced intermediate solution | 120 |
| 5.7 | Solution terms for the intermediate solution for sustaining peace (SP) across types of conflict | 124 |
| 5.8 | Solution terms for the enhanced intermediate solution for peacebuilding conditions and sustaining peace (SP) across conflict regions | 129 |
| 6.1 | Perceptions of (inter)national peacebuilding institutions in Sierra Leone | 148 |
| 6.2 | Results of the 2002 parliamentary elections in Sierra Leone | 156 |
| 6.3 | General and personal security in Sierra Leone | 157 |
| 6.4 | Local perceptions of the Sierra Leonean peace process regarding international commitment | 158 |
| 6.5 | Local perceptions of the Sierra Leonean peace process regarding transitional justice | 166 |
| 6.6 | The effect of peacebuilding actors in Sierra Leone | 167 |
| 7.1 | Estimated military and police forces in South Africa, January 1994 | 185 |
| 7.2 | Composition of the National Assembly after the 1994 general elections in South Africa | 187 |
| 7.3 | Composition of the South African National Defence Force by former force (November 1996) | 190 |

# Preface

This book has been in the making for several years. The journey started in 2013, when I had just finished my MA in Peace and Conflict Studies and was thinking about what to do next. As with many academic projects, my Master's thesis had raised more new questions about the conditions for successful peacebuilding than it was able to answer. And I was encouraged by my supervisor Tanja Brühl to tackle these new questions in a subsequent PhD project at the Goethe University in Frankfurt. I am forever grateful to Tanja for creating an incredible working environment in our team and for giving me the space and guidance to freely think about and implement my research ideas. I had already been introduced to Qualitative Comparative Analysis (QCA) in a workshop by Claudius Wagemann and Carsten Schneider at the ECPR Summer School in Ljubljana and was fortunate enough to have Claudius as my second supervisor. His office door was always open to discuss solutions for my frustration with calibrations that did not turn out the way I expected or consistency and coverage scores that were too low for any meaningful interpretation. During my PhD, a series of workshops followed that had a formative influence on my academic work: a dynamics of civil war workshop with Jeffrey Checkel and Scott Gates at the Peace Research Institute Oslo (PRIO); an introductory process tracing workshop with Rasmus Pedersen and Hilde van Meegdenburg at the ECPR Summer School in Budapest; an advanced QCA workshop with Carsten Schneider and Ioana-Elena Oana at the ECPR Winter School in Bamberg; and a short course on causal case studies with Derek Beach at the American Political Science Association (APSA) annual meeting. I want to thank these teachers and mentors, without whom this book would not have been possible.

I am also grateful for opportunities provided to me by a PhD scholarship from the Polytechnic Society Frankfurt am Main, a fellowship from the German Fulbright Commission, and the funding of a PhD travel stipend by the German Academic Exchange Service (DAAD). Thanks to this generous funding, parts of this book were written in New York, Freetown and Monrovia. In 2015, I was able to spend ten months as a visiting researcher at Columbia University's Department of Political Science and benefited greatly from the supervision of Michael Doyle. Most of the conceptual work on the sustaining peace scale and the analytical framework of this book was written in various libraries and coffee shops all over the city. During my stay at Columbia University, I was also fortunate to benefit from discussions with a number of colleagues, including Page Fortna, Michael Gaouette, Richard Gowan, Edward Luck and Dirk Salomons. For my case studies, the fieldwork in Liberia and Sierra Leone was funded by the DAAD and allowed me to spend three months travelling both countries and conducting around 40 semi-structured interviews with a range of (inter)national peacebuilding actors as well as public opinion surveys. I am grateful to all my respondents and research partners in Sierra Leone and Liberia for their time, patience and willingness to participate in this research project. Special thanks are due to my local research assistants Alie Hassan Kargbo, Cynea Ireland, Joseph B. Eastman, Jospeh Moove, Nehemiah Bryant, Princess P. Dabieh Nimeke and Sieh Kargbo for invaluable support with my fieldwork.

I had the pleasure of working with great teams during and after my PhD, whose feedback and support contributed to the successful completion of this project. In Frankfurt, I was part of the best possible PhD group and benefited immensely from our fruitful exchanges across topics and empirical methods. My deepest thanks go to Marika Gereke, Eva Ottendörfer, Anne Peltner and Samantha Ruppel for making me rethink my own approach and prompting me to clarify many aspects of my research. After the completion of my PhD, the team of Andrea Liese gave me a new academic home in Potsdam and supported me in my efforts to turn my dissertation into a book project. The book proposal was written in Potsdam, and I am grateful for comments and suggestions by Maria Debre, Thomas Dörfler, Mirko Heinzel, Andrea Liese, Nina Reiners and Thomas Sommerer. In 2021, my dissertation won the United Nations Association of Germany (DGVN) Best Dissertation Award as well as the third place in the Aquila Ascendens Young Researcher Award for Security Policy, and I would like to thank the jury members of both award committees for recognizing my valuable and lasting contribution to peacebuilding scholarship.

Throughout my work on this book, I was fortunate enough to receive feedback from several colleagues. Alongside my fellow team members in Frankfurt and Potsdam, these included the participants of various workshops of the German Association for Peace and Conflict Studies Methods Section. For fruitful exchanges about empirical methods and several drafts of my manuscript, I am grateful to Christoph Dworschak, Belén Gonzáles, Felix Haass, Roos van der Haer, Anna-Lena Hönig, Clara Neupert-Wentz, Constantin Ruhe, Adam Scharpf and Nils Weidmann. For feedback on the QCA-related parts of the book, I would like to thank the participants of several QCA expert workshops in Zurich, above all Benoît Rihoux, Charles Ragin, Claude Rubinson, Carsten Schneider and Eva Thomann. I further thank the four anonymous reviewers that Bristol University Press elicited during two rounds of reviews. Their constructive and critical comments encouraged me to undertake substantial revisions which strengthened the final version of this book. I also want to express my gratitude to my editor, Stephen Wenham, for supporting this project from the initial stages and for steering the manuscript towards publication, as well as the people involved at Bristol University Press for their assistance. Some ideas of this book have already been published, partly abridged, partly with a different focus in *Peace, Conflict & Change* (Leib 2016), *International Peacekeeping* (Leib and Ruppel 2021), the *International Journal of Transitional Justice* (Leib 2022) and *Vereinte Nationen* (Leib 2023). Replication data and the online appendix for this book are available at my dataverse: https://doi.org/10.7910/DVN/K70 AWW. All remaining errors are my own.

Finally, I want to express my deepest gratitude to my family for all their loving support. My husband, Sebastian, accompanied and supported me throughout the twists and turns of my PhD and finally this book project. He happily embraced tying our holiday plans to conference locations and understood that fixed working hours are nonexistent in academia. And our daughter, Juna, who turned our world upside down last year in the best possible way. I dedicate this book to them.

1

# Introduction: The Challenges of Institutional Peacebuilding

In 2018, Liberia celebrated the 15th anniversary of the comprehensive peace agreement (CPA), ending 14 years of vicious civil wars, the withdrawal of the United Nations Mission in Liberia (UNMIL) after 15 years of service, and the first peaceful transfer of power in 74 years. Liberia has often been hailed as a success story for international peacekeeping and the implementation of peace agreements. In a tweet about the closure of UNMIL, the mission declared it made an invaluable contribution to restoring peace to Liberia.[1] This assessment seems to be valid, as Liberia has demobilized and reintegrated the former armed factions, rebuilt the armed forces and national police, re-established the rule of law, held three peaceful elections and amended the Constitution since the CPA was signed in 2003. However, despite these landmark achievements, Liberia is still fragile: the economy is weak; corruption is rampant; and national institutions are too centralized and lack basic infrastructure.

Other troubling developments can be found in other post-conflict countries. In El Salvador, where the 1992 agreement between the government and the Farabundo Martí National Liberation Front (FMLN) led to a consolidation of democracy, increasing trust in state institutions and improvements in human rights compliance, drug-related violence has increased exponentially in the last decade, threatening to undermine the reform process (Joshi and Wallensteen 2018: 3). In Cambodia, the successful postwar transition and economic recovery after the signing of the Paris Agreements in 1991 has contributed to the consolidation of a one-party regime under Prime Minister Hun Sen and widespread corruption. In South Sudan, the CPA signed in 2005 between the government of Sudan and the Sudan People's Liberation Movement/Army (SPLM/A) provided the foundation for the creation of the independent state of South Sudan in 2011; however, the newly independent country has not been able to consolidate the peace and has instead suffered

1

from ethnic violence and recurring civil war, despite strong support from the international community.

As these examples demonstrate, the fate of post-conflict societies does not follow any type of linear logic once the warring factions have signed a peace agreement. While most countries that negotiated a peace agreement to end intrastate armed conflicts between 1989 and 2016 experienced no recurrence of armed conflict, the degree of post-conflict peacefulness varies with regard to social, political and economic factors, as highlighted by the preceding examples. The causal mechanisms underlying such peacebuilding processes are complex as local conditions may vary from one conflict to the next, and peacebuilding episodes can involve various constellations of local and international actors and strategies (Paris 1997). Analysing these peacebuilding processes thus requires a research design that can uncover different recipes for their success.

Peace agreements demonstrate an important commitment by conflict parties to a specific framework for post-conflict reconstruction and represent critical junctures in the way that they intend 'to institutionalize peace following the tenuous conditions in the immediate aftermath of armed conflicts' (Joshi and Wallensteen 2018: 5); however, it remains unclear how we can capture these apparent differences between qualitatively distinct levels of peace in post-conflict settings and the best approaches to ensure the establishment of high-quality and sustaining peace in societies that recover from large-scale armed conflicts. Both questions are at the centre of this book, which is guided by the main hypothesis that the establishment of high-quality sustaining peace in post-conflict societies is the result of different equifinal interactions between individual institutional peacebuilding measures that define and regulate post-conflict order. For example, international interventions and security sector reform (SSR) focus on maintaining or restoring security, discouraging combatants from returning to war, and might be interacting in a security-first peacebuilding approach (Walter 2002; Fortna 2004a; Marten 2004; Barnett et al 2007; Toft 2010). Comprehensive SSR might also interact with inclusive power sharing, as both institutions address commitment problems by rewarding former rebels and government forces for maintaining a peace agreement, either through political or military incentives and power (Clark 2001; Pugh 2002).

## The research puzzle and main argument

For a long time, international peace and conflict research focused mainly on interstate wars and great power rivalries, but since the mid-1990s there has been an increase in publications on the causes and consequences of intrastate conflicts and civil wars. This development was preceded by a change in international warfare and the dramatic increase in civil wars. Following the end of the Cold War, the number of armed conflicts had initially decreased substantially, a trend praised by some scholars as the demise of war and the beginning of a more peaceful world (Goldstein 2011; Pinker 2011). Since its peak in the early 1990s, the total number of armed conflicts has globally declined by more than one third.[2] This downward trend can partly be explained by the almost complete absence of classic interstate wars in the 21st century, which makes civil wars within nation states the predominant form of warfare today. A second explanation for this general decline is that more old wars have ended than new wars have begun, supporting the main argument of this book: successful peacebuilding is an important device for the reduction of armed conflicts.

For the past decade, the world has seen a new peak in the number of state-based conflicts, matched only by the early 1990s and reversing the promising previous trends (see Figure 1.1; Pettersson et al 2021). For example, the number of active civil wars tripled from four to 12 between 2007 and 2016. In 2020, the Uppsala Conflict Data Program (UCDP) recorded a record-high number (56) of active state-based armed conflicts, and the years since 2014 have had the highest numbers of armed conflict since 1946.[3] While the early peak in armed conflicts in 1991 corresponded with a similar peak in the number of peace agreements signed within these conflicts and a subsequent decrease in the number of conflicts in the late 1990s and early 2000s, a similar trend is not evident for the most recent rise in armed conflicts (Pettersson et al 2019). In addition, the share of internationalization of armed conflicts – conflicts that see military involvement of external actors supporting one or both warring sides – has been growing steadily from nine in 2012 to 25 in 2020. This development makes the resolution of conflicts even more difficult because external military support and the presence of foreign troops pose a serious threat to conflict resolution and make conflicts longer and bloodier (Lacina 2006; Balch-Lindsay et al 2008).

Currently, fewer wars end in outright victory and, consequently, there has been an increase in the number of peace agreements signed after armed conflicts. The peace following these settlements is in most cases extremely fragile, and post-conflict countries face a higher risk of renewed warfare. The foundation for successful peacebuilding after armed conflicts and thus the way out of the 'conflict trap' (Collier et al 2003) has to be established in the de-escalation phase, but it is precisely at this point that the efforts of state and civil society actors often fail. Successful peacebuilding after armed conflicts and the therewith-associated way out of the conflict trap are thus central themes of peace and conflict research (Bigombe et al 2000).

Knowledge of the conditions for successful peacebuilding is still limited, which is especially surprising in light of the enormous political importance of this issue. Part of the problem lies in the inconsistency of peacebuilding evaluation and the application of divergent peace concepts. As a result,

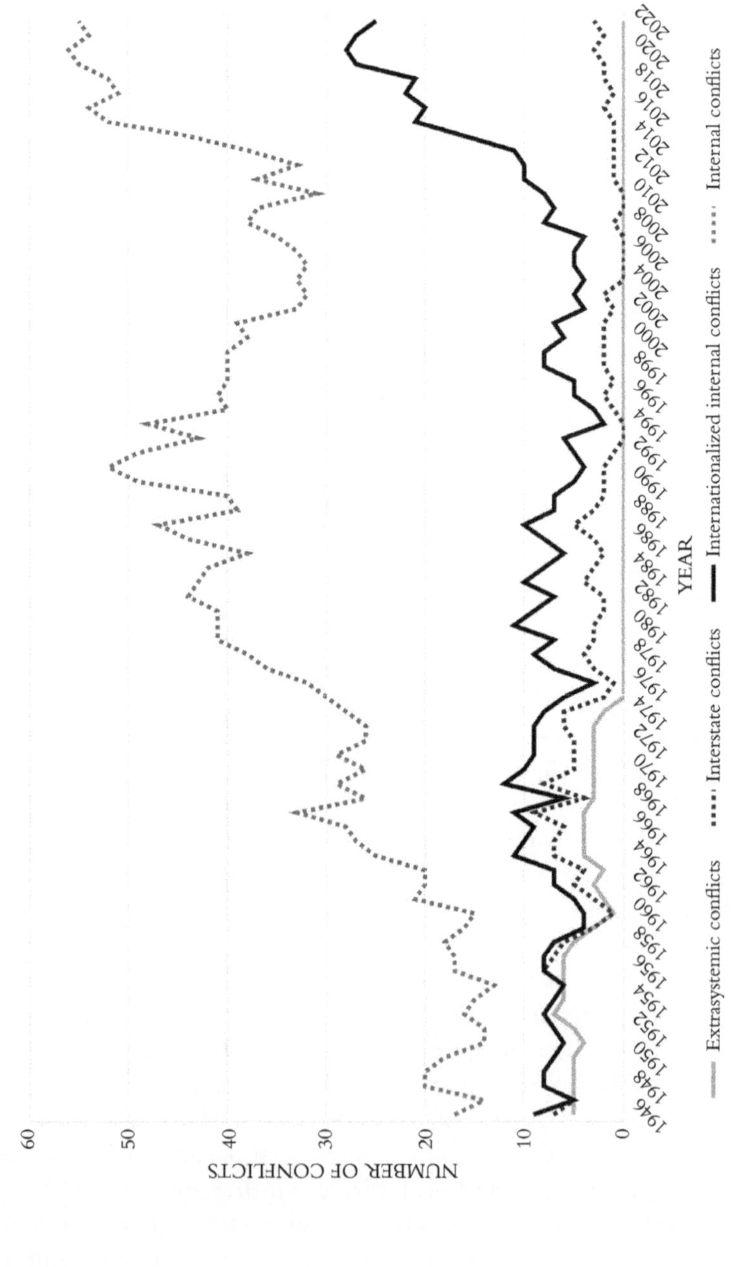

**Figure 1.1:** State–based armed conflicts by type, 1946–2020

there is still a lack of an agreed-upon framework for what can be marked as a success or failure of a peace process beyond the absence of war (Joshi and Wallensteen 2018).

Following former United Nations (UN) Secretary-General Boutros Boutros-Ghali (1992, para 21), peacebuilding is understood as 'action to identify and support structures which will tend to strengthen and solidify peace in order to avoid a relapse into conflict'. As such, the overall aim of peacebuilding is to reduce the risk of recurring armed conflict, while simultaneously paving the way for sustaining peace and development. Recent peacebuilding literature focuses on the many institutional options available to strengthen a fragile post-conflict peace and emphasizes types of institutions, which increase the likelihood that conflict will not resume (Williams and Sterio 2020; Dorussen 2022). For example, the deployment of UN peacekeeping operations has been shown to reduce the risk of conflict recurrence (Walter et al 2021), while the inclusion of power-sharing provisions in peace agreements is believed to strengthen post-conflict peace by mitigating the commitment problem (Walter 2002; Hartzell and Hoddie 2007), and transitional justice is put forward as a key element of peacebuilding interventions in post-conflict societies to promote peace and reconciliation (Teitel 2000; Olsen et al 2010; Loyle and Appel 2017). However, what is still missing is substantial knowledge about the interaction of these factors and the dynamics and mechanisms resulting in sustaining peace. Thus, the main argument put forward here is that the previous focus on single peacebuilding institutions is misplaced because sustaining peace is likely the result of multiple institutional combinations. Hence, the research question guiding this book is the following: which (configurations of) peacebuilding institutions are necessary and/or sufficient for sustaining peace and how do they exert their influence in post-conflict countries?

Throughout this book, I work with a broad understanding of peacebuilding institutions – formal rules, norms and policy structures that organize and constitute social relations in post-conflict societies – which are expected to interact, resulting in alternative causal paths that structure the post-conflict political order and lead to sustaining peace (Keohane 1988: 383). To address the research question, the subsequent study examines 54 peacebuilding episodes initiated through peace agreements between 1989 and 2016. I construct an original dataset that encompasses a variety of information about the level of post-conflict peacefulness in these countries and the institutional frameworks that have been put in place to ensure a successful transition. This data allows me to draw a comprehensive picture of institutional configurations and patterns of peacebuilding success after armed conflicts and civil wars.

Overall, this book contributes to the advancement of peacebuilding studies through the following theoretical, conceptual and methodological innovations. First, by developing and operationalizing the concept of sustaining peace as a suitable measure for the analysis of peacebuilding success which goes beyond the traditional notion of negative peace, I respond to calls by Regan (2014) and Diehl (2016) for direct engagement with the issue of peace and its causes and advance prior work by Wallensteen (2015). Second, this book calls for the vigorous inclusion of set-theoretic methods into the study of peacebuilding processes to uncover configurational patterns and dependencies, which lead to a realistic picture of the underlying processes. In this regard, I outline multiple equifinal and configurational patterns of peacebuilding success through the transparent application of Qualitative Comparative Analysis (QCA) and develop an analytical model of peacebuilding success based on the differentiated (non)implementation of peacebuilding institutions. Third, I subject this model to empirical plausibility tests by analysing the mechanisms behind the two sufficient institutional patterns for sustaining peace in the cases of post-conflict Sierra Leone and South Africa, through the means of process tracing.

## Current theories of conflict transformation and peacebuilding

The literature on civil wars, armed violence and international peacebuilding is so extensive that it is impossible to present it in its entirety. While there seems to be increasing consensus about patterns of civil war onset and termination (for example, Dixon 2009), there is considerably less agreement on the causal dynamics of postwar transitions to peace, successful peacebuilding and the factors causing a relapse to war.

Some trends of peacebuilding success or post-conflicts risks have been identified (Call and Cousens 2008; Williams and Sterio 2020). Data on armed conflicts show the overall pattern of conflict termination has changed. Today, fewer wars end in outright victory and, consequently, there has been an increase in the number of peace agreements signed after armed conflicts (Einsiedel 2014; Pettersson and Wallensteen 2015). Until the end of the 1980s, conflicts ended in military victories four times more often than in peace agreements. Today, the relationship has been reversed, and more than twice as many conflicts end in peace agreements or ceasefires than they do in victories. The end of the Cold War brought a more favourable setting for solving many longstanding conflicts, which has made negotiated settlements the dominant form of conflict resolution in the post-Cold War era, often setting the stage for the subsequent peacebuilding phase (see Figure 1.2); however, many of the peace processes following victories or negotiated settlements remain fragile and 'an unfortunate number of wars that end have recurred' (Call and Cousens 2008: 5). In addition, the last several years have also seen the disturbing development of fewer conflicts ending in an

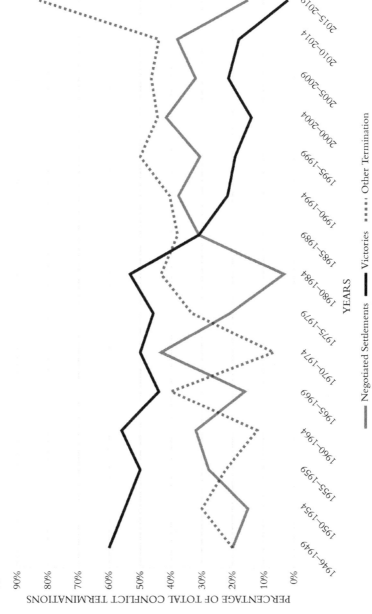

**Figure 1.2:** Type of conflict termination, 1946–2019

**Figure 1.3:** Conflict recurrence rate by type of termination, 1989–2019

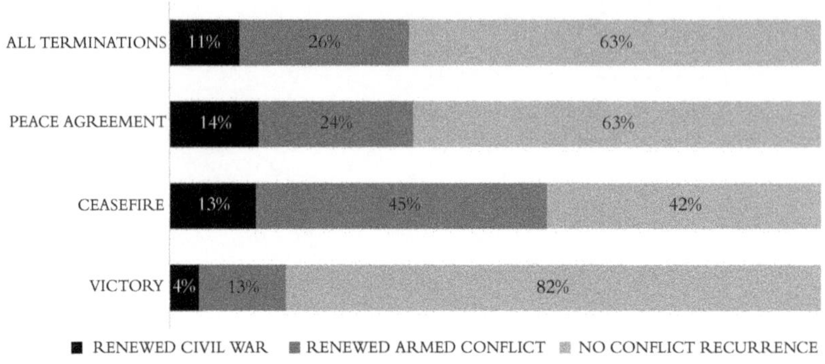

| | RENEWED CIVIL WAR | RENEWED ARMED CONFLICT | NO CONFLICT RECURRENCE |
|---|---|---|---|
| ALL TERMINATIONS | 11% | 26% | 63% |
| PEACE AGREEMENT | 14% | 24% | 63% |
| CEASEFIRE | 13% | 45% | 42% |
| VICTORY | 4% | 13% | 82% |

official termination, while the vast majority enter a phase of low activity before the conflicts erupt again.

Conflict recurrence is hardly surprising, as civil wars usually exacerbate the factors that led to the original outbreak of the armed conflict: state capacities deteriorating, poverty increasing, intergroup relations becoming more hostile and so on. If we take a look at all officially terminated intrastate armed conflicts between 1989 and 2019, 11 per cent have relapsed into a civil war within five years, 26 per cent went through another armed conflict, and peace remained stable in 63 per cent (see Figure 1.3); however, the recurrence rate differs considerably between the individual types of conflict termination. Conflicts that ended with the victory of one party were almost twice as likely not to experience a conflict recurrence (82 per cent) as those that ended with a ceasefire (42 per cent). The figures for peace agreements are somewhat better, with the recurrence rate being 38 per cent, including armed conflicts and civil wars. However, the absence of a renewed conflict does not indicate the quality of peace or the possibilities for political participation of the general public in those post-conflict settings. Even though conflicts ending in military victories recur less frequently (Licklider 1995), they are usually associated with high human losses or retributive violence, which, from a moral viewpoint, speaks against the endorsement of this form of conflict resolution.

Without any grand theories dealing with post-conflict peacebuilding in international relations (IR), the research field is characterized by a growing collection of midrange theories, which provide a myriad of potential explanations as to why and how armed conflicts are resolved, endure or recur, without representing an explicit theory of peacebuilding (Checkel 2015). Current theories of conflict transformation and peacebuilding focus on the institutional setup in post-conflict countries and assume that the establishment of certain peacebuilding institutions reduces a country's risk of reversion to civil war, thus supporting the establishment of sustaining peace.

*Peacebuilding institutions advocating for sustaining peace*

Peacebuilding scholars usually focus on the institutional options that can be put in place to increase the likelihood that conflict will not resume and to strengthen a fragile post-conflict peace (Williams and Sterio 2020). We have evidence that multiple types of international conflict resolution efforts can reduce a country's risk of reversion to civil war and thus support the establishment of sustaining peace (Call and Cousens 2008). In particular, four institutions are likely to affect the chances of sustaining peace: international commitment, political power sharing, security sector reform and transitional justice.

A large debate has materialized around the influence of third-party interventions and international commitment to civil war settlements and peace processes. International interventions are a typical reaction to ongoing violent conflicts and can have a significant influence on peace processes and their outcome. The possible involvement of intergovernmental organizations or individual states ranges from mediation over sanctions to military interventions. As mediators, they can help to solve difficult negotiation problems and support combatants in achieving an agreement (Bercovitch and Rubin 1992; Bercovitch 1996). Peacekeeping forces can support the peace process by enforcing the terms of a peace agreement and enabling both sides to disarm, without fear of their opponent cheating (Dorussen 2022). Most studies can provide statistical evidence of the positive effects of UN peace operations on reducing the risk of recurrent violence (Walter et al 2021), shortening the conflict duration (Gilligan and Sergenti 2008) and weakening the severity of hostilities (Hultman 2010; Hultman et al 2013). According to Doyle and Sambanis (2006), the inherent risk of renewed conflict can be counteracted by a comprehensive peace agreement and the deployment and monitoring of its implementation by a multidimensional peace operation. Hartzell et al (2001) support the claim that the survival rate of peace agreements is strongly influenced by the deployment of a peacekeeping mission. Walter (2002) demonstrates that external security guarantees are a necessary condition for fully implemented peace agreements, while Fortna (2004a) finds that the character of a third-party peacekeeping mission is an important determinant of postwar stability. Given this theoretical approach, one expects that comprehensive international commitment towards the peacebuilding process enables the establishment of sustaining peace.

Scholars have argued that power sharing, usually understood as 'including political opponents in a joint executive coalition government' (Binningsbø 2013: 89), has been introduced in many post-conflict societies as a political solution to overcome deep divisions between the formerly warring parties and to enhance the durability of peace (Walter 2002; Hartzell and Hoddie 2007; Jarstad and Nilsson 2008). The argument is that power-sharing provisions contribute to sustaining peace by preventing the government and the rebels from singlehandedly controlling any area of political power, excluding their opponents from decision making. Power-sharing institutions define the way in which competition within divided societies should take place. They facilitate the transition from civil war to democratic governance and sustaining peace by reassuring opposition and minority groups that their interests will be considered through the participation of their representatives in the governmental decision-making process. Given this theory, political power sharing is understood as a governing system that is beneficial for post-conflict societies by providing warring factions with access to political power, enabling the establishment of sustaining peace.

Proponents of a security-centred approach to peacebuilding argue that the establishment of a professional, effective and accountable security sector that ensures the security of the civilian population is a prerequisite for a process of conflict transformation and the rebuilding of the state (Perito 2020). The remnants of a wartime military and security apparatus usually pose great risks for any peace process, as they jeopardize internal security in societies, already devastated by conflict (Schnabel and Ehrhart 2005). One of the central objectives of peacebuilding interventions is to address patterns of violence and insecurity by supporting basic safety and security and by building resilient and legitimate state institutions. The goal of SSR is to restructure and retrain security actors in a way that they become an asset, not a liability, for the peacebuilding process (Berdal 1996; Chalmers 2000; Toft 2010). This reform includes the integration and transformation of military, paramilitary, rebel and police forces into adequate, legitimate and democratic security structures and actors. The disarmament and demobilization of former combatants help to restore security, and reintegration programmes offer them an alternative to a life with the gun. The theory thus predicts that the complete implementation of different SSR provisions creates resilient security institutions and enables the establishment of sustaining peace.

Finally, there is a growing consensus that justice is essential to sustaining peace, and transitional justice (TJ) measures are increasingly viewed as key elements of peacebuilding interventions (Loyle and Appel 2017; de Hoon 2020). Regardless of how armed conflicts are resolved, post-conflict societies are usually faced with questions of reconciliation, as almost everyone – whether civilian or combatant – is affected by violence and traumatic experiences. TJ is a response to systematic violations of human rights and constitutes an important institutional approach to promoting peace and reconciliation (Olsen et al 2010). In one form or another, TJ measures are currently included in most peace processes and have come to 'dominate debates on the intersection between democratization, human rights protections, and state reconstruction after conflict' (McEvoy 2007: 412). Despite the increase in academic literature and practical applications of TJ,

**Table 1.1:** Alternative theoretical assumptions and their expected causal direction

| Theory | Causal direction | Theoretical assumption |
| --- | --- | --- |
| International commitment | Supportive | The comprehensive commitment of international actors towards the peacebuilding process enables the establishment of sustaining peace. |
| Political power sharing | Supportive | Inclusive power sharing provides warring factions with access to political power and enables the establishment of sustaining peace. |
| Security sector reform | Supportive | The complete implementation of different SSR provisions creates resilient security institutions and enables the establishment of sustaining peace. |
| Transitional justice | Ambiguous | Holistic transitional justice approaches may both enable and impede the establishment of sustaining peace. |

scholars disagree about its effectiveness. Many argue that TJ promotes peace in the aftermath of conflict by addressing grievances through truth telling, apologies and compensation, by fostering respect for human rights or by deterring perpetrators from future violence (Wiebelhaus-Brahm 2009; Loyle and Appel 2017). In contrast, sceptical voices find little or even contradictory evidence for the peace-promoting role of TJ, arguing that 'digging up the past' and identifying perpetrators can trigger renewed conflict (Mendeloff 2004; Snyder and Vinjamuri 2004). Against this ambiguous background, the theory predicts that the implementation of transitional justice measures may both enable and impede the establishment of sustaining peace.

The preceding discussion reveals a range of alternative explanations as to why some peacebuilding interventions end successfully while others do not. Table 1.1 lists these alternative theoretical assumptions and their expected causal direction.

## What is missing from the theories

As this review has pointed out, there is some general agreement about the mechanisms linking peacebuilding institutions to renewed warfare or successful peacebuilding after armed conflicts. However, regardless of these trends, we still know remarkably little about the best ways to accomplish sustaining peace after armed conflicts or how to avoid the conflict trap. Part of the problem lies in the inconsistency of peacebuilding evaluation and the application of divergent concepts of peace. Additionally, very few studies have addressed issues of complexity and conditionality when it comes to explaining successful peacebuilding. What is still missing is substantial knowledge about the interaction of these institutional factors and the dynamics that result in sustaining peace. So far, no empirical study has bridged the gap between peacebuilding factors by testing these competing theoretical expectations in a single comparative analysis of successful peacebuilding patterns. Because peacebuilding represents a complex problem, it is assumed to also require complex answers. The main argument put forward here is that this previous focus on single peacebuilding institutions is misplaced, because sustaining peace is more likely the result of different institutional configurations, which can be tested in a comparative analysis.

# The research design in a nutshell

This section briefly presents a summary of the entire research design to clarify my line of argument and to make it easier for the reader to understand the following discussions and analytical illustrations made throughout the book.

## Core argument and analytical approach

Because I argue that peacebuilding success is most likely the result of different institutional configurations and their development over time, I establish an appropriate analytical framework by merging a liberal institutionalist peacebuilding approach with insights from historical institutionalism and bargaining theory to explain the establishment of sustaining peace in post-conflict societies.

International peacebuilding approaches usually focus on the (re)construction of institutions and state capacity, which are expected to form the basis for effective and legitimate governance in post-conflict societies (Williams and Sterio 2020). The analytical framework thus focuses on the institutional configurations within those approaches and the overarching contexts and interacting processes that shape and reshape the peacebuilding process (Pierson and Skocpol 2002). Following the 'liberal peace' approach towards peacebuilding, which is most prominently pursued by the UN (Paris 2010), peacebuilding institutions are considered as important causal conditions that are at the heart of any peacebuilding process and generating sustaining peace. Here, the term 'institutions' is used broadly, describing formal rules, norms and policy structures that organize and constitute social relations in post-conflict societies (Keohane 1988), and that are expected to interact, resulting in alternative causal patterns that structure the post-conflict political order and lead to sustaining peace. The liberal institutionalist perspective provides the solid foundation for the overall analytical framework, as it provides 'the "software" that drives the "hardware" of many international organizations', states and international nongovernmental organizations (NGOs) in the peacebuilding arena (Mac Ginty 2010: 396).

Historical institutionalism, as a second component of the analytical approach, is used to explain the interaction of various peacebuilding institutions and how post-conflict political order is constructed and influenced by the conflict environment. It guides the subsequent analysis by focusing on two critical phases along the temporal sequence of peacebuilding processes: (1) the peace agreement that ends violent conflict, predefines the institutions included in the post-conflict political order, and acts as a critical juncture for the following peace process; and (2) the actual path-dependent peacebuilding period, including the implementation of the peace agreement to create sustaining peace through institution building (see also Barma 2017: 23). Because historical institutionalism assumes that causal conditions may not operate independent of each other regarding the origin and impact of institutions, but rather bundle together, resulting in alternative causal paths to similar outcomes, it is highly compatible with a set-theoretic approach towards the analysis of institutional conditions for successful peacebuilding. Peacebuilding interventions are thus understood as critical junctures or transformative moments which establish 'certain directions of change and foreclose others in a way that shapes politics for years to come' (Collier and Collier 1991: 27). Lastly, bargaining theory is consulted to explain the stability of post-conflict peace. Especially in cases of negotiated settlements, bargaining continues after the conflict has ended, as the organizational structures of the belligerents usually remain intact, which makes them, in theory, capable of continuing the fight at a later point in time. As a result, institutions must be set up to keep the former conflict parties from breaking the agreement.

Figure 1.4 presents a summary of the holistic framework for the analysis of peacebuilding processes. To arrive at the establishment of a peacebuilding intervention, which is seen as a critical juncture for the peace process, the belligerents first have to agree on a negotiated solution ending the armed conflict. The bargaining phase is generally characterized by cost-benefit analyses and information asymmetries between the warring factions and might be supported by international mediation efforts to reduce uncertainty (see Chapter 3 for more details). If the bargaining process is successful, it results in a negotiated peace agreement that also includes the relevant peacebuilding institutions to be set up in the subsequent implementation phase. In line with the historical institutionalist approach, the signing of a peace agreement acts as a critical juncture and constitutes the starting point for the path-dependent peacebuilding process in which the implementation of a peace agreement represents 'a period of significant change' (Collier and Collier 1991: 29). Four peacebuilding institutions are considered relevant for the establishment of sustaining peace, as they address commitment problems and account for the importance of national reconciliation: third-party commitment, security sector reform, political power sharing and transitional justice. Finally, it is assumed that the implementation of different

**Figure 1.4:** The holistic institutional framework for the study of peacebuilding processes

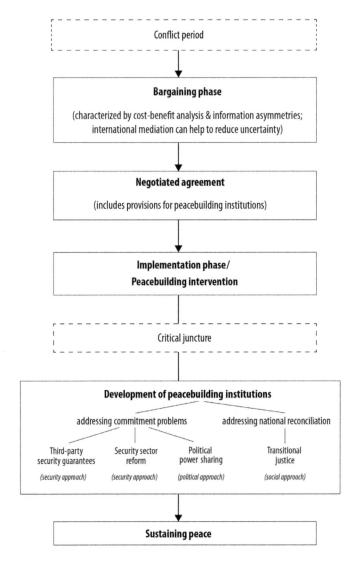

combinations of these four peacebuilding institutions will lead to the establishment of sustaining peace.

*Timeframe and case selection*

The peacebuilding dataset includes all peace processes after intrastate armed conflicts that were ended by a peace agreement between 1989 and 2016.

Setting the starting point for case selection in 1989 accounts for the fact that the end of the Cold War fundamentally changed international warfare and altered the context for conflict resolution and peacebuilding by giving rise to multiple processes, such as the emergence of new states with contested boundaries, the proliferation of cheap weapons, and the withdrawal of superpower support (Kalyvas and Balcells 2010). Closing the case selection in 2016 is necessary in order to allow for a subsequent consideration of the peacebuilding period spanning five years. Many studies utilize this five-year timeframe, as it represents the most critical stage for successful peacebuilding (Call 2008). Putting the research focus on conflicts that ended with a peace agreement makes sense for several reasons: (1) it accounts for the dominance of negotiated settlements as the main termination type of armed conflicts since the end of the Cold War; (2) in those cases, the conflict parties committed to a peace process and the peace agreements represent a common ground for the peacebuilding process; (3) it creates a small, bounded population of cases that are as causally homogeneous as possible; (4) we can learn a lot from these peacebuilding initiatives: both from those agreements that have failed to end conflicts successfully and from those that have proven more sustainable; and (5) data availability for a comparative research design is much better if one focuses on the subset of postwar transitions that began with a peace agreement.[4]

Case selection is based on the UCDP/PRIO Armed Conflict Dataset (Davies et al 2023). I follow the UCDP coding rules and define a state-based conflict as 'a contested incompatibility that concerns government and/or territory where the use of armed force between two parties, of which at least one is the government of a state, results in at least 25 battle-related deaths in a calendar year' (Pettersson 2023: 1).[5] The sample is then further narrowed down according to the type of conflict and only includes internal conflicts, fought between a government and at least one rebel group, and internationalized internal conflicts, which, in addition, see the involvement of foreign governments with troops in support of at least one side. Each post-conflict peacebuilding episode represents an observation for the comparative analysis. I exclude armed conflicts that were ongoing at the end of the analysis period (31 December 2016) and cases that were not terminated by a peace agreement. Data on peace agreements are compiled from different sources, including the UCDP Peace Agreement Dataset, the Peace Accords Matrix (PAM)[6] and UN Peacemaker[7], and is then merged with the information about the selected conflicts from the UCDP/PRIO Armed Conflict Dataset. The final dataset includes 54 peacebuilding episodes in 38 countries initiated between 1989 and 2016.[8] Of those 54 peacebuilding episodes, 31 occurred after less intense armed conflicts and 23 after civil wars. The sample is regionally skewed towards peace processes occurring in Africa (57 per cent), followed by Asia (17 per cent), Europe (17 per cent) and the Americas (9 per cent). However, this skewedness is representative for the overall tendency of armed conflicts to occur disproportionally in Sub-Saharan Africa (Pettersson and Wallensteen 2015).

## Model development and verification

There is little generalized knowledge about the complex interactions of individual peacebuilding institutions. Because the cases under investigation represent peacebuilding episodes, this book is closely linked to research on civil war occurrence, duration and termination, as well as to the more recent debates about post-conflict reconstruction and sustainable conflict resolution. Due to the wide range of theoretical and empirical studies, it is reasonable to proceed deductively, with the first step of the research process of reviewing the current state of research to determine a set of potentially relevant explanatory factors for the following comparative research (see Table 1.2).

In the second step, I perform a fuzzy-set QCA on the explanatory factors to identify peacebuilding patterns that are necessary or sufficient for sustaining peace. QCA is perhaps the most formalized set-theoretic method and focuses on explicit connections between explanatory conditions (Ragin 1987, 2008; Rihoux and Ragin 2009; Schneider and Wagemann 2012; Mello 2021; Oana et al 2021). It has been chosen as the method of analysis because it can handle three aspects of causal complexity that are central to the research question: equifinality; conjunctural causality; and asymmetric causal relations. *Equifinality* carries the assumption that there are different, mutually non-exclusive explanations and patterns contributing to sustaining peace. *Conjunctural causation* refers to the fact that in complex fields, such as peacebuilding, the effects of individual conditions can only unfold in combination with others. Finally, due to *asymmetric causal relations*, the explanation of sustaining peace is based on other configurational patterns

**Table 1.2:** Summary of the multi-method research design

|        | Method                            | Result                                                                                                          |
|--------|-----------------------------------|---------------------------------------------------------------------------------------------------------------|
| Step 1 | Deduction                         | Identification of potential explanatory factors from the current theoretical and empirical peacebuilding debate. |
| Step 2 | Concept formulation               | Development of a suitable empirical measure for the analysis of peacebuilding success.                          |
| Step 3 | QCA (model development)           | Development of a configurational model of peacebuilding success.                                                |
| Step 4 | Process tracing (model testing)   | Empirical test of the model based on the two case studies of the peacebuilding processes in Sierra Leone and South Africa. |

than the absence of sustaining peace. The fuzzy-set variant of QCA is chosen to allow for multiple membership degrees of cases in sets. In a third step and based on the QCA results, I then develop a configurational model of peacebuilding institutions and sustaining peace, which builds on the state of art in peacebuilding research.

In the fourth step, the patterns of the configurational model will be tested for their explanatory power regarding the research question. This empirical verification is done by means of process tracing. Because set-theoretic methods like QCA are essentially case-based methods, they provide good entry points for the integration of case studies. But where QCA focuses on explicit connections between explanatory conditions, process tracing will be applied to open up the black box and take a closer look at the mechanism between the explanatory configurations (assisted accountability; spoils-of-peace) and the outcome of sustaining peace. Here, the general goal is to analyse how the peacebuilding conditions interact with each other in order to lead to the outcome. Process tracing is a distinct within-case method that makes it possible to trace a mechanism that links a cause (or conjunction of causes) with an outcome to generate an inference about causal mechanisms (George and Bennett 2005; Gerring 2008; Goertz 2017; Beach and Pedersen 2019; van Meegdenburg 2022). Here, it will be used to give us a better understanding of how peacebuilding institutions produce sustaining peace in the ideal typical peacebuilding episodes in Sierra Leone and South Africa, and what the steps of the causal process in between those conditions and the outcome are: the goal is to unpack the causal mechanisms between certain configurations of peacebuilding institutions and sustaining peace.

In summary, this book has several research objectives: to solve the research puzzle of contradictory findings about the impact of peacebuilding institutions by outlining equifinal and configurational patterns of peacebuilding success; to develop and operationalize the concept of sustaining peace as a suitable measure for the analysis of peacebuilding success; to develop an analytical model of peacebuilding success based on the differentiated (non) implementation of peacebuilding institutions; and to subject this model to an empirical plausibility test.

## The plan of the book

The book is structured in the following way. Chapter 2 offers a conceptual contribution to peacebuilding studies by providing an operational indicator for peacebuilding success that permits the systematic evaluation of different levels of peace – with a clear focus on societies emerging from large-scale armed conflict – which can then be used for comparative analyses of peacebuilding success. In order to analyse successful peacebuilding, we first need to define what 'success' means, including how it has previously been defined and measured. I build on these ideas and present the theory-centred, empirically guided and systematized concept of sustaining peace as a multidimensional peace measure to facilitate the comparative study of the conditions for peacebuilding success.

Chapter 3 lays the foundations for the subsequent analyses by presenting the analytical framework for the analysis of peacebuilding success, which consists of combining historical institutionalist and bargaining theory with a liberal institutionalist peacebuilding approach. It also presents a set of explanatory conditions and their expected impacts on the establishment of sustaining peace: four peacebuilding institutions that define the post-conflict structure of society emerging from armed conflict.

The main ideas of the set-theoretic multi-method approach to peacebuilding are presented in Chapter 4, which highlights why a set-theoretic multi-method approach is particularly well suited to address the question of successful peacebuilding and how QCA and process tracing can be meaningfully combined.

Chapter 5 reports the QCA findings, looking for configurations of peacebuilding conditions associated with sustaining peace. The results for the analysis of the four selected peacebuilding institutions and their relations to sustaining peace are presented in the form of a configurational model of peacebuilding institutions and sustaining peace. The robustness of these findings is checked by taking a closer look at the variations in peacebuilding patterns in a comparative cluster analysis and separate examinations of set relations across conflict types and regions.

Chapters 6 and 7 use the qualitative method of process tracing to test the causal mechanisms that link the sufficient patterns from the configurational model to the outcome of sustaining peace. Chapter 6 studies the mechanism behind the most empirically relevant assisted accountability approach in the ideal typical case of the peacebuilding process in Sierra Leone. The peacebuilding approach included a strong parallel focus on security and justice, with a comprehensive TJ component being implemented alongside the presence of a multidimensional peacekeeping mission and extensive international support. Chapter 7 conceptualizes the spoils-of-peace peacebuilding mechanism on the theoretical level and traces its implementation in the ideal typical case of South Africa. The peacebuilding approach in South Africa did not rely on strong international support, but instead focused on the simultaneous adoption of a wide range of policy instruments, including a political power-sharing system and the transformation of the security sector.

Lastly, this book concludes with a summary of the main findings regarding peacebuilding institutions and their impact on successful peacebuilding and a critical discussion of the research approach. The last chapter also discusses what the findings imply for the role and workings of the UN and other international organizations in the field of peacebuilding more broadly. Finally, it addresses promising avenues for future research and develops policy recommendations for a wider audience interested in peacebuilding and the establishment of sustaining peace.

2

# How to Assess Peacebuilding Success: Conceptualizing the Sustaining Peace Scale

The increase in demand and expectations about the role of the UN in peacebuilding was combined with the question of accountability, challenges of assessing the impact of peace missions, and judgement of whether the peace missions were successful. A main issue is that any peace concept, generally used as a measure for peacebuilding success, is multidimensional and normatively charged. In addition, from the first stages of modern peace research, the central task of coming up with a definition of peace has been linked to one essential question: 'Is peace researchable' (Boulding 1964)? Even though there has been a longstanding and extensive scholarly discussion of the concept of peace (Galtung 1969; Czempiel 1977a; Boulding 1978; Rapoport 1992; Wallensteen 2015), few efforts synthesized multiple conceptual ideas or provided systematic and measurable definitions (Goertz et al 2016). As a result, peace research has no clarified concept of peace (Czempiel, 2006). The theoretical debate focuses mainly on the distinction of broader and narrower conceptions of peace, while in empirical analyses, peace is predominantly defined negatively, as the absence of war or violence. Most of the extensive scholarly literature concentrates on the absence of war rather than positive conceptions of peace. What is still missing is a clear concept of peace in postwar situations that moves beyond the inadequate not-war conceptualization (Goertz et al 2016).[1]

This chapter is a conceptual contribution about ways to measure and analyse peace that goes beyond the absence of violence. The goal is to provide an operational indicator that permits the systematic evaluation of different level of peace – with a clear focus on societies emerging from large-scale armed conflict – which can then be used for comparative analyses of peacebuilding success. To analyse successful peacebuilding, we first need to define *success*. Therefore, this chapter starts by acknowledging previous work done on the core ideas of peace. Because any discussion about the establishment of peace in post-conflict societies is inseparably connected to international peacebuilding efforts and the activities of the UN, the review also includes a more application-oriented discussion of the tools for the maintenance of peace and security. The subsequent section discusses prominent analytic measures for peace that have been used in comparative research. At the end of this chapter, I build on these debates and present the theory-centred, empirically guided and systematized concept of sustaining peace as an actual empirical measure of a multidimensional peace concept that facilitates the comparative study of the conditions for peacebuilding success. The chapter concludes with a summary of the debate and the added value of the sustaining peace scale for peacebuilding research.

## Concepts of peace and their measurement in contemporary scholarship

The conceptual debates on the matter of peace reach back to the classic works of the Greek and Roman philosophers, who perceived peace as a praised but temporary state, while war was a normal aspect of political life (Mallet 2017). Later, Machiavelli points to the general peacefulness of republics and localizes its causes in the equal distribution of values, leading to the sufficient satisfaction of citizens' needs. With a similar argument, Montesquieu defines peace and moderation as the 'spirit of republics' (Czempiel 1996: 80). The modern debate about the substance of peace begins with the work of Immanuel Kant. Kant's concept of a *perpetual peace* is based on the idea that states with republican constitutions tend to be peaceful with each other (Hoesch 2015).

Over time, philosophical and pragmatic conceptions of peace have changed and diversified. Although these early scholars recognized the centrality of peace, it was not until the end of the Second World War that peace studies emerged as an academic discipline with its own conceptual tools. Peace research and the range of definitions have revealed several patterns, which informed the theoretical and conceptual development of the sustaining peace scale introduced later on.

### *The notion of negative and positive peace*

In 1954, Quincy Wright and Fred Cottrell shared a prize offered by the Institute for Social Research in Oslo for the best paper on the relevance of research to the problems of peace. Peace, as Cottrell (1954: 99) defines it, 'is a situation in which governors of states limit their use of physical coercion to actors that are not likely to encounter extended, organized, and effective physical resistance'. Wright (1954) understands peace as a condition of stability arising from an adaptive equilibrium among numerous forces in the world community (military, legal, social and psychic) that push either towards war or towards peace. Wright was also the first to introduce a distinction between negative and positive aspects of peace, and understood negative peace as the elimination of violence and positive peace as 'the condition of a community in which order and justice prevail, internally among its members and externally in its relations with other communities' (Wright 1964: 864).

While a central part of Wright's work dealt with a systematic understanding of positive peace, Johan Galtung (1964, 1969) emphasizes the idea of multiple levels of peace. For Galtung, peace and violence are linked to each other in a continuous state: peace can be regarded as the absence of violence. Violence, in turn, can be direct and personal – human beings are physically hurt or killed – or indirect and structural, in which case the violence 'is buil[t] in the structure and shows up as unequal power and consequently as unequal life chances' (Galtung 1969: 171). Therefore, structural violence is also referred to as social injustice. Building on this distinction between personal and structural violence, peace, perceived as the absence of violence, also becomes two-sided.

*Negative peace* is synonymous with the absence of direct violence and the cessation of armed hostilities. Thus, peacebuilding approaches to achieve negative peace must aim at the removal of conflict 'by solving it or, more modestly, by transforming the conflict so that the parties can handle it in a nonviolent way' (Galtung 2008: 92). In contrast, *positive peace* adheres to the absence of any form of structural violence and is built around such ideas as harmony, cooperation, and integration. The role of peace research is to consider the negative and the positive aspects of peace (Galtung 1985). While Galtung's definition of positive peace is highly relevant and very exact, it is at the same time extremely broad (that is, the meaning of social justice), which results in a lack of clarity for measurement.

Kenneth Boulding (1978) makes another important contribution to the study of peace. Boulding articulates a theory of multicausal war–peace systems with the competing notions of *strain* and *strength*. In contrast to Wright and Galtung, he concentrates mainly on the concept of peace as the absence of war, and regards peace and war as alternating conditions of the relationship between social and political entities. The model is based on four general phases of war and peace that differ in the combination of strength and strain in the system and which can be expressed as a war–peace cycle. This cycle moves from unstable peace towards unstable war, leading to a phase of stable war, where war is virtually interminable. As the war proceeds, the war system can become weak and come under strain. At the same time, the underlying peace strength and the pressure for peace can rise, as people get tired of war. At this point, the cycle moves again towards unstable peace. If the peace system can remain dominant – because the strength is sufficiently larger than the strain – there is stable peace, which 'is a situation in which the probability of war is so small that it does not really enter into the calculations of any of the people involved' (Boulding 1978: 13). Even though Boulding never fully develops the operational components of either the stable war or stable peace systems, 'his argument did lay out the fragility of either system under conditions where the internal dynamics where not sufficiently robust to withstand the strains imposed on it' (Regan 2018: 83). This seems important in the context of civil wars because the stress and strengths of peace systems may influence whether war occurs or peace sustains.

The German peace researcher Ernst-Otto Czempiel (1977b) argues that in order to be useful in scholarly discussions, a definition of peace needs to be clearly conceptualized and multidimensional. Writing in the context of the Cold War, Czempiel (1977a) argues for using the term 'peace' exclusively for determining patterns of relationships in international politics. He derives his peace concept from a classical definition of nonwar and understands peace as an interpersonal relationship pattern characterized by increasing justice and diminishing violence. Czempiel rejects the strict dichotomization between negative and positive peace: conflict is perceived as a general condition and normal state of social relationships and peace; as such, it is not a conflict-free situation, but a state in which nonviolent conflict resolution methods are used. For him, peace is a continuous pattern in international relations (Czempiel 1977a: 29–30). Following the matrix in Table 2.1, peace is a state of the international system in which violence – directly or indirectly – diminishes and social justice increases. Czempiel sees peace as a process with negative and positive peace as the endpoints of this continuum. Like Galtung, Czempiel propagates an understanding of peace that goes beyond the negation of physical violence and includes additional value dimensions.

**Table 2.1:** Czempiel's matrix for the 'development' of peace within the framework of the international system

| | Patterns of the international system | | | |
| --- | --- | --- | --- | --- |
| | **Enmity** | **Coexistence** | **International organization** | **Integration** |
| Methods of conflict resolution | War, blockade | Pressure, compromise | Adaptation | 'Justice' |
| Instruments of conflict resolution | Weapons | Economic power | Conferences | Majority decisions |
| | Nonpeace | Development of peace from | | |
| | | negative to increasingly positive peace | | |

Source: Adapted from Czempiel (1977a: 30)

Almost every early identified definition of peace mentions the absence of violence as a necessary condition for peace, and a common argument given for focusing research on the explanations of war has always been that this research would eventually lead to conclusions for peace (Wallensteen 2012); however, knowing the factors that might lead to war is not the same as knowing the conditions for peace. More recently, there have been some efforts to establish peace concepts that go beyond the absence of war and move towards a notion of positive peace. A focus on justice is shared by John Paul Lederach (1999), who proposes the concept of *justpeace*, which refers to conflict resolution approaches aimed at reducing direct violence, while at the same time increasing justice in human relationships. He defines justpeace in three ways: (a) as a structure of human relationships characterized by high justice and low violence; (b) as a form of governance that responds to human conflict through nonviolent means as a first and last resort; and (c) as a whole system responsive to the interdependence of relationships.

To move the focus away from research on explanations of war and towards advancing the study of peace, Peter Wallensteen (2012) calls for a Correlates of Peace Project.[2] For him, peace has to be understood as being broad and inclusive. It is not only a matter of being without war for a certain period of time, but also includes maintaining conditions that do not produce war in the first place. Wallensteen's idea of *quality peace* includes 'the creation of postwar conditions that make the inhabitants of a society ... secure in life and dignity now, and for the foreseeable future' (Wallensteen 2015: 6). He also discusses several possible measurements for the elements of his definition of quality peace, but does not narrow them down to a limited set of indicators that could constitute an operational measure. Wallensteen is interested in conceptually advancing the academic discussion about peace, and his notion of quality peace represents a big step for peace research; however, his definition still relates to an understanding of peace as the absence of war recurrence and is associated with a previously terminated war, thus defined for postwar situations. To operationalize Wallensteen's definition of quality peace, recent studies rely on his concept as an underpinning and propose measures that should allow us to study peace directly rather than through war (Goertz et al 2016; Davenport et al 2018). These measures will be discussed later on in this chapter.

Some conclusions can be drawn from the discussion of various peace definitions and their conceptual development over time. First, all definitions have in common that they agree on the absence of violence as the lowest common denominator and a necessary condition for any understanding of peace. Second, several authors have proposed definitions that reflect a continuous understanding that progresses on a qualitative continuum of peace. This understanding of a peace–conflict continuum is central to the analyses in this book. Third, while some definitions have limited potential for operationalization, most do not, and without strong operational measurements, it is impossible to study the conditions under which peace can be built and maintained.

## Empirical measurements for peace

The expanded conceptualization of peace has subsequently led to methodological attempts to apply the notions of positive peace or quality peace in empirical studies of postwar societies. There have been few efforts to synthesize the different conceptions of peace and even fewer to provide systematic and measurable definitions. The discussion has never moved to systematic conceptualization, measurement and the production of data (Goertz et al 2016).

At the narrow end of definitions, peace is essentially about the absence of violence and is usually measured by means of war recurrence between the same combatants. Even though increasing scholarly attention has been devoted to the topic of war recurrence, the results on the rate of recurrence remain inadequate and contested.[3] Most studies use a five-year lapse to measure war recurrence and include the argument that between one quarter and one third of all ended conflicts revert to warfare (Collier et al 2008). Fortna (2004a) finds a recurrence rate of 41 per cent for civil wars that ended between the mid-1940s and the mid-1990s, and Walter (2004) endorses these findings with a similar relapse rate of 38 per cent. Call (2008) included only civil wars that were followed by a peacebuilding mission and accounts for a success rate of 60 per cent, which translates into a recurrence rate of 40 per cent. Similar results were provided by Hartzell et al (2001), who account for a recurrence rate of 37 per cent for five years for the peace agreements they examined.

All of these quantitative studies focusing on negative peace and the associated literature generally rely on a *battle–death view* of armed conflict, which defines wars in terms of the number of people killed. Negative peace is thus an event-based notion of the absence of armed conflict in which the event is the individual incidence of battle-death; however, 'such an approach is fundamentally unable to deal with peace, except as the absence of fatalities' (Goertz et al 2016: 4). Whereas war can be conceptualized as an event, peace resembles a process of multiple stages and characteristics. There is even less agreement on which characteristics constitute the essential core of sustaining peace.

There have been some efforts to establish peace measures that go beyond the absence of war. The comprehensive work *Making War and Building Peace* by Michael Doyle and Nicholas Sambanis (2006) still represents, to this point, the most serious quantitative effort to measure peacebuilding success beyond the absence of violence. The authors argue that self-sustaining peace should be the standard used to evaluate the success or failure of peace processes and apply two short-run measures of peacebuilding success to build on the conceptual work of Boulding (1964), and include the absence of low-level violence and a degree of political openness. Their lenient and negative standard focuses on the absence of large-scale violence and is conceptualized as *sovereign peace*: it 'requires an end to civil war, undivided sovereignty, no residual violence ... and no mass-level human rights abuses by the state' (Doyle and Sambanis 2006: 73). Their second peace measure, *participatory peace*, requires negative sovereign peace plus a minimum level of political openness, which they coded based on the Polity index. Out of their sample, 70 per cent were participatory peace failures and only 30 per cent were successes. Achieving only sovereign peace seems to be easier, with 56 per cent failures and 44 per cent successes. Following this moderate standard, peacebuilding success would thus be assessed by looking at the recurrence of hostilities and the quality of postwar governance.

In their book *The Puzzle of Peace*, Gary Goertz, Paul F. Diehl and Alexandru Balas (2016) move beyond defining peace as the absence of war and develop a broad explanation for an increasing peacefulness of the international system. To study peace in the international system, Goertz et al (2016) systematically conceptualize peace along a continuum of state relationships that can range from very hostile to very peaceful. The resulting interstate peace scale consists of five levels: (a) severe rivalry; (b) lesser rivalry; (c) negative peace (which constitutes the transition point of the peace scale); (d) warm peace; and (e) security communities. While severe rivalries are defined by a militarized foreign policy and the expectations of future conflicts, security communities are characterized by the absence of major territorial claims, institutions for conflict management, high levels of functional interdependence, and satisfaction with the status quo. The essential contribution of the study by Goertz et al lies in moving the discussion and conceptualization of peace away from being synonymous with the decline or absence of war; peace should be considered multidimensional and included in systematic studies on the causes of both negative and positive peace.

In a collaborative effort, Christian Davenport, Erik Melander and Patrick Regan (2018) explore the meaning of quality peace by providing three distinct measurements of a peace continuum that can be used in comparative research. Drawing on the work by Quincy Wright, Kenneth Boulding and Johan Galtung, Regan argues that 'peace is an equilibrium condition where resort to violence is minimal and where the highest quality of peace exists when the idea of armed conflict approaches the unthinkable' (Regan 2018: 79–80). As such, the quality of peace shifts along a continuum that is closely connected to the perceived risk of armed violence. Regan's *perceptual indicator of peace* focuses on risk from an economic vantage point and uses black market exchange rates and bond prices to capture a society's perception of risk regarding the current quality of peace (Regan 2018: 99). Drawing on a bond index by JPMorgan Chase and black market currency data, the indicator captures the underlying conflict risk in any society, but is unable to directly capture the conditions associated with peace or conflict.

The *relational indicator of peace* by Christian Davenport includes two components. First, peace should be seen as a dyadic, two-way relationship between distinct groups, one of which usually is the state, which can range from genocidal and warlike (opposition) to full, respectful and voluntary integration (mutuality). Second, peace should be considered on multiple levels (for example, international, regional, national and community) simultaneously because a country could be peaceful at one level of analysis and conflictual at another. Peace exists 'where a shared identity is imagined and pursued' and mutual respect for each other's identities exists (Davenport 2018: 153). Davenport conceptualizes the various levels of his peace scale and discusses existing databases that could be used to analyse his relational argument, yet he did not convert them into an index that would be applicable in comparative research.

Finally, Melander proposes a *Clausewitzian concept of quality peace* and defines his continuum through three elements: (a) violent means; (b) political compellence; and (c) violent emotion. On the lowest extreme point, war is defined as the instrumental use of extreme violence. At the opposite end of the scale, quality peace is understood as the 'conduct of politics with respect for the physical person of one's adversary, using consensual decision making, on the basis of strong equality values' (Melander 2018: 113). On the operational level, the different elements of the scale are measured by the absence of war, plus high respect for physical integrity rights, democratic political institutions and widespread respect for women's social rights. The final scale classifies countries on eight levels of quality peace and a first application of the data shows that Western countries overall experience high or very high-quality peace, while the quality of peace is generally very poor in Africa, the Middle East and South Asia. While the procedural approach proposed by Melander can include various dimensions in an operational indicator, it still relies on aggregate measures. Additionally, his proposed level of quality peace represents different concepts or categories, rather than a scaled continuum.

## The United Nations and peace

The UN is probably the most striking embodiment of the idea of peace in our time (Harfensteller 2011). Its core assignments, as declared by the UN Charter (1945: 2), are to 'save succeeding generations from the scourge of war' and to unite 'our strength to maintain international peace and security'. Even though peace is not directly defined in the Charter, the provisions provide sound reasons for assuming a fairly restrictive (or negative) interpretation of peace as the absence of international wars and not civil wars (White 2002). In contrast, the *Declaration on a Culture of Peace*, adopted by the UN General Assembly (UNGA) in 1999, hints at a much wider understanding of peace, recognizing 'that peace not only is the absence of conflict, but also require a positive, dynamic participatory process where dialogue is encouraged and conflicts are solved in a spirit of mutual understanding and cooperation' (UNGA 1999). The meaning of peace thus seems to have expanded over time and has moved away from solely defining it as the absence of war. This section traces the development of this wide understanding of peace and reflects on the question of what UN peace currently means, as well as the extent to which it differs from the original concept from 1945.

## *The concept of peace in the United Nations Charter and during the Cold War*

Even though 'peace' is the most frequently used term in the UN Charter, mentioned in 52 passages, it is never precisely defined in the treaty (Gareis and Varwick 2014). According to the records of the United Nations Conference on International Organization (UNCIO), peace was understood narrowly as the absence of war and military aggression with the nation state acting as the primary reference point. Peace was a passive state rather than an active process that had to be maintained among nations (Harfensteller 2011).

The UN founders agreed that the UN Security Council (UNSC) would bear the chief responsibility for the maintenance of world peace and security. Because of this monopoly on the use of force, in the early years, the UNSC's role in the UN system has often been defined as that of a 'policeman'. Unfortunately, the great powers never agreed on any kind of military force to be placed at the disposal of the UNSC. As a result, the UNSC could not fulfil its role during the Cold War, and 'the international policeman is walking around trying to keep nations from fighting each other, not only without a gun, but without even a club to help him do his job' (Lie 1949: 51). In its early years, the UNSC adopted 'a very restrictive approach to peace. It did this by placing the concept of threat to the peace solely in the context of interstate conflicts as a prelude to a determination of a breach of the peace' (White 2002: 50).

The scope and limits of the UNGA with regard to the maintenance of peace and security were the subject of intense discussions during the San Francisco Conference.[4] In the end, the UNGA was designed as a 'world forum of public opinion', with a discursive role in questions concerning peace and security (UNCIO 1945: vol IX, p 33). The UNGA is allowed to discuss any matters relating to international peace, but its power of decision is constrained in two ways: first, UNGA resolutions are not binding according to international law; and, second, the right to adopt resolutions is suspended in cases currently being discussed by the UNSC. Regarding the UN peace framework, the UNGA undertook efforts to conceptually frame peace and restrict it to certain characteristics. One of the first records of this attempt is the *Essentials of Peace* resolution, adopted in 1949, where the UNGA defines the requirements for an *enduring peace*: in addition to the absence of interstate aggression, these requirements also include the respect of human rights and 'efforts to achieve and sustain higher standards of living for all people' (UNGA 1949). Overall, most UNGA resolutions passed during the Cold War include narrow conceptions of peace that focus on the absence of war.

In the provisions in the UN Charter, the position of the UN Secretary-General (UNSG), as the chief civil servant in the field of international peace and security, was not designed to be an exceptionally big role. Most duties, such as the management of the UN Secretariat, are administrative. In contrast to the rather passive UNSG concept of the League of Nations, the UN Charter allocates the right of the UNSG to 'bring to the attention of the Security Council any matter which in his opinion may threaten the maintenance of international peace and security' (UN 1945: Article 99). In 1945, the UNSG's powers were limited to a modest reporting function, but the vague formulations in the Charter implied major possibilities for future UNSGs 'to shape the office and specify the Civil Servant's role' (Harfensteller 2011: 121). While the first UNSG, Trygve Lie (1946–1952), added some flesh to the UN's conflict resolution instruments and expanded his responsibilities in the realm of maintaining peace and security (Gaglione 2001), his successor, Dag Hammarskjöld (1953–1961), significantly contributed to shaping the role of the UN and establishing the UNSG's role as a political authority, especially in the field of peacekeeping.

### Embracing a broader concept of peace and security

Since 1990, there has been a fundamental conceptual change in UN peace and security policy as well as 'dramatic changes in both the volume and the nature of United Nations activities in the field of peace and Security' (UNSG 1995: para 4). Currently, the peace concept applied by the UNSC in its resolutions has broadened, especially regarding a wide concept of threats to peace. Examples for these nontraditional threats to peace include the deliberate targeting of civilian populations, the proliferation of small arms and light weapons, and the support of terrorist acts. Closely related to this development are the gradually broadening of the *security* concept during the 1990s and the emergence of the new concept of *human security*, which represents a renouncement of the state-centred concept of security towards a focus on the individual human life.[5]

Since the end of the Cold War, the UN concept of peace has widened from a narrow notion of negative peace to include the protection of human rights. Before 1990, the UNSC only considered two cases of human rights violations as a threat to peace: South Africa and Rhodesia (Frowein and Krisch 2002). After 1990, the repression of the civilian population was, for the first time, considered a threat to peace and security in the case of Iraq and followed by many situations where the UNSC condemned human rights violations as threats to peace, such as the conflicts in Sierra Leone and East Timor.[6] Today the UNSC 'focuses on the permanent absence of violence, building on stable societal structures of deeply fragmented societies after civil war' (Harfensteller 2011: 179). It has created a rich portfolio for its task of maintaining international peace and security under the authority of Chapters VI and VII of the UN Charter, developing a coherent approach to conflict prevention, conflict resolution and post-conflict peacebuilding.

The UNGA also continued its efforts to conceptually frame peace, underlining that 'peace not only is the absence of conflict, but also requires a positive, dynamic participatory process where dialogue is encouraged and conflicts are solved in a spirit of mutual understanding' (UNGA 1999). After the end of superpower rivalries, the UNGA talked about the emergence of new threats and later coined the new phrase 'global threats and challenges', which include 'international terrorism ... transnational organized crime, regional conflicts, poverty, unsustainable development, illicit drug trafficking, money-laundering, infectious diseases, environmental degradation, natural disasters' (UNGA 2003). Even though the UNGA urged the 'build[ing of] consensus on major threats and challenges' (UNGA 2005: para 8), a common definition regarding threats to peace has not yet been issued.

When Boutros Boutros-Ghali (1992–1996) became UNSG, the international system and the UN were undergoing tremendous changes. He released a landmark report that would significantly shape the future work of the UN. *An Agenda for Peace* (UNSG 1992) outlined ambitious aims for the future development of the UN and marked a new 'modus operandi for the UN in preventing and resolving conflict and in keeping and building peace' (Burgess 2001: xvi). To cope with the increased demand in UN peacekeeping operations, Boutros-Ghali restructured the UN Secretariat and created the Department for Peacekeeping Operations (DPKO), which provided increased institutional capacity for peacekeeping.

Like his predecessor, Kofi Annan (1997–2006) strongly influenced agenda setting at the UN and framed new ideas relating to peace and security. Reform of the UN was the centrepiece of his tenure as UNSG. He argued for a new understanding of peace and security based on a 'broader, more comprehensive concept of collective security: one that tackles new and old threats and addresses the security concerns of all states' (UNSG 2004: para 5). Regarding the field of the maintenance of peace and security, the establishment of the High-Level Panel on Threats, Challenges and Change and the adoption of the Responsibility to Protect (R2P) at the 2005 World Summit constitute Annan's biggest achievements.[7]

Ban Ki-moon (2007–2016) took up his predecessor's efforts to streamline the organization's work in various fields and to establish the UN as a servicing institution in a global world. He was also a vehement supporter of the R2P and provided considerable doctrinal specifications and strategies for its implementation (UNSG 2009a).

António Guterres took over the office as SG in 2017, during a time of immense challenges for the UN and world politics. He has made several proposals to reform the UN, the biggest one being the restructuring of the UN Secretariat (UNSG 2017): he proposed the establishment of a unified peace and security pillar, which is made up of the Department of Political and Peacebuilding Affairs (DPPA) and the Department of Peace Operations (DPO), within the secretariat.

The UN peace framework has become more comprehensive and currently consists of several normative dimensions and principles connected to a focus on peace and reveal an increasingly holistic view of peace. Those dimensions are democracy and good governance, justice and the rule of law, human rights and humanitarian law, the R2P, disarmament and sustainable development (Harfensteller 2011). Additionally, peace is no longer understood as a fixed status quo that might last for some time, but rather as a process, over time, with different possible stages.

## *The United Nations peacebuilding architecture*

In contrast to sanctions and blockades, the founders did not envision peace operations as a conflict resolution tool, so these operations are not part of the UN Charter. Peacekeeping essentially emerged from the failure of collective security as an acceptable and nonaggressive UN military presence during the Cold War, when the UN could not perform the collective security function for which it was originally created (Durch 1993). Traditional peacekeeping is based on the principles of consent from the conflict parties, impartiality and minimum use of force. Being freed from Cold War restrictions, peacekeeping moved from this traditional base towards complex and multidimensional missions, which combine traditional peacekeeping functions with the oversight of elections, the disarmament and demobilization of the armed forces involved in the conflict, human rights monitoring, and even the temporary administration and sovereignty over a country. Peace operations have become the tool of choice for conflict resolution, and parties in a conflict often formally request peace operations in peace agreements and ceasefires. Currently, the UN is the largest provider of international peace operations, with nearly 78,000 civilian and uniformed personnel serving in 11 peacekeeping operations across three continents (in addition to 22 special political missions).

As a reaction to this increased demand after the Cold War, the UNSC mandated that UNSG Boutros-Ghali prepare an analysis of the UN's peacekeeping actions. The resulting *Agenda for Peace* defined the various approved UN conflict resolution tools along a conflict continuum, ranging from preventive diplomacy to peacemaking, peacekeeping and peacebuilding. *Peacebuilding* is associated with the post-conflict phase and is defined as 'action to identify and support structures which will tend to strengthen and solidify peace in order to avoid a relapse into conflict' (UNSG 1992: para 21). This book follows the agenda's line of argument and understands peacebuilding as a range of efforts aimed at political, institutional, social and economic transformations in postwar societies for the purpose of sustaining peace.

The surge in demand for peace operations soon pointed to a large gap in the UN's institutional structure. The DPKO was overloaded with financial, logistical and human pressures, resulting in post-conflict situations that received too little attention (Barnett et al 2007). To close this institutional gap, Annan called for the creation of an intergovernmental Peacebuilding Commission (PBC) and a Peacebuilding Support Office (PBSO) within the UN Secretariat – institutionalizing peacebuilding at the highest international level.

At the same time, the DPKO was able to make progress towards establishing doctrines guiding UN peace operations in the field. The *United Nations Peacekeeping Operations Principles and Guidelines*, often referred to as the Capstone Doctrine, marked an important step towards clarifying the nature and purpose of UN peace operations and defined peacebuilding as 'a range of measures targeted to reduce the risk of lapsing or relapsing into conflict by strengthening national capacities at all levels for conflict management, and to lay the foundation for sustainable peace and development' (DPKO 2008: 18).

Since 2005, the work of the UN's peacekeeping and peacebuilding institutions has been regularly reviewed. The 2009 report highlighted the need for national ownership of the peace process and identified the most urgent and important peacebuilding objectives: (a) establishing basic safety and security; (b) building confidence in a peace process; (c) delivering basic services and initial peace dividends; and (d) restoring core government functions (UNSG 2009b). The 2014 report of the High-Level Independent Panel on Peace Operations highlighted several deficits regarding the sustainment of peace and acknowledged 'a widening gap between what is being asked of United Nations peace operations today and what they are able to deliver', as peace operations are often deployed in difficult environments where there is little or no peace to keep and they are thus unable to respond effectively (UNGA 2015). In 2016, the UNGA and the UNSC jointly adopted twin resolutions on the review of the UN peacebuilding architecture, in which they expressed their commitments towards building and sustaining peace (UNGA 2016; UNSC 2016). According to the resolutions, sustaining peace should be 'broadly understood as a goal and a process to build a common vision of a society, ensuring that the needs of all segments of the population are taken into account' in order to prevent the outbreak, escalation, continuation and recurrence of conflict (UNGA 2016: 2).

In his 2018 peacebuilding report, António Guterres stressed that sustaining peace is first and foremost a responsibility of UN member states, while the fragmentation of peacebuilding efforts across the UN system 'undermines its ability to support member states in their efforts to build and sustain peaceful societies and to respond early and effectively to conflicts and crises' (UNSG, 2018: para 7). He introduced a set of mutually reinforcing reforms to ensure coherence and accountability across the development, management and peace and security pillars of the UN Secretariat. The effect of these newest reforms remains to be seen, but peacebuilding has been officially linked to the purposes and principles of the UN charter and has been institutionalized at the highest organizational level. With the twin resolutions of 2016, the notion of sustaining peace has become part of the UN discourse, which 'makes emerging peacebuilding research on the success and failures of peace processes particularly relevant' (Joshi and Wallensteen 2018: 8).

## A way forward: conceptualizing sustaining peace

Despite the steady growth of research into the success or failure of peace processes and the increasing interest in identifying factors for successful peacebuilding, there are still no general explanations. There are also no measurements for peace that go beyond the absence of war. This book responds to calls by Regan (2014) and Diehl (2016), who draw attention to the need of comprehensive peace measures and the direct analysis of peace and its causes.

While the conceptual debate of defining peace beyond the absence of violence has gained some momentum during the last few years, little progress has been made in terms of providing actual measures for multidimensional peace concepts. The most common way of defining peace is still the absence of war; however, while the absence of war is a common denominator for many post-conflict countries, the characteristics and qualities of the subsequent peace vary considerably (Höglund and Söderberg Kovacs 2010). This book contributes to the emerging research agenda by providing a fine-grained and nuanced picture of peace in societies that emerge from armed conflicts. Building on Boulding's (1978) relational war–peace cycle, Czempiel's (1977a) multidimensional notion of peace as a continuous process pattern and Wallensteen's (2015) discussion of quality peace, the proposed sustaining peace scale breaks the dichotomy of negative-versus-positive peace and defines particular elements of quality, beyond the absence of war.

Hence, this book adopts a quality peace perspective (Joshi and Wallensteen 2018) by focusing on the post-conflict process of changes in three basic dimensions: (a) security; (b) political; and (c) socioeconomic.[8] The following sections discuss the definition, conceptualization and empirical relevance of the sustaining peace scale as a means to measure peacebuilding success.

### Definition

The fundamental purpose of peacebuilding remains the establishment of conditions for stable and lasting peace in countries that experienced armed conflicts or civil wars. Thus, the aim is to generate a definition that enables the analysis of various steps of peacebuilding success and simultaneously makes allowances for the characteristics of post-conflict societies. As has been mentioned earlier, in most empirical analyses, peace is defined negatively, as merely the absence of war or violence: 'what is missing from these analyses, and even from their critics, is a clear conception of what it means for actors to be at peace, which moves beyond the inadequate not-war conceptualization' (Goertz et al 2016: 3). This is particularly crucial, since peace is much more than the absence of war.

A separate definition for sustaining post-conflict peace has not been previously developed, even though the fragile peace after armed conflicts is very distinctive from the well-established peaceful societies in, for example, Western Europe. A peace concept based on post-conflict characteristics would allow for specific analyses and a clear assessment of peacebuilding efforts undertaken by the UN and various international actors. As has been discussed in the previous section, there have been efforts to establish peace concepts that go beyond the absence of war (Wallensteen 2015; Davenport et al 2018; Goertz et al 2016), but an operationalized peace concept for the analysis of post-conflict situations is still missing. To fill this gap, this book considers peace as a continuum and introduces a broad range of possible states of post-conflict peacefulness.

In keeping with its central aim – avoiding relapse into war – peacebuilding is considered to be successful if it results in sustaining peace. Relating to the UN's broad understanding of *sustaining peace* as a process to build a common vision of a society (UNGA 2016), the following concrete definition of sustaining peace has been established: sustaining peace is defined as the absence of violence or fear of violence, combined with an adapted level of political and socioeconomic development, which, taken together, create and sustain peaceful societies that emerge from armed conflicts. The concept of sustaining peace thus moves beyond the notion of nonrecurrence of armed conflict and towards a notion of peace that, in addition to the security dimension, incorporates political, economic and social changes in societies emerging from armed conflict.

## Concept structure of sustaining peace

In order to analyse the mechanisms of sustaining peace, it is necessary to define the constitutive elements of the phenomenon and translate the theoretical definition to a conceptual structure. The concept formation is based on set theory and set logic, as the structure of necessary and sufficient conditions forms the basis for building concepts. Additionally, following fuzzy logic, I assume that dimensions are continuous and that a dichotomous dimension would represent a special case. Like most comprehensive concepts, sustaining peace is multidimensional and multilevel in nature and follows the three-level structure, suggested by Goertz (2006), as a way to construct concepts.[9] According to this structure, a concept consists of basic level, secondary level, and indicator or data level. With regard to the combination of different levels, the multilevel concept of sustaining peace is structured by necessary and sufficient conditions (Sartori 1970).

The concept of sustaining peace will be put forward by: (a) presenting the different level of the structure; (b) considering the number of dimensions at each level; and (c) discussing the substantive content of each of the dimensions at each level. The basic level is based on the theoretical definition of sustaining peace and conceptualized as a continuum between the positive and negative poles. Building on previous work by Boulding (1978) and Czempiel (1977a), I describe sustaining peace as a multicausal war–peace system based on a continuous relationship pattern, characterized by increasing justice and diminishing violence. Defining sustaining peace as a process pattern is both precise, in that it absolutely separates peace from any form of violence, and fundamental, in that it perceives the basis of sustaining peace in justice as an essential prerequisite. Following Figure 2.1, sustaining peace is a continuous state in which violence – directly or indirectly – diminishes and social justice increases.

At the positive pole of the continuum, sustaining peace is present when there is no residual violence, human and political rights are evenly respected, and societies sustain reasonable economic development and gender equality. In contrast, sustaining peace is completely absent at the negative pole, which is characterized by the recurrence of civil war and missing respect for political or social rights. This negative pole is identical to traditional measures of peacebuilding failure. The grey zone between these two poles includes cases that are characterized by negative peace (that is, no conflict recurrence), but where political and social rights are frequently violated. The underlying continuum between the negative and positive poles of the sustaining peace concept is based on six degrees of sustaining peace.

**Figure 2.1:** The sustaining peace continuum

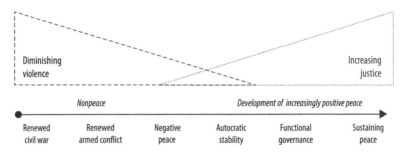

**Figure 2.2:** The three-level concept structure of sustaining peace

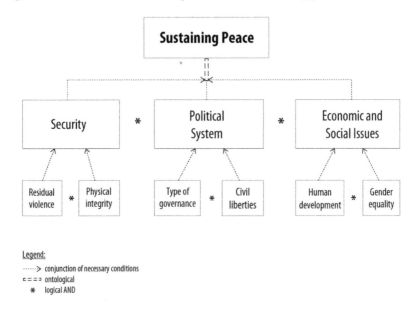

The multidimensional character of the concept becomes apparent at the secondary level, which consists of three constitutive dimensions, forming the ontological analysis of this concept (Goertz 2006). Sustaining peace has been defined as a relationship with three necessary and sufficient conditions: (a) the guarantee of security and absence of personal violence; (b) effective and legitimate political system; and (c) reasonable economic and social development (see Figure 2.2). These three dimensions are attributed to the claim of moving beyond the inadequate not-war conceptualization, and each represents an extension of the concept towards a notion of positive peace. The security dimension constitutes the basis for peaceful relations, the political system allows for the inclusion of citizens in the political process, and the economic and social dimension is scratching at the elements of positive peace.

The security dimension evaluates whether a post-conflict country can restore and maintain its monopoly on the legitimate use of physical force and discourage the combatants from returning to war. Focusing on the absence of large-scale violence represents a minimalist standard of peace and is closest to Galtung's (1969) concept of negative peace. The creation of a secure environment goes along with the guarantee of personal security, as both are necessary for any measure of peace. The political dimension takes the quality of postwar governance into account and is concerned with the legitimacy and effectiveness of postwar governments, and whether they respect the civil rights of their citizens. The socioeconomic dimension goes one step further by indicating that some economic and social variables can constitute strong risk factors for war recurrence. Thus, in order for a post-conflict situation to be classified as sustaining peace, there must have been some improvement regarding the societal conditions that had reinforced the previous violent conflict (Hartzell 2014). Taken together, these three necessary dimensions are sufficient components of sustaining peace.

The next and last level of the concept structure is called the *indicator* or *data* level and involves the actual operationalization of the concept. Data are gathered for six indicators, which permit the categorization of a fine-grained scale that allows for the classification of individual cases on the concept scale. The indicator level provides a solid empirical foundation for the theoretical definition of sustaining peace. The concept structure is formalized – or translated into a quantitative measure – by the mathematics of (fuzzy) logic and set theory, implying the necessary and sufficient structures of the secondary and indicator levels are mathematically modelled by logical AND (minimum) or the intersection in set theory.

The indicators *residual violence* and *physical integrity* are associated with the security dimension and evaluate whether a country can provide physical security for its citizens by means of the potential recurrence of armed conflict and the government's respect for physical integrity rights. The political dimension assesses the type of governance and whether a postwar government respects the political rights of its citizens. The indicator *civil liberties* reflects the extent to which the rights (freedom of religion, freedom of movement and freedom from forced labour) of a country's citizens are protected by their government. Derived from the democratic peace theory, it is assumed that the threshold for violent action to combat oppositional uprisings and violent conflict escalation is lower in autocracies than in democracies (Doyle 1986, 1996; Geis et al 2007). The indicators of the socioeconomic dimension evaluate how well a state guarantees the equality of its citizens and provides for a reasonable development. *Economic development* has been identified as essential for successful peacebuilding

(Collier et al 2003) and *gender equality* represents an indispensable part of peaceful social relations.

## The sustaining peace scale

Since the concept structure is formalized by means of set-theoretic reasoning, the continuous nature of the sustaining peace concept can be expressed by six qualitative degrees of peacefulness: (a) renewed civil war; (b) renewed armed conflict; (c) negative peace; (d) autocratic stability; (e) functional governance; and (f) sustaining peace (see Table 2.2). In this way, sustaining peace is calibrated along a continuum rather than as an all-or-nothing state (Regan 2014; Goertz et al 2016). This calibration leads to two conceptual points that distinguish this scale from previously applied indicators used to measure peacebuilding success: (a) peace is defined as much more than the absence of war; and (b) peace is understood as a relationship, not an event. This section describe the essential components for each category of the sustaining peace scale, discusses the indicators or characteristics, and presents examples that will be used as anchor cases (Ragin 2000).

### Nonpeace

The left side of the scale can be characterized as the most hostile post-conflict environment, where peace is completely absent and belligerents have engaged in another high-intensity civil war. The nonpeace level of the scale focuses on the security dimension, as issues of security are critical and can derail the entire peace process (Joshi and Wallensteen 2018). Security concerns are especially acute after the armed conflict has come to an end because commitment problems might cause the peace process to fail: 'commitment problems occur because neither the government nor the rebels can credibly commit themselves to uphold the negotiated settlement in the future' (Mattes and Savun 2009: 739). However, in the event of conflict recurrence, the intensity of renewed violence matters, as sporadic incidences of violence against civilians are qualitatively different from armed conflicts or full-blown civil wars. *Missing peace* is defined as the recurrence of civil war. Following the coding of the UCDP/PRIO Armed Conflict Dataset, a conflict is defined as a civil war if it results in at least 1,000 battle-related deaths in a given year. The indicator of residual violence thus measures whether a subsequent civil war has been fought by the same combatants and for the same goals.

An anchor case for missing peace is the peace process after the civil war in Angola (1975–1995), which was fought between the government of Angola and the União Nacional para a Independência Total de Angola (UNITA) over government control. After the end of the Cold War, several rounds of peace talks resulted in the Lusaka Protocol (1994), which established a government

**Table 2.2:** Conceptualization of the sustaining peace scale

| | Sustaining peace scale | | | | | |
|---|---|---|---|---|---|---|
| | Nonpeace | | Negative peace | | Development towards positive peace | |
| Indicator | Missing | Armed conflict | Negative peace | Autocratic stability | Functional governance | Sustaining peace |
| **Security dimension** | | | | | | |
| 1. Residual violence | Occurrence of civil war | Occurrence of armed conflict | Sporadic violent incidences | Absent | Absent | Absent |
| 2. Physical integrity | | | Not respected | Frequently violated | Limited amount of violations possible | Generally respected |
| **Political dimension** | | | | | | |
| 3. Type of governance | | | | Autocratic | Minimally democratic | Democratic |
| 4. Political and civil liberties | | | | None or very restricted | Restricted or unevenly protected | Moderately protected |
| **Socioeconomic dimension** | | | | | | |
| 5. Human development | | | | Low | Low | Medium |
| 6. Gender equality | | | | | Low level of women empowerment | Moderate/high level of women empowerment |
| Anchor cases | Angola (1975–1995) | Burundi (1994–2006), Papua New Guinea (1990) | Liberia (1989–1990), Sudan (1983–2005) | Angola (1998–2002), DRC (2005–2008) | Mozambique (1977–1992), Nepal (1996–2006) | Guatemala (1965–1995), Liberia (2000–2003) |

of national unity and provided for the demobilization of UNITA; however, the accord was not supported by UNITA leader Jonas Savimbi. Due to failing disarmament, UNITA was suspended from the government in 1998, and the civil war returned, with massive offensives by the Angolan military to recapture territory held by UNITA.

The *armed conflict* level of the sustaining peace scale captures post-conflict episodes that are not re-escalating as full-blown civil wars, but are still characterized by significant violence and insecurity. It is the severity element that distinguishes this category from missing peace. In line with the UCDP/PRIO definition, an episode is categorized as renewed armed conflict if the subsequent use of armed force between the same combatants and for the same goals results in at least 25 battle-related deaths in a calendar year.

Anchor cases include the post-conflict episode after the Burundian Civil War (1994–2006) and the territorial conflict over Bougainville in Papua New Guinea (1990). In Burundi, the conflict over the distribution of governmental power between the Tutsi minority and Hutu majority led to an armed conflict, resulting in nearly 9,000 conflict-related deaths. After many failed negotiation efforts, the Comprehensive Ceasefire Agreement signed between the government and the Palipehutu Forces nationales de liberation (FNL) terminated the conflict and stipulated the demobilization and transformation of the rebel organization into a political party; however, splinter groups of the FNL soon continued the violence on a low-scale level until the conflict was finally ended by a full peace agreement in 2009. In Bougainville, an island located in the far east of Papua New Guinea, the Bougainville Revolutionary Army (BRA) fought an armed struggle for independence, until the Papua New Guinean government withdrew and set up a blockade of the island in 1990. As civilians on Bougainville suffered severely under the blockade, conflict soon resumed.

### Negative peace

Between a backslide into renewed civil war or armed conflict and the development towards a notion of positive peace lies what has been referred to in various studies as negative peace (Galtung 1969), stable peace (Boulding 1978) or cold peace (Miller 2001). Following Galtung (1969), *negative peace* is defined as the absence of physical violence during the peacebuilding episode. The absence of residual violence is an indication for a state's ability to maintain peace within its borders and to provide basic physical and human security to its citizens. In addition to battle-related deaths, research has also focused on the deliberate use of violence against civilians as a war strategy and has measured the number of civilians killed to identify cases of specific civilian targeting (Eck and Hultman 2007; Wood et al 2012). Those sporadic violent incidences might still occur, even though armed conflict has stopped.

The negative peace level of the scale thus captures peacebuilding episodes which are characterized by a sustained absence of overt militarized conflict.

A second indicator is added to the security dimension to capture the personal effects of physical security. It addresses whether state-based political violence, which is defined as the absence of respect for physical integrity rights, extends to a country's population (Clark and Sikkink 2013). If those individual rights are not respected by a post-conflict government, the peacebuilding episode cannot move beyond the state of negative peace. Physical integrity rights are based on international humanitarian law and include an individual's protection from arbitrary physical harm and coercion by their government (Cingranelli and Richards 1999). Government violations of these rights, sometimes called 'state sanctioned terror' (Fariss 2014: 301), usually include extrajudicial executions, beatings and torture, disappearances, arrests and political imprisonment. It is expected that the level of government respect for different types of human rights increase with a development towards sustaining peace.

The first anchor case for the negative peace level is represented by the peacebuilding episode after the first Liberian Civil War. In 1989, Charles Taylor's National Patriotic Front of Liberia (NPFL) launched a brutal rebellion against the authoritarian government of Samuel K. Doe, who was subsequently tortured and murdered by Taylor's henchmen. While Liberia was then officially governed by an Interim Government of National Unity (IGNU) protected by UN and Economic Community of West African States (ECOWAS) forces, Taylor maintained control of the vast majority of Liberian territory, which he ruled as 'Greater Liberia' (Reno 1993). While the country was officially at peace, political violence, looting and displacement continued to affect much of the civilian population, making this peacebuilding episode a textbook example for negative peace. The second anchor case is the peacebuilding episode after the territorial conflict over South Sudan (1983–2005) in which the Sudan's Peoples Liberation Movement/Army (SPLM/A) fought against the Khartoum regime for secession of the region, until the Comprehensive Peace Agreement signed in 2005 established a government of national unity and provided for a referendum to be held in 2011. Even though the overall situation improved, tensions remained high in the region and violent incidences occurred regularly.

*Development towards positive peace*

On the positive peace side of the scale, two additional dimensions are added to the concept, taking the type of governance and socioeconomic changes in societies emerging from conflict into account. As sustaining peace is multidimensional, these two dimensions are crucial for the quality of the resulting peace. Governance issues have been included in many peacebuilding studies and democratic political systems, and strong inclusive institutions are generally expected to contribute to the duration of peace (Walter 2015). With regard to the third dimension of the sustaining peace scale, the lack of economic wellbeing remains a main cause of armed conflicts (Collier et al 2003; Fearon and Laitin 2003), and economic reconstruction should be a priority for post-conflict societies. This reconstruction usually includes the restoration of devastating war economies into market economies and the creation of economic opportunities for the broad population to create potentials for economic growth (Castillo 2008). Regarding post-conflict security, all cases situated on the right side of the scale experience the complete absence residual violence, including both armed conflict and the deliberate use of violence against civilians.

The *autocratic stability* level captures cases in which armed conflict and one-sided violence are absent, but the government frequently violates the physical integrity rights of its citizens. On the political dimension, those post-conflict states are governed by autocratic regimes, which commonly restrict or suppress political competition and political and civil freedoms. Regarding economic reconstruction and human development, those cases can experience low to medium levels of development and even economic growth; however, the autocratic type of governance remains the distinctive characteristic of this level as it has a very strong impact on the quality of post-conflict peace.

The peacebuilding episode after the Angolan Civil War (1998–2002) serves as an anchor case for autocratic stability. In 2002, the Angolan government troops made significant advances on UNITA, and in February, Savimbi and other rebel generals were killed in a government ambush (Arnson and Zartman 2005: 120). The parties agreed to a ceasefire and soon initiated the demobilization of UNITA and its transformation into a political party; however, the power is concentrated in the president, who represents the ruling People's Movement for the Liberation of Angola (MPLA). Angola is classified as 'not free' by the Freedom House Index, as parliamentary elections usually suffer from serious flaws and state authorities repress political dissent. In addition, physical integrity rights are frequently violated, with human rights abuses,[10] including cruel and excessive punishment (torture and beatings) and unlawful killings by police and other security personnel.

The *functional governance* level captures post-conflict episodes characterized by political systems transitioning towards democracy, where personal and civil liberties might still be restricted and human development and gender equality have only been achieved at a low level. Regarding post-conflict security, conflict-related and one-sided violence against civilians are absent, but government violations of physical integrity rights sometimes occur. Post-conflict states on this level are at least minimally democratic, but the government might only weakly respect and still restrict civil liberties.

Regarding the socioeconomic dimension, post-conflict states can suffer from a weak economy and low human development. The scale is expanded at this level by a sixth indicator, to also capture the aspect of gender equality. For the development towards an inclusive and egalitarian post-conflict society, men and women need to be given the same rights and abilities to participate in political processes. At the level of functional governance, women's empowerment[11] is still low, so overall, women have fewer opportunities to participate in societal decision making or to hold formal political positions.

The civil war in Mozambique (1977–1992) and the subsequent peacebuilding episode represents an anchor case for functional governance. The conflict was fought between the Frente de Libertação de Moçambique (FRELIMO) government and the Resistência Nacional Moçambicana (RENAMO) armed opposition until a peace agreement was reached in 1992. The UN Operation in Mozambique (ONUMOZ) was subsequently deployed to oversee the implementation of the agreement and multiparty elections, which were won by FRELIMO. Since then, the ruling party has dominated politics and has established a significant control over state institutions. In addition, Mozambique is still one of the poorest and most underdeveloped countries, ranking number 180 out of 189 on the Human Development Index, which depicts a risk of future conflict (UNDP 2019).

At the positive extreme or endpoint of the peace continuum, post-conflict societies experience *sustaining peace*. This level corresponds to the UN's broad understanding of sustaining peace, which aims at building peaceful societies based on good governance and the strong rule of law, sustainable economic growth and social development, gender equality, and respect for human rights and fundamental freedoms. Post-conflict states at this level of the scale usually work on addressing root causes of the conflict and establishing mechanisms to prevent the recurrence or escalation of conflict, while the society moves towards recovery, reconstruction and development. Six related core characteristics define the level of sustaining peace: (a) absence of armed conflict and one-sided violence; (b) government respect for physical integrity rights; (c) democratic governance; (d) at least moderate respect for civil liberties; (e) reasonable human development; and (f) a moderate level of gender equality. While these categories are still miles away from Galtung's (1969) ideal of positive peace, they represent a realistic and achievable starting point for societies emerging from armed conflict. If peacebuilding initiatives in a post-conflict situation can lead to sustaining peace, the endeavour should be coded as a success.

An anchor case that illustrates the sustaining peace level is the peacebuilding episode after the second Liberian Civil War (2000–2003), which was fought between Charles Taylor's government forces and the two rebel groups Liberians United for Reconciliation and Democracy (LURD) and Movement for Democracy in Liberia (MODEL). Peace talks, facilitated by ECOWAS, resulted in the signing of the Accra Comprehensive Peace Agreement in August 2003, which provided for a two-and-a-half-year transitional government, before elections were held at the end of 2005. The new government under President Ellen Johnson-Sirleaf continued the demobilization and reintegration of the former rebel factions and implemented a comprehensive reform of the security sector. Overall, the post-conflict environment has been relatively stable and secure, and physical integrity rights are generally respected. In addition, women's organizations have played an important role during the peace process, and women's participation in the National Legislature of Liberia had risen to 13.5 per cent in 2011 (Cole 2001). Liberia's economy is still heavily dependent on foreign aid and foreign direct investments, but after the end of the second Civil War, gross domestic product (GDP) growth increased significantly alongside life expectancy and overall education levels.

Overall, the sustaining peace scale allows for a fine-grained assessment of a country's post-conflict peace and enables substantial analyses regarding the success of peacebuilding efforts. The three dimensions of the sustaining peace scale are interconnected and depict a country's post-conflict capacities. Sustaining peace has been achieved when there is: (a) no residual violence; (b) human and political rights are evenly respected; and (c) the society manages to sustain a reasonable economic development and gender equality. Successful peacebuilding is thus understood as the creation of sustaining peace.

## A descriptive outline of sustaining peace in post-conflict settings

This section takes a closer look at how successful peacebuilding approaches are in terms of establishing sustaining peace after armed conflicts and civil wars, and provides a first empirical overview of peacebuilding success after negotiated settlements. Based on the sustaining peace scale, it presents data on 54 intrastate peacebuilding episodes, initiated between 1989 and 2016, through the signing of a peace agreement. The selected cases were examined for their five-year post-conflict performance using the indicators for the three dimensions of sustaining peace discussed earlier.

As has been highlighted previously, most peacebuilding analyses use the nonrecurrence of civil war or armed conflict as an indicator of success. It is thus wise to take a look at the outcomes of the selected peacebuilding episodes (see Figure 2.3). Out of the 54 postwar transitions, only one relapsed into civil war (2 per cent). If this type of negative peace was taken as the indicator of success, it would leave us with a success rate of 98 per cent, which represents a huge deviation from the 28 per cent measured with the sustaining peace scale. The picture gets a little better when one includes the 13 cases that relapse into armed conflict, but this more comprehensive measure of negative peace still results in a success rate of 74 per cent.

**Figure 2.3:** Comparison of different measures for peacebuilding success according to the selected data

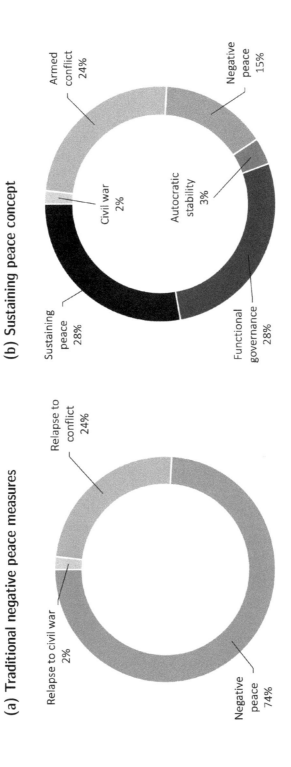

(a) Traditional negative peace measures

(b) Sustaining peace concept

The sustaining peace scale divides this ill-defined negative peace category into four distinct states of post-conflict peacefulness – negative peace (15 per cent), autocratic stability (4 per cent), functional governance (27 per cent) and sustaining peace (27 per cent) – providing a nuanced picture of peacebuilding processes and their outcomes. The sustaining peace scale thus provides a novel way to analyse post-conflict peacebuilding and expands the current analytical spectrum. Taken together, traditional indicators measuring negative peace miss a lot of information regarding post-conflict transitions and cannot differentiate between different levels of peace. The sustaining peace scale can highlight these differences and provides a realistic picture of peacebuilding success.

According to the case distribution across the whole spectrum of the sustaining peace scale, 58 per cent of the peacebuilding episodes demonstrate outcomes on the positive side of the scale (including autocratic stability, functional governance and sustaining peace), meaning they are rather members of the sustaining peace concept than nonmembers; however, only 15 cases (or 27 per cent) exhibit a complete membership in the concept and satisfy all criteria of the sustaining peace scale. The data are not disproportionally skewed towards one side of the scale, but instead are balanced between the two poles. However, a closer look at the regional composition of the different outcome values provides evidence of an uneven distribution of sustaining peace in the world (see Figure 2.4). Only five African cases can achieve complete membership in sustaining peace, while half of the peacebuilding episodes in Africa are found in the lower part of the scale.

Eighty per cent of the peacebuilding episodes in the Americas experienced either sustaining peace or functional governance, and the same

**Figure 2.4:** Patterns of peacebuilding success across regions, 1989–2016

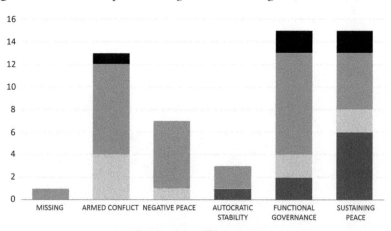

is true for eight out of nine European cases, of which six even resulted in sustaining peace. The Asian sample presents mixed results, as four out of nine peacebuilding episodes either resulted in sustaining peace and functional governance or in renewed armed conflicts. Altogether, sustaining peace seems to be more likely after internal armed conflicts in Europe or the Americas, with Asian and African peacebuilding episodes displaying mixed results. This regionally unbalanced distribution of successful cases will also play a role in later chapters when it comes to performing cluster analyses. For the moment, peacebuilding success differs across regions and further research is needed to uncover the relevant determinants explaining this difference.

The success of peacebuilding episodes might also vary over time. Figure 2.5 provides an overview about the absolute number of peacebuilding episodes initiated in intervals from 1989 until 2016. Obviously, two details are striking, namely that most peacebuilding episodes were initiated between 1989 and 1999 (59 per cent) and that the success rates are mixed. Since its peak in the early 1990s, the number of armed conflicts has globally declined by more than one third, which also resulted in a decline of initiated peacebuilding episodes.

Regarding the average distribution of peacebuilding success, the second interval (1995–1999) performs best, with 83 per cent of peacebuilding episodes initiated during that time resulting in a successful implementation (autocratic stability, functional governance or sustaining peace). In comparison, the odds for successful peacebuilding were less promising for conflicts that ended between 2010 and 2016, as 80 per cent of them resulted in negative peace or renewed armed conflict. The success rates of peacebuilding episodes thus vary over time, with earlier peacebuilding processes being more likely to experience sustaining peace. It is especially striking that since 2005, none of the cases was able to achieve complete peacebuilding success.

As this first empirical application has demonstrated, the sustaining peace scale provides a new way to analyse post-conflict situations and expands the current analytical spectrum. It is primarily designed to facilitate the application of set-theoretic methods within peacebuilding research, but could easily be adapted for qualitative or statistical analyses. Within the realms of this chapter, it was only possible to provide a preliminary overview. To unravel the underlying mechanisms leading to sustaining peace, further empirical studies are needed to identify the relevant factors.

## Summary

The starting point of this conceptual chapter was the question of how best to assess successful peacebuilding after intrastate wars and armed conflicts. While nearly all reviewed definitions of peace and peacebuilding success

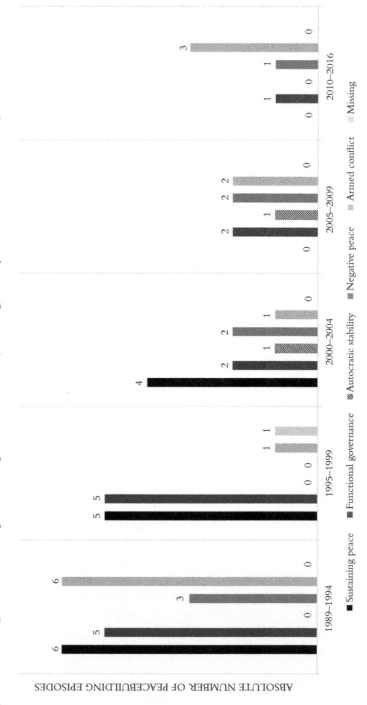

**Figure 2.5:** Average distribution of peacebuilding success over time (according to the year of conflict termination)

agree on the absence of violence as the lowest common denominator for any understanding of peace, what exactly this *peace* includes remains contested. Overall, any peace concept is invariably normatively charged and, at best, multidimensional, in that it includes more than just the absence of armed conflict. While most of the early concepts have only limited potential for empirical operationalization, current efforts of applying the notion of positive or quality peace in empirical studies of postwar societies and their peacebuilding transitions appear promising for differentiated analyses of peacebuilding success and distinct policy recommendations.

The peace discourse within the UN has also acknowledged the need for a comprehensive peace concept and differentiated criteria for peacebuilding success. Overall, the UN peace framework has become more comprehensive and now consists of several normative dimensions and principles (such as democracy, justice and the rule of law, human rights and the R2P) that are connected to its peace core. Additionally, peace is no longer understood as a fixed status quo that might last for some time, but rather as a continuous process over time, including multiple possible stages. With the twin resolutions of 2016, the notion of sustaining peace has become institutionalized in UN discourse and practices, and is generally understood 'as a goal and a process to build a common vision of a society, ensuring that the needs of all segments of the population are taken into account' to prevent the outbreak, escalation, continuation and recurrence of conflict (UNGA 2016: 2).

Building on the UN's understanding of sustaining peace and previous academic discussions reflecting a continuous understanding of peace (Czempiel 1977a; Boulding 1978), I introduced the sustaining peace scale as a measure for peacebuilding success that breaks out of the dichotomy of negative versus positive peace by defining particular elements of quality beyond the absence of war. In this book, peacebuilding approaches are successful if they lead to the establishment of sustaining peace, which has been defined as the absence of violence or fear of violence combined with an adapted level of political and socioeconomic development, which, taken together, create and sustain peaceful societies that emerge from armed conflicts. This concept moves beyond the traditional notion of nonrecurrence of armed conflict and towards a notion of peace that, in addition to the security dimension, incorporates political, economic and social changes in societies emerging from armed conflicts.

The aim of this chapter has been to establish the conceptual groundwork for the following empirical analyses. The sustaining peace scale forms the basis for answering the research questions raised in this book. The multiple levels of peacefulness allow me to make significantly more nuanced assessments than the simple absence-of-war concept. The scale has been introduced as a richer concept of peace that takes the specific characteristics of post–conflict situations into account and can be used to analyse the conditions and mechanisms of successful peacebuilding. However, the concept of sustaining peace is operating on the macrolevel and is thus unable to cover local peace processes or to adequately determine how civilians in post-conflict societies are affected by the peace process or whether they are experiencing meaningful changes in their lives (Richmond 2006; Mac Ginty 2010).

3

# Liberal Peacebuilding, Path Dependence and Commitment Problems

As there are currently no grand theories in International Relations (IR) about the termination of intrastate conflicts or post-conflict peacebuilding, the field is characterized by 'a growing collection of partial, mid-range theories, which are largely the result of the analytic and methodological choice in favor of process and mechanisms' (Checkel 2015: 77). No explicit theory of peacebuilding exists, and scholarly and practical understandings of the term differ considerably with regard to the approaches used, the scope of activities and the timeframes (Barnett et al 2007). Additionally, various theoretical perspectives have offered a myriad of potential explanations as to why and how armed conflicts are resolved, endure, or recur (Fearon and Laitin 2003; Collier and Hoeffler 2004; Walter 2004; Ross 2006; Toft 2010; Cederman et al 2011; Mason et al 2011).

This book adopts a liberal intuitionalist perspective towards the study of peacebuilding interventions, treating peacebuilding agents as rational actors, emphasizing the temporal dimension of peacebuilding, and arguing that temporal processes might generate and reinforce actor preferences, power relations and material interests. International peacebuilding approaches usually focus on the establishment of new institutions and state capacity, which are expected to form the basis for effective and legitimate governance. The focus is on the institutional configurations in those approaches and the interacting processes that shape the peacebuilding process (Pierson and Skocpol 2002). Hence, peacebuilding institutions are considered as important causal conditions at the heart of peacebuilding processes, being able to generate sustaining peace. The term 'institutions' is used broadly to describe formal rules, norms and policy structures that organize and constitute social relations in post-conflict societies, and which are expected to interact, resulting in alternative causal paths that structure the post-conflict political order and lead to sustaining peace (Keohane 1988). The combined analytical framework is highly compatible with a set–theoretic approach toward the analysis of conditions for successful peacebuilding.

The aim of this chapter is to establish the analytical framework of this book by merging a liberal institutionalist peacebuilding approach with historical institutionalism (HI) and bargaining theory to explain the establishment of sustaining peace in post-conflict societies. Therefore, it starts with an outline of liberal peacebuilding, its different sectoral activities and the critical debate surrounding it. The second section introduces HI and its value for peacebuilding research. I argue for an institutionalist understanding of peacebuilding, where interventions are understood as critical junctures, setting up political institutions that develop in a path–dependent manner. Third, the bargaining model of war is discussed as a rationalist explanation for problems inherent to durable settlements of armed conflicts, which must be addressed by peacebuilding operations. The three approaches are then combined into an analytical framework used for the selection of the causal conditions included in the empirical analysis. The last section discusses institutional peacebuilding conditions that define post-conflict structures of societies emerging from armed conflict and their expected impact on the establishment of sustaining peace. The chapter concludes with a summary of the main points.

## Underlying assumptions and conceptual foundations of a peacebuilding theory

The theoretical framework for the arguments made in this book is based on the large body of literature on peacebuilding and the so-called liberal peace, which is most prominently pursued by the UN (Paris 2010). Even though the approach has been identified as being in a state of crisis, its rhetoric still has primacy in the area of conflict resolution and peacebuilding. Most peace operations and international interventions in post-conflict countries are still framed by a neoliberalizing agenda. Thus, it is important to understand the central components of this 'chief organizing idea and operational system' (Mac Ginty 2006: 190) behind current peacebuilding operations to analyse the nature and underlying mechanisms of this approach and to identify factors for success. In line with the current UN discourse, this book adopts a broad definition of peacebuilding as the range of efforts aimed at political, institutional, social and economic transformations in postwar societies for the purpose of sustainable and positive peace (UNGA 2015). As such, the overall aim of peacebuilding is to reduce the risk of recurring armed conflict, while simultaneously paving the way for sustaining peace and development.

## The blueprint of liberal peacebuilding

At the end of the Cold War, when communism had been defeated and with it 'the total exhaustion of viable systematic alternatives to Western liberalism' and any opposing model for post-conflict support, liberal peace became the 'final form of human government' and the dominant peacebuilding approach (Fukuyama 1989: 3–4). As a result, the single paradigm of liberal internationalism has guided the work of most international actors engaged in peacebuilding (Paris 1997). This paradigm rests on the assumption that the best sponsor for peace within and between states is the combination of liberal democratic governance and a market-oriented economy.

The rationale for promoting liberal principles in other countries goes back to the writings of Immanuel Kant (1903 [1795]). Kant's concept of a *Perpetual Peace* is based on the idea that states with liberal-democratic constitutions would tend to be peaceful with each other (Hoesch 2015). To empirically test Kant's proposition, scholars have found strong empirical evidence that democracies indeed rarely go to war against each other, resulting in a liberal zone of peace (Doyle 1983). These empirical findings have resulted in the formulation of the democratic peace theory.[1] While it is widely accepted that democracies are peaceful in relation to each other, there is still scepticism as to whether they are more peaceful overall. Nevertheless, the empirical findings of studies of democratic peace have prompted international organizations (IOs) and individual states to advocate the promotion of democracy as a method of supporting peacebuilding within states (Paris 1997). Shortly after the end of the Cold War, the UNGA embraced Western democratic principles (UNGA 1991), and in 1994, the UNSC defined, for the first time, the interruption of democracy in Haiti as a threat to international peace and security and authorized the use of force (UNSC 1994a).

Most UN peacebuilding missions undertaken in the 1990s were governed by the paradigm of liberal peace and worked towards the common goal of 'peace through political and economic liberalization' (Paris 1997: 63). Following liberal assumptions, they aimed to transform war-shattered states into market democracies by promoting economic reform, constructing democratic political institutions, civil society building, respect for human rights, rule of law and good governance. Peacebuilding operations generally involve a wide range of international actors, such as the UN, regional organizations, NGOs, international financial institutions and development agencies. As such, 'the international community's approach to building sustainable peace in war-torn states rests upon the notion that an engineered process of simultaneous statebuilding and democratization can bring modern political order to post-conflict states' (Barma 2017: 1). Liberal peacebuilding[2] is still the dominant framework in contemporary peace operations, and there are not any real alternatives: 'the liberal peace is operationalized in highly standardized formats. It becomes a peace from IKEA; a flat-pack peace made from standardized components' (Mac Ginty 2008: 144–145).

Peacebuilding initiatives are usually launched to support a post-conflict society's transition towards sustaining peace. As such, the overall aim of peacebuilding is to reduce the risk of recurring armed conflict while simultaneously paving the way for stable peace and development (Björkdahl et al 2016); however, there is a great division in the specific approaches applied to institutionalize peace (Barnett et al 2007). External actors apply different strategies and use a wide range of policy instruments, which are based on divergent assumptions regarding peacebuilding priorities and can be broadly divided into four sectoral peacebuilding categories: (a) providing security; (b) establishing the socioeconomic framework for sustaining peace; (c) establishing the political framework for sustaining peace; and (d) supporting justice, reconciliation and national healing processes. These sectoral activities are neither ideal types nor mutually exclusive, but must be seen as complimentary. In reality, peacebuilding operations often adopt some or all of these approaches simultaneously.

Activities in the security sector focus on maintaining or restoring security and discouraging combatants from returning to war. Peacebuilding thus continues important peacekeeping functions by focusing on the creation of a secure environment for the affected population and on the restoration of the state's monopoly on the use of force (Marten 2004). It goes beyond peacekeeping in several ways: 'peacebuilding activities directly attempt to reduce the means available, and the incentives, for actors to return to conflict' (Barnett et al 2007: 49). To create post-conflict stability, security sector activities usually include demining; the disarmament, demobilization and reintegration (DDR) of former combatants; security sector reform (SSR); the removal of small arms and light weapons (SALW); and the development of conflict assessment and early warning systems. But the emphasis on the national security apparatus may strengthen authoritarian or semi-authoritarian structures, which have a counterproductive impact on other areas of peacebuilding.

The goal of peacebuilding activities in the second sectoral category is the development of the socioeconomic infrastructure necessary to facilitate economic development. This approach follows the Washington Consensus,[3] which emphasizes political and economic freedoms, democratization and the introduction of elements of a free market economy. Peacebuilding priorities include the (re-)creation of physical infrastructure, privatization and market opening, comprehensive economic reforms and the promotion of economic growth. The objective of socioeconomic strategies is to improve the living conditions of the conflict-affected population as quickly as possible so as to reduce the potential for further conflict.

The political sector focuses on building or restoring key state functions 'that have the capacity to generate basic public goods and possess a modicum of legitimacy' (Barnett et al 2007: 49). Because most post-conflict states lack the capacity to deliver basic public goods, peacebuilders either replace the state or collaborate with it to rebuild basic institutions and infrastructure and to promote democratization. The main focus of this peacebuilding dimension is thus on building effective and legitimate state institutions, at the national and local levels, that are capable of providing essential government services and to promote human rights and fundamental freedoms. It is crucial that all relevant parties involved in the conflict be represented in these institutions, usually ensured through power-sharing agreements. The challenge is that this strategy underestimates the destabilizing effects that can be associated with a rapid democratization in post-conflict societies and that its elite-oriented, top-down perspective implies a certain tendency to de facto favour forces that are more interested in securing their positions of power than they are in facilitating a sustainable peace process (Schneckener 2005).

The last peacebuilding sector focuses on reconciliation and justice, and transcends the previous approaches, as it attempts to build the state's and society's abilities to manage conflict peacefully by emphasizing local bottom-up processes (Lederach 1995, 2005). In addition to creating a general culture of peace, in which conflicts are solved by nonviolent means, the goal is to 'develop civil society organizations and a viable private sector that have the capacity to represent diverse societal interests and constrain the power of state' (Barnett et al 2007: 50). To achieve that goal, peacebuilding activities are concerned with trauma counselling and healing for war victims, the facilitation of a dialogue between leaders of antagonist groups, projects for reconciliation, strengthening civil society organizations, and grassroots dialogue. As such, a liberal peacebuilding approach considers a vibrant civil society as an essential component of liberal democracies, thus arguing that international support should be given to local actors.

In practice, most international actors involved in peacebuilding operations apply multiple strategies simultaneously or use a mix of activities; however, liberal peacebuilding remains the dominant approach and post-conflict reconstruction nearly always entails the 're-engineering' of societies emerging from civil war along liberal lines to prevent their return to conflict (Tschirgi 2004). This mixture of activities and strategies is also evident in the mandates of current multidimensional peacekeeping operations, which, in addition to traditional monitoring tasks, aim at economic reconstruction and institutional transformation (Doyle and Sambanis 2006). The implementation of Western ideals in post-conflict states sparked an ongoing debate over the so-called liberal peace and the question of local agency in the peacebuilding process, which will be discussed in the next section.

## Peacebuilding and its critics

With the Cold War coming to an end, the UN was able to take on an active role as mediator and peacebuilder, intervening in support of national peace processes in (post-)conflict countries, with the aim of ending violence and rebuilding states after armed conflicts. While during the early 1990s, UN peace operations were rather successful in supporting peace processes in El Salvador, Cambodia, Namibia and Mozambique, a few years later, the cataclysmic failures of the UN and the international community to establish sustaining peace in Somalia, Rwanda or the Balkans demonstrated the limits of externally driven peacebuilding interventions and damaged the belief in the liberal peace approach, leading to a reorientation in the liberal peace debate. This reorientation has three aspects: (a) the UN undertook critical analyses on the mistakes made within the UN system; (b) conflict resolution scholars focused on analysing effective ways of conducting peacebuilding missions;[4] and (c) critical scholars advocated for a new understanding of peacebuilding, empowering local[5] people as primary actors in the peace process.

While the liberal peace paradigm is still the dominant form of internationally supported peacebuilding, for critical scholars, it 'reflects the practical and ideological interests of the global north' (Mac Ginty 2010: 393). According to Oliver Richmond (2006: 298), the existing superficial peacebuilding consensus, whereby 'like-minded liberal states coexist in a western-oriented international society and states are characterized by democracy, human rights, free markets, development, a vibrant civil society and multilateralism' is in itself contested, both academically and in practice. As a result, liberal peacebuilding has attracted criticism from a variety of theoretical perspectives and has evolved into one of the central debates in contemporary IR (Pugh 2005; Duffield 2007; Chandler 2015; Richmond and Mac Ginty 2015).

According to Paffenholz, 'the local turn in peacebuilding advocates a major shift in focus from international peace builders to local people as the most important drivers of peace' (Paffenholz 2015: 868). Critical peacebuilding scholarship has focused its attention on the *local* in order to produce a counternarrative to the liberal peace. The first local turn in peacebuilding began with the work of John Paul Lederach (1997), who promoted local ways of facilitating sustainable reconciliation in conflict-affected societies. As a reaction to the drastic failures of international peacebuilding interventions in the 1990s, critical scholars argued that only local actors from within conflict-affected societies could build sustaining peace in their own countries. According to Lederach's integrated peacebuilding framework, external interveners should modify their roles to supporting local actors (such as NGOs, civil society organizations and community leaders) at the middle level of society because they have the biggest peacebuilding potential by influencing peacebuilding at the top (the national level) and the bottom (the grassroots level). Overall, Lederach's theory presents the first comprehensive argument for a shift to the local in peacebuilding research and practice; however, the framework has also been criticized by scholars for its uncritical perception of the local, the lack of power analysis and its limited attention to the processes within the political system of the conflict-affected society (Bendaña 1996; Fetherston 2000; Miall 2004; Mac Ginty 2010; Paffenholz 2010, 2014).

The second local turn evolved as a critical reaction to the failures of international liberal peacebuilding projects in Afghanistan and Iraq, which aimed to support sustaining peace, democracy and state institutions, but had damaging effects and demonstrated the limitations of states from the Global North imposing their will on others (Chandler 2010). This current local turn builds on the works of postcolonial and poststructuralist scholars, such as Foucault (1980), Bhabha (1994) and Scott (1990), to analyse local power and resistance against the dominant discourse and practice of international liberal peacebuilding. The aim is to analyse power structures, international domination and local forms of resistance to establish a postliberal peace founded on emancipatory local agency (Richmond 2011; Chandler 2015). While moderate critics, such as Paris argue that the damaging effects of peacebuilding were caused by the process of liberalization itself, fundamental peacebuilding critics, such as Autesserre (2014), Duffield (2001) and Jabri (2013), challenge the very foundations and structures of the liberal peace, and deconstruct it as a neocolonial approach of governing the 'borderlands' of a standardized 'peaceland'. The local turn thus focuses on the 'everyday peace' and emancipation of ordinary people by pointing to the need of including oppressed voices from conflict zones and emphasizing their agency in peacebuilding and a subaltern view of peace (Mac Ginty 2013; Mac Ginty and Richmond 2013).

The controversies around liberal peacebuilding and the local turn have led to the introduction of new concepts, such as *hybridity* and *hybrid peace*.[6] While IOs often promote liberal peace as the 'only game in town', alternative Indigenous, traditional or customary practices of conflict resolution exist in many societies. The concept of hybrid peace specifically acknowledges traditional institutions and norms that deviate from the predominant Western liberal model of peacebuilding. Accordingly, peacebuilding is seen as a dynamic and multidirectional process, including a multitude of local and international actors, leading to unique understandings of peace in each society. Actual peacebuilding strategies thus need to be adapted for each context, instead of using a one-size-fits-all approach. Hybrid peace usually combines legitimate and accountable democratic institutions and formal practices with informal systems, such as ethnic, traditional or hereditary rule, usually empowering local actors such as chiefs or traditional and religious leaders (Jarstad and Belloni 2012). A major contribution of the hybridity debate lies in highlighting that building sustaining peace is an inherently conflictual process which 'entails competing ideas, political contestation and transformation of power relations' (Björkdahl and Höglund 2013: 289).

Acknowledging the valuable contributions of critical peacebuilding scholarship, this book adopts a moderate liberal institutionalist position, which holds that liberal peacebuilding, despite its limitations, still has a moderate success rate in terms of ending violence and managing violent conflicts (Paris 2010). There are several reasons for adopting this perspective: First, despite the claims of the critics, the principles represented by liberal peacebuilding (freedom, democracy, human rights and so on) are worth pursuing. Second, so far, there is no viable alternative to some form of liberal peacebuilding because liberal peace critics have yet to come up with applicable alternatives. Third, the critique itself fails to escape liberal paradigms and to systematically address its Eurocentrism (Heathershaw 2013; Sabaratnam 2013). Fourth, a peacebuilding concept that is grounded in a liberal perspective can also resort to the critical debate and take local contexts into account.

## Institutional structures and peacebuilding research

The study of processes, effects and approaches to peacebuilding operations has developed significantly over the last 30 years. A large, emerging body of empirical and theoretical work, from scholars and practitioners, has contributed to a better understanding of peacebuilding structures and approaches. Some studies have also focused on the processes of peacebuilding and the institutional provisions included in peace agreements; however, they have largely overlooked the conjunctural nature of the causal interaction between peacebuilding interventions and different institutional structures that determine whether sustaining peace is established and enduring. Less consideration has been given to the actual dynamics of peacebuilding processes and potential path dependencies caused by contextual factors. This book adopts an institutionalist lens for the study of peacebuilding operations, viewing it as a 'hyperpolitical undertaking that interacts over time with the reconstruction of political order in post-conflict states' and local institutions (Barma 2017: 3).

International approaches towards peacebuilding usually focus on the establishment of new institutions and state capacity, which should form the basis for effective and legitimate governance. I put the focus exactly on the institutional configurations within those approaches and the interacting processes that shape and reshape the peacebuilding process (Pierson and Skocpol 2002). Because *institution* is an inherently fuzzy concept in IR, I follow Keohane in broadly defining institutions as referring to 'a *general pattern or categorization* of activity or to a *particular* human-constructed arrangement, formally or informally organized' (Keohane 1988: 383). More precisely, I focus on peacebuilding institutions and practices that 'can be identified as related complexes of rules and norms, identifiable in space and time' (Keohane 1988: 383).

### Historical institutionalism

Many political science scholars have analysed how institutions influence political behaviour and shape political processes; however, being dissatisfied with the behaviouralist treatment of institutions as mere arenas of group competition within which political behaviour is driven by calculated self-interest, the new institutional turn in political science brought attention to the relative autonomy of institutions as political actors and the ways in which they order political life (March and Olsen 1984). Historical institutionalism evolved outside of IR's main paradigms as an answer to the question of why institutions persist, despite dramatic changes in the international order. It represents a 'research tradition that examines how temporal processes and events influence the origin and transformation of institutions that govern political and economic relations' (Fioretos et al 2016: 3). Historical institutionalists analyse macrostructures, arguing that temporal processes might generate and reinforce actor preferences, power relations and material interests. While early scholars focused on answering 'big questions' (Pierson and Skocpol 2002) such as the occurrence of revolutions and social movements, the development of the modern state, or regime transformation and democratization, today's studies deal with virtually all types of institutions at the local, national and international levels.

In general, HI takes history seriously, meaning that historically grounded investigations analyse processes over time: 'because theoretically grounded assertions of causal relationships imply temporal relationships among variables (either that one precedes the other or that both happen essentially at the same time)', examining temporal sequences can contribute to causal inference (Pierson and Skocpol 2002: 699). Historical institutionalists conceive of institutions as the products of struggle among unequal actors, examine multiple institutions in interaction and pay close attention to how 'multiple institutional realms and processes intersect with one another, often creating unintended openings for actors who trigger change' (Pierson and Skocpol 2002: 706). Historical institutionalism takes its explanatory leverage from analysing political processes over long periods of time, focusing especially on the temporal development of institutions. To understand dynamic processes and the stability of institutions, HI makes use of three core concepts: (a) path dependence; (b) critical junctures; and (c) sequencing (Rixen and Viola 2016).

The concept of path dependence originates in economics and has been integrated into HI in order to find answers to the question of why institutions persist, even after they are no longer effective. It generally describes a situation in which reversing an institutional practice (or path) becomes more difficult over time and implies that outcomes are the result of previous decisions and events which had a significant causal impact. A certain path or behaviour is reinforced through endogenous institutional conditions, which increase the positive returns of this behaviour over time and make the adoptions of alternatives less attractive (Arthur 1994; David 2007). While scholars share a general understanding of path dependence, they disagree on the causal mechanisms behind those processes and whether path dependence requires some sort of contingency (Mahoney 2000; Pierson and Skocpol 2002). The opposite process, path undermining, is a more recently recognized phenomenon and happens when a choice, decision or institutional rule leads to decreasing returns for this behaviour which then leads to the unravelling of the institution (Greif and Laitin 2004).

The concept of critical junctures is essential for HI as they constitute the starting point for path dependence.[7] Critical junctures are generally defined as '*relatively* short periods of time during which there is a *substantially* heightened probability that agents' choices will affect the outcome of interest' (Capoccia and Kelemen 2007: 348). They can be decisions or events that interrupt long periods of stasis or institutional stability and thus lead institutions on one path of development, rather than another (Rixen and Viola 2016). Following causal logic, the choices made during those critical junctures have lasting effects and constitute the starting point for many path-dependent processes. In their seminal work on the political development of eight Latin American countries, Collier and Collier (1991) argue that the timing of a critical juncture would be especially consequential to subsequent politics. Using a similar comparative approach, Mahoney (2001: 6) defines *critical junctures* as key 'choice points when a particular option is adopted from among two or more alternatives'. He specifically focuses on the connection between critical junctures and path-dependence, explaining that 'junctures are "critical" because once an option is selected, it becomes progressively more difficult to return to the initial point when multiple alternatives were still available' (Mahoney 2001: 6–7). At a critical juncture, agency thus matters most, and choices can trigger path-dependent processes that constrain future choices (Capoccia and Kelemen 2007).

Finally, as a third tool, HI considers the historical sequencing of events as important for the outcome of change processes, as the timing and sequence of particular events can matter a great deal: 'Steps in a sequence are irreversible because institutional rules cause forgone alternatives in early rounds to be dropped from the range of possible later options' (Pierson and Skocpol 2002: 702). Mahoney (2000: 509) develops the notion of a *reactive sequence*, which are 'chains of temporally ordered and causally connected events', in which 'the overall chain of events can be seen as a path leading up to' the outcome under investigation. Subsequent institutional choices are thus partly constrained by prior decisions, following a certain causal chain. While path dependence can be considered as a modus of sequencing, 'sequencing can also characterize other dynamic processes which may not be characterized by increasing returns, but for which the exact order of the unfolding of decisions or events matters for the outcome' (Rixen and Viola 2016: 13).

## *Analysing peacebuilding from a historical institutionalism perspective*

The strong emphasis on interaction effects in HI makes it pertinent for peacebuilding research. Historical institutionalism assumes that causal conditions may not operate independently of each other with regard to the origin and impact of institutions, but rather bundle together, resulting in alternative causal paths to similar outcomes. Scholars in this tradition tend to analyse institutions and a broader context to discover the impact of configurations of institutions on outcomes of interest (Katznelson 1997, 2009). The theoretical HI perspective is thus highly compatible with a methodological set-theoretic approach towards the analysis of conditions for successful peacebuilding as both share a common understanding of configurational causation and equifinal patterns leading to the same outcome.

The literature on the building of political order and state institutions has shown that the sequencing of institutional choices is central for a substantive interpretation of the outcome. Historical institutionalists also use sequencing arguments to highlight conjunctures or 'interaction effects between distinct causal sequences that become joined at particular points in time' (Pierson and Skocpol 2002: 702). Institutions are considered important causal conditions at the heart of peacebuilding processes, as they can generate sustaining peace. Peacebuilding institutions are thus understood as formal rules, norms, and policy structures that organize and constitute social relations, and they will be examined with regard to the constraints and opportunities they create for political action in post-conflict societies. Peacebuilding institutions are also path-dependent products of a political struggle over power and are deeply embedded in the respective social context: 'when we view peacebuilding efforts in temporal perspective it becomes clear that the formal institutions they transplant into post-conflict states interact with the patterns of the past instead of serving as a break with them' (Barma 2017: 29). So far, peacebuilding has mostly been studied from a probabilistic logic, which usually treats peace operations as exogenous treatments to post-conflict situations and assesses their impact regarding whether they have met their objectives. By adopting an HI approach, a temporal and conjunctural understanding towards the development of institutions is included into the analysis, thus 'opening it up to endogenous change shaped by the interaction of specific actors' (Barma 2017: 28).

I make the argument for an institutionalist understanding of peacebuilding, where interventions are understood as critical junctures and a path-dependent approach to the study of peacebuilding processes is considered. A peacebuilding operation can be understood as 'a transformative moment' from its inception (via peace settlements) through to its completion, 'encompassing its implementation on the ground' through transitional institutions (Barma 2017: 29). Following this logic, a peacebuilding mission can be treated as a decisive point that, like a classic HI critical juncture, 'establish[es] certain directions of change and foreclose[s] others in a way that shapes politics for years to come' (Collier and Collier 1991: 27). Such interventions, influenced by international and national actors, can be seen as structural phenomena, in which different institutions reshape the politics within post-conflict countries, and which, as critical junctures, offer contingent choices for actors involved in the transformation. This central feature of contingency is especially important for peacebuilding interventions, in which 'uncertainty as to the future of an institutional arrangement allows for political agency and choice to play a decisive causal role in setting an institution on a certain path of development', shaping the institutional arrangements within the country over a long period of time (Capoccia 2015: 148).

The historical institutionalist approach is used to explain the interaction of different peacebuilding institutions and how post-conflict political order is constructed. It guides the subsequent analysis, with a focus on three critical phases along the temporal sequence of peacebuilding processes: (a) the peace agreement that ends violent conflict and predefines the institutions included in the post-conflict political order; (b) the actual peacebuilding period, including the implementation of the peace agreement to create sustaining peace through institution building; and (c) the aftermath of international interventions, including long-term effects in the post-conflict country. Emphasizing the temporal dimension of peacebuilding by viewing political processes 'in time' (Pierson 2004) is essential to uncovering elements of the causal mechanisms and unintended consequences underlying peacebuilding interventions. Through its temporal and configurational causal logic, HI is ideally suited to be combined with set-theoretic methods in a configurational analysis of the impact of peacebuilding institutions on the establishment of sustaining peace in post-conflict societies.

## Bargaining theory, commitment problems and post-conflict peacebuilding

To arrive at the establishment of a peacebuilding intervention, adversaries first have to agree on a negotiated solution to end the armed conflict. Especially after negotiated settlements, as Quinn et al (2007) argue, it is necessary to dissolve dual sovereignty (that is, when an opposition group has the organizational capacity and popular support to challenge the government's sovereignty) to prevent the recurrence of armed conflicts. Scholarly discussion around the settlement of armed conflicts and the conditions leading to conflict recurrence have mostly been influenced by the bargaining framework, which 'has become the dominant approach in the quantitative-empirical literature when investigating questions of conflict resolution as well as the stability of the post-conflict order' (Bussmann 2018: 166–167). The bargaining model of war understands the initiation, execution, termination and consequences of war as parts of a single bargaining process over scarce goods 'such as the placement of a border, the composition of a national government, or control over natural resources' (Reiter 2003: 27).

The bargaining model can also be used to explain the stability of postwar peace. Bargaining theory is usually applied to the study of civil war to understand the chances of renewed fighting and the duration of peace. The rationalist bargaining model of war regards armed conflict as one policy tool available to rational actors who seek to resolve a dispute; however, the basic assumption is that because fighting is risky, costly and thus always inefficient ex post facto, peaceful settlements have better utility for conflicting parties than the gamble of war (Powell 2002; Reiter 2003). Accordingly, adversaries should be able to agree in advance on a peaceful bargain that reflects exactly what they would have negotiated at the end of war, but without actually being subjected to the costs of fighting; however, civil wars are still common, and scholars have identified two main explanations for bargaining failure – information asymmetries and commitment problems.

Previous research suggests information asymmetries and incentives for misrepresentation might influence the occurrence and duration of civil wars (Cetinyan 2002; Rauchhaus 2006; Walter 2006; Mattes and Savun 2010). The government and the rebels may lack important information about each other's fighting capabilities, external support or the willingness to suffer the costs of fighting. Information asymmetries can also be an obstacle for the settlement of civil wars, when, for example, warring parties have incentives to withhold information about their military capabilities during the negotiation process to get a better deal (Walter 1999). Uncertainty and information asymmetries may thus persist, despite the conclusion of a negotiated settlement, and could account for bargaining failure (Mattes and Savun 2010). As a result, peace agreements ending civil wars are less likely to be fully implemented until information problems are resolved (Findley 2012). A similar argument is brought forward by Smith and Stam (2004), who argue that the more battles are fought, the more information is revealed, which leads to expectations and information about the capabilities of the two sides to converge. As the convergence of expectations about the capabilities of each side increases with the duration of war, peace will last longer after longer wars with more revealed information: 'Information about the conflict duration and distribution of power is relevant to the conflict actors beyond the time of conflict ending and will influence decisions on whether to stick with the negotiated terms or whether to restart fighting' (Bussmann 2018: 158).

As a second explanation, commitment problems have been identified as an important cause of bargaining failure in civil wars (Fearon 1995; Walter 1997, 2002; Hartzell and Hoddie 2003, 2007): commitment problems describe situations in which mutually preferable bargains are unattainable 'because neither the government nor the rebels can credibly commit themselves to uphold the negotiated settlement in the future' (Mattes and Savun 2009: 739). While the issue of information asymmetry is more relevant during the earlier phases of conflict, warring factions find it extremely difficult to overcome commitments problems in the later stages, when they have decided to settle a conflict and establish a post-conflict order (Walter 2002). In general, commitment problems can occur on both sides. The government might not trust the rebels to end their military campaign once they are given concessions. Similarly, the rebels may be afraid of the government exploiting the situation once they are disarmed. As a result, the implementation of peace agreements can leave both sides potentially vulnerable in the event that the opponent dishonours the deal (Bussmann 2018). Scholars have suggested two mechanisms that can be applied to address these commitment problems: (a) security guarantees from third parties; and (b) the adoption of power-sharing institutions. Third-party guarantees ensure the rebel groups that the terms of the agreement will be fulfilled once they have given up their weapons and are demobilized (Walter 1997, 2002). Power-sharing institutions reduce the government's ability to dominate the rebel group once it has demobilized (Hartzell and Hoddie 2003, 2007). Both approaches can be crucial by providing mechanisms that ensures compliance and send costly signals of the conflict parties' intentions.

Especially in cases of negotiated settlements, bargaining will continue after the war ends, as the organizational structures of adversaries usually remain intact, which makes them, in theory, capable of continuing the fight at a later point in time. We can thus expect the bargaining framework to be relevant for peacebuilding processes, highlighting the institutions that have to be set up to keep the former conflict parties from breaking the agreement. Taken together, the combination of historical institutionalist and bargaining theory with a liberal peacebuilding approach leads to a holistic analytical framework for the analysis of peacebuilding success (see Figure 1.4). The following section will complete the analytical framework by discussing the relevant peacebuilding factors included in the comparative analysis.

## Peacebuilding institutions and the prospect for sustaining peace

Institutions can have a powerful influence on the shape and outcome of peace processes. There is an abundance of theoretical approaches for the explanation of peacebuilding success, and most consider the influence of particular types of institutions on the likelihood that conflict will not resume (Binningsbø et al 2012). This book adopts a comprehensive yet disaggregated view on peacebuilding processes, as initially applied by Mross et al (2022). In one of the few QCA studies engaging with peacebuilding, the authors find that peacekeeping and support for politics and governance are important components of effective post-conflict support, while only combined international support across all main areas of post-conflict peacebuilding is sufficient in difficult conflict contexts (Mross et al 2022: 6).

The general assumption behind the configurational approach adopted in this book is that sustaining peace is most likely the result of a complex interaction of different institutional options. Empirically, this assumption can never be truly tested, unless one can claim to know all possible peacebuilding factors and include them in a model (Bara 2014). This restriction makes a limitation to the most relevant factors necessary to allow for a subsequent set-theoretic analysis. To avoid an overly complex model leading to inexplicable results, the choice of relevant peacebuilding institutions will be guided by the following three selection principles (Amenta and Poulsen 1994; Berg-Schlosser and de Meur 2009).

By accounting for theoretical relevance, I transfer the logic of the bargaining framework of war to the study of peacebuilding processes to deduce three theoretically relevant peacebuilding institutions for the establishment of sustaining peace: (a) international commitment; (b) political power sharing; and (c) security sector reform. While third-party commitment and SSR have their origins in the security dimension of peacebuilding approaches and focus on the creation of stability, political power sharing is attributed to the political peacebuilding sector, with a focus on the restoration of state institutions. Compared with the peacebuilding sectors discussed previously, the bargaining model does not provide accountability measures resulting from negotiated settlements. To account for the importance of national reconciliation on the establishment of sustaining peace, TJ measures are included as a fourth peacebuilding institution. A limitation to these four theoretically relevant factors reflects the general debate without letting the model grow too complex (see also Mross et al 2022).

Empirical relevance is considered as a second criterion to balance relevance and inclusiveness of the comparative framework. I draw on existing scholarship to identify explanatory factors shown to be coherently linked to peacebuilding success and the consolidation of sustaining peace. This

**Figure 3.1:** The selection process of relevant peacebuilding institutions

process of elimination leaves only the most relevant factors. By accounting for configurative relevance, I assume that the four peacebuilding institutions derive their theoretical and empirical relevance independently from each other, in a conjunctural or combinatorial manner. Sustaining peace is likely the result of many institutional combinations, in which the contribution of single conditions is dependent on the presence or absence of other conditions.

These selection principles lead to the delineation of a holistic peacebuilding model that takes account of multiple sectoral approaches that also form the basis of many current multidimensional peacebuilding interventions, making the model and the subsequent analyses highly relevant for policy (see Figure 3.1). The general assumption behind this configurational peacebuilding model is that all four explanatory conditions exert a positive influence on the causal mechanisms and increase the likelihood of successful peacebuilding.

*Peacekeeping and international commitment*

One of the most significant developments with regard to the management of international conflicts has been the development of peace operations, which have been deployed in international conflicts under the auspices of the UN, regional organizations like the EU, the African Union (AU) or ECOWAS, coalitions of the willing, and states acting individually or collectively outside the control of the UN (Bellamy and Williams 2005). As a result, scholarly literature on third-party interventions is both broad and deep (Liebel 2015). Most research focuses on how military instruments affect conflict duration and termination, with mixed evidence pointing to a complex picture (Regan et al 2009).

Peace operations and third-party commitment can produce negative and positive effects. The potential positive outcomes usually relate to democratization, economic development, the promotion of human rights and political stability. Peace agreements that receive a great deal of support from third parties are more likely to be adhered to and are more successful than agreements where conflict parties are left on their own, while trying to keep the peace (Walter 2002; Fortna 2004b; Doyle and Sambanis 2006). However, according to critics, third-party interventions may lead to negative outcomes – for example, prolonged war, indirect social consequences, such as human rights abuses, and the derailment of long-term conflict resolution (Liebel 2015). According to Luttwak (1999: 44), interventions can block 'the transformative effects of both decisive victory and exhaustion' and thus disrupt a process that could, if left alone, lead to long-term conflict resolution.

From a theoretical and empirical perspective, and despite the criticism, extensive international commitment – the intervention of IOs and/or individual states in violent conflicts and peace processes – represents the single most important explanatory factor influencing the prospects of sustaining peace (Walter et al 2021). International actors, such as the UN, NATO, the EU or the AU can play a crucial role in bringing civil wars to an end. Their possible involvement ranges from mediation over sanctions to peacekeeping interventions. As mediators, they can help to solve difficult negotiation problems and support combatants in achieving an agreement (Bercovitch and Rubin 1992; Bercovitch 1996). Peacekeeping forces can support the peace process by enforcing the terms of a peace agreement and enabling both sides to disarm without fear of their opponent cheating the agreement (Mason et al 2011). Overall, international commitment to peacebuilding in war-torn states is a complex attempt to manipulate the preferences of warring parties, the costs of continued fighting and the benefits from a stable settlement. International commitment can encompass all forms of international attempts to interfere with ongoing conflicts, but the most common policy tools include sanctions, mediation and peacekeeping.

### Sanctions and sieges

With the end of the Cold War, international sanctions became some of the most used strategic tools to initiate conflict resolution (Felbermayr et al 2020). The aim of sanctions is to bring about change in target state policies and they have been explicitly used to influence the outcomes of domestic struggles (Hufbauer et al 2007). With the imposition of comprehensive trade sanctions against Iraq in 1990, the UNSC ushered in a 'sanctions decade' where it frequently used all collective coercive measures originally envisioned in Chapter VII of the UN Charter (Cortright and Lopez 2000). For example, there are currently 15 ongoing sanctions regimes imposed and monitored by the UNSC, while the US has administered sanctions programmes against 39 countries and nonstate entities.

However, the use of sanctions is not without controversy, as evidence of their effectiveness as a viable conflict resolution tool is ambiguous (Allen 2005; Peksen 2019; Meissner and Mello 2022). Studies have shown that multilateral sanctions under the authority of IOs are more effective than those by a single country or ad hoc coalitions, since they are less vulnerable to free-riding and defection problems (Bapat and Morgan 2009; Early and Spice 2015). According to the traditional punishment theory of sanctions, the harm caused by international sanctions directly translates into increased domestic political pressure that forces rulers to comply with external demands (Lektzian and Souva 2007). A different approach considers sanctions as a form of persuasion and a tool for encouraging the targeted regimes to reconsider their policy options. According to the bargaining model, sanctions work best as part of a carrot-and-stick diplomacy, increasing the costs of defiance, while simultaneously offering benefits for cooperation; however, target states might survive sanctions regimes by developing new trade and investment ties with third-party countries (Early 2015; Peksen and Peterson 2016).

Overall, sanctions might at times be counterproductive foreign policy tools bringing about unintended consequences for the civilian population of the targeted country, resulting 'in more authoritarianism, increased state repression, poor governance, worse public health conditions, widespread poverty, and higher levels of income inequality in target countries' (Peksen 2019: 643). In a rare QCA study on sanctions' negative externalities, Meissner and Mello (2022) find three recipes for unintended consequences of sanctions: (a) comprehensive sanctions combined with the involvement of a permanent member of the UNSC; (b) sanctions with a long duration; and (c) sanctions regimes targeting autocratic regimes that are not economically isolated. Regarding positive externalities and using a bargaining framework, Escribà-Folch (2010) demonstrates that when international institutions, such as the UN, are involved in sanctions, the likelihood that a civil war ends through a negotiated settlement significantly increases. Especially when combined with military interventions, sanctions can contribute to conflict management strategies that result in more stable settlements (Lektzian and Regan 2016). Economic sanctions are thus usually part of coercive diplomacy packages and are more often used alongside other policy instruments than in isolation to extract concessions. With regard to UN sanctions, Biersteker et al (2018: 408) report that they 'are never applied in isolation' and are most often accompanied by diplomatic and mediation efforts, peacekeeping and the threat or use of force.

## *Mediation*

Over the last two decades, mediation has become one of the most extensively used conflict resolution tools (Bercovitch and Kadayifci 2002). It is a distinct process of conflict management, where 'the disputants seek the assistance of, or accept an offer of help from, an individual, group, state or organization to settle their conflict or resolve their differences without resorting to physical violence' (Bercovitch et al 1991: 8). It is consensual, which means that the conflict parties and the third parties must believe that it will provide some net benefit (Beardsley 2011). In some cases, adversaries might also agree to mediation as a stalling tactic to regroup and recruit so that they can achieve a stronger position on the battlefield (Toft 2010). To overcome the commitment problem, third parties can offer monitoring or enforcement during agreement implementation (Walter 1997).

Mediation by IOs (UN and regional organizations) is usually correlated with success (Wallensteen and Svensson 2014). In a study on mediation in Cambodia and Haiti, Nguyen (2002) finds the best conflict outcome was achieved when the regional actors worked in close collaboration with the UN and major powers. Gurses et al (2008) conclude the presence of mediation is associated with longer-lasting peace after civil wars. Overall, mediation should be considered as a broad process that supplements other conflict management and intervention tools (Bercovitch and Kadayifci 2002). Third-party mediation and diplomatic engagement can contribute to successful peacebuilding by strengthening the political process in countries exiting civil conflicts (Papagianni 2010).

### Peacekeeping operations

A large debate has developed about the influence of peacekeeping operations on civil war settlements and peace processes (Walter et al 2021). Most studies reviewed provided statistical evidence for the positive effects of UN peace operations on reducing the risk of recurrent violence (Walter 2002; Fortna 2004b; Doyle and Sambanis 2006), shortening the conflict duration (Gilligan and Sergenti 2008) and weakening the severity of hostilities (Hultman 2010; Hultman et al 2013), yet the literature also shows that peacekeeping is limited in improving human rights, shortening periods of violence and reducing rebel violence against civilians (Beardsley and Gleditsch 2015). Peacekeeping forces can support the peace process by enforcing the terms of a peace agreement and enabling both sides to disarm, without fear of their opponent cheating on the agreement (Mason et al 2011). Hartzell et al (2001) find support for the claim that the survival rate of peace agreements is strongly influenced by the deployment of a peacekeeping mission. Looking at the spatial dimension of conflict, peacekeeping forces can affect the geographical spread of intrastate conflict trough containment, especially when the missions are robust in terms of troop strength (Beardsley and Gleditsch 2015).

Overall, most studies identify a positive impact of peace operations which seem to increase the chances of long-term peace and reduce the level of violence against civilians and the number of battle-related deaths (Brosig and Sempijja 2017). Peacekeepers can reduce the severity of fighting and mitigate a conflict's effects on civilians, while at the same time helping to overcome commitment problems blocking a sustainable peace settlement: 'peace lasts substantially longer when international personnel deploy than when states are left to maintain peace on their own' (Fortna 2004a: 517). In conclusion, it is expected that comprehensive international commitment (including sanctions, mediation and peacekeeping) towards the peace process supports the establishment of sustaining peace.

*Security sector reform*

The provision of security is a core function of any state. However, in situations of armed conflict, security institutions might not be able to protect individuals or communities against violence or they 'may marginalize, exclude, or even prey on the very population they are entrusted to protect' (UNSG 2013: para 8). The remnants of a wartime security apparatus pose great risks for any peace process, as they jeopardize internal security in societies already devastated by conflict (Schnabel and Ehrhart 2005). A secure environment and a functioning security system that ensures the security of the civilian population are prerequisites for a process of conflict transformation and the rebuilding of any institution. A central objective of peacebuilding interventions is addressing patterns of violence and insecurity by supporting basic safety and security, and by building resilient and legitimate state institutions. Peacebuilding interventions thus regularly support the transformation of wartime security systems in an environment characterized by general mistrust, an overabundance of weaponry and little or no control over the military and the police.

The strong academic and practical interest in stable security institutions warrants the inclusion of SSR as a means to consolidate peace after conflicts (Toft 2010). In general, core security actors in post-conflict societies include military and paramilitary forces, police and gendarmeries, reserve or local security units (such as civil defence forces, national guards and militias), presidential and border guards, intelligence and security services (both military and civilian), judicial and penal systems, and the civil structures responsible for management and oversight (Chalmers 2000; Schnabel and Ehrhart 2005). No single model of a security sector exists, as 'states and societies define and pursue security according to their particular contexts, histories, cultures and needs' (UNSG 2008: para 15). There is still no consensus on a common definition of SSR or on what the objectives and priorities of international interventions should be (Hendrickson and Karkoszka 2005). The UN has emphasized the importance of a comprehensive approach to security to support sustaining peace, and I follow its definition, according to which SSR:

> describes a process of assessment, review and implementation as well as monitoring and evaluation led by national authorities that has as

its goal the enhancement of effective and accountable security for the State and its people without discrimination and with full respect for human rights and the rule of law. (UNSG 2008, para 17)

The goal is to restructure and retrain security actors in a way that they become assets, not liabilities, for the peacebuilding process. This process includes the integration and transformation of military, paramilitary, rebel and police forces into legitimate and democratic security structures.

In addition to institutional reforms of the security sector, SSR usually includes DDR of former combatants. Effective DDR of warring parties can help to restore security, which is necessary for the successful implementation of peace agreements after civil wars (Berdal 1996; Spear 2002). The disarmament of combatants serves two purposes: (a) the elimination of the means by which the civil war was fought and the prevention of a recurring war; and (b) the creation of a stable environment, whereby confidence building between the combatants will be strengthened (Spear 2002). The demobilization of former combatants represents the cornerstone for successful peacebuilding as it offers former combatants an alternative to life with the gun (Stedman 2002). Third parties often play an important role in supporting and verifying security sector reforms and are often even accountable for them. In summary, it can thus be assumed that the complete implementation of different levels of SSR provisions enables the establishment of sustaining peace.

## *Democratic institutions and power sharing*

Power sharing, usually understood as 'including political opponents in a joint executive coalition government', is a dominant approach to conflict resolution (Binningsbø 2013: 89). It has been introduced in many post-conflict societies as a political solution to overcome deep divisions between formerly warring parties. There is a growing body of literature on power-sharing provisions negotiated in peace agreements and their effects on the durability of peace (Walter 2002; Hartzell and Hoddie 2003, 2007; Mukherjee 2006; Jarstad and Nilsson 2008; Mattes and Savun 2009). Most of these studies use the same broad approach to power sharing as did Arend Lijphart, the theoretical father of the concept, distinguishing between types of power sharing: political, military, territorial and economic (Lijphart 1977). Political provisions usually regulate the distribution of power in the central government, military provisions deal with the integration of armed forces, territorial provisions provide for some form of decentralization, and economic provisions concern the distribution of wealth and income. In general, power-sharing institutions define how decisions are to be made within a divided society and how the power should be distributed.

Several studies have examined the effects of power-sharing provisions on the durability of peace, though solely on the basis of promises included in the agreements (Walter 2002; Hartzell and Hoddie 2003). More recent literature also includes the implementation of those provisions (Jarstad and Nilsson 2008; Joshi et al 2015; Ottmann and Vüllers 2015). In general, the argument is that power-sharing provisions contribute to sustaining peace by preventing the government and the rebels from singlehandedly controlling any area of political or military power and excluding their opponents from political decisions. The provisions are designed to ensure that the combatant groups and the local population will not become victims of discrimination and violence in the post-conflict state (Mattes and Savun 2009). In studies of the separate effects of types of power sharing, most results indicate that military and territorial provisions significantly reduce the risk of recurring conflict (Hoddie and Hartzell 2005; Mukherjee 2006). In contrast, Walter (2002) argues that power sharing on its own is insufficient to achieve peace, and it needs to be coupled with third-party security guarantees.

The central aim of power sharing is to avoid conflict and, ultimately, to achieve peace. Power-sharing institutions 'minimize the security threats belligerents face when ending a civil war by allocating rights and limiting the exercise of power' (Hartzell and Hoddie 2007: 27). In peacebuilding literature, most studies look at the effects of power-sharing provisions negotiated in peace agreements, stating that the inclusion of these provisions strengthens post-conflict peace. In these studies, power sharing is understood as a peacebuilding tool used in post-conflict countries and defined as any arrangement between the government of a state and a rebel faction or societal group with promises to establish institutions mandating joint control over power at the national or subnational level of government (Ottmann and Vüllers 2015). This rather narrow definition focuses on political arrangements dealing with two dimensions: (a) political power sharing at the national level; and (b) territorial power sharing at the subnational level.[8] The notion of political power-sharing institutions is based on the consociational model introduced by Arend Lijphart (1977), according to which the inclusion of power-sharing provisions in bargained agreements should be useful in stabilizing the transition to sustaining peace in countries emerging from civil wars. In divided societies, minority groups seek a negotiated settlement, providing them with some guarantee of access to power. The central mechanisms for sharing political power are electoral or administrative proportional representation and proportional representation in the executive branch of a national government. In territorial conflicts, ethnic groups can be granted the power to govern themselves by creating an autonomous region (Rothchild and Roeder 2005).

Power-sharing institutions facilitate the transition from civil war to sustaining peace by reassuring opposition and minority groups that their interests will be taken into account through the participation of their representatives in the governmental decision-making process. Thus, power sharing is understood as a governing system that is beneficial for post-conflict societies (Binningsbø 2013). Accordingly, to be sufficient for sustaining peace, political power sharing must be fully implemented during the peace process.

## Reconciliation and transitional justice

A last research area focuses on the various forms of justice and accountability available in post-conflict situations. There is a growing consensus that justice is essential to sustaining peace and TJ measures are therefore increasingly viewed as a key element of peacebuilding interventions (UNSG 2004b). Regardless of how armed conflicts have been resolved, post-conflict societies are usually faced with questions of reconciliation and accountability: 'a transitioning society needs to find a precarious equilibrium in which perpetrators are held accountable, but opportunities for restorative justice are not eliminated' (Joshi and Wallensteen 2018: 15f). TJ is a response to systematic or widespread violations of human rights and constitutes an important institutional approach to promote peace and reconciliation (Olsen et al 2010; Binningsbø et al 2012).[9] It is concerned with judicial and nonjudicial measures to deal with the past of violent conflicts or a violent regime and to redress the legacies of massive human rights abuses (Buckley-Zistel 2008). The most prominent TJ measures include truth commissions, trials and criminal prosecution, reparations, amnesties and vetting.[10] In intrastate conflicts, almost everyone – whether civilian or combatant – is affected by violence and traumatic experiences. By means of a clear break with the past, the concept of TJ wants to promote the work-up and social reconciliation as well as to ensure the prevention of future outbreaks of violence.

While TJ originally emerged from debates over how best to deal with transitions from authoritarian rule to democracy in Latin America, post-conflict justice (PCJ) focuses specifically on processes 'implemented in the post-conflict period to address wrongdoings that occurred during a previous episode of conflict' (Loyle and Appel 2017: 690). Despite the increase in academic literature and practical applications of PCJ, scholars disagree about its effectiveness. Many scholars argue that PCJ promotes peace in the aftermath of conflict by addressing grievances through truth telling, apologies and compensation, fostering respect for human rights and the rule of law, or deterring perpetrators from future violence (Goldstone 1996). In contrast, sceptical voices find little or even contradictory evidence for the peace-promoting role of TJ, arguing that 'digging up the past' and identifying perpetrators can trigger renewed conflict (Mendeloff 2004; Snyder and Vinjamuri 2004; Lie et al 2007). While early studies focused on identifying and justifying the use of TJ, contemporary scholarship is particularly engaged in investigating the impact of PCJ measures on diverse outcomes (Wiebelhaus-Brahm 2009). In one form or another, TJ measures are now included in most peace processes and have come to 'dominate debates on the intersection between democratization, human rights protections, and state reconstruction after conflict' (McEvoy 2007: 412). Some scholars have even classified the unprecedented increase since the mid-1980s in efforts to address human rights abuses as a 'revolution in accountability' or a global 'justice cascade' (Sriram 2005; Sikkink 2011). Despite the steady increase in practical implementation, explicit comparative studies of TJ impact on the peace process are still rare and arguments thus lack empirical foundations.

Overall, TJ includes a set of tools aimed at confronting and dealing with human rights abuses and atrocities that usually occur in the context of armed conflicts. The motive for including TJ provisions in peace agreements is that TJ would help remove perpetrators from political influence and that the recognition of victims would lead to fewer grievances in the future, thus leading to sustaining peace. Previous studies suggest that the entire repertoire of TJ measures is supportive of the establishment of peace, when initiated at the right moment and combining the right tools. Based on the literature review, causal expectations about the influence of TJ are ambiguous, and holistic TJ measures may both support and impede the establishment of sustaining peace.

## Theoretical expectations regarding peacebuilding conditions

As this review of peacebuilding institutions has pointed out, there is some general agreement regarding the mechanisms linking peacebuilding approaches to renewed warfare or successful peacebuilding. We can formulate theoretical expectations for the four conditions corresponding to the empirical trends illustrated earlier. A glance at the summary in Table 3.1

**Table 3.1:** Explanatory peacebuilding conditions and their expected impact on sustaining peace

| Condition | Assumed causal direction |
| --- | --- |
| International commitment | Supportive, extensive international commitment enables the establishment of sustaining peace |
| Security sector reform | Supportive, comprehensive security sector reform enables the establishment of sustaining peace |
| Power sharing | Supportive, inclusive power sharing (including political and/or territorial provisions) enables the establishment of sustaining peace |
| Transitional justice | Ambiguous, holistic transitional justice approaches may both enable and impede the establishment of sustaining peace |

reveals that nearly all peacebuilding conditions are considered supportive to the peacebuilding process and enable the establishment of sustaining peace. Only TJ can have a supportive and an impeding impact on the establishment of sustaining peace, as the accountability process might trigger renewed conflict. These inferred theoretical expectations will be relevant for the set-theoretic analysis implemented in Chapter 5 and should thus be kept in mind.

## Summary

In light of the absence of an explicit peacebuilding theory, the aim of this theoretical chapter was to provide an analytical framework for the subsequent analysis of peacebuilding success. To this end, I have drawn on several theoretical approaches that can be meaningfully combined in the sense of a complimentary peacebuilding approach. The framework is based on a moderate liberal institutionalist position, which holds that peacebuilding based on the notion of liberal peace, despite its limitations, still has a moderate success rate in ending violence and establishing sustaining peace. In line with the historical institutionalist approach, peacebuilding institutions are broadly understood as formal rules, norms and policy structures that organize and constitute social relations in post-conflict societies that are expected to interact, resulting in alternative causal paths that structure the post-conflict political order and lead to sustaining peace.

The framework focuses on three critical and path-dependent phases along the temporal sequence of peacebuilding processes: (a) the peace agreement that ends violent conflict and defines the peacebuilding institutions included in the analysis; (b) the actual peacebuilding period, including the implementation of the peace agreement, which will be the focus of the comparative analysis; and (c) the aftermath of international interventions, including long-term effects in the post-conflict country, which will be discussed in detail in the case studies of the peacebuilding process in Sierra Leone and South Africa. Lastly, the bargaining framework is assumed to be relevant for peacebuilding processes, substantiating the need for institutions to be set up to keep the former conflict parties from breaking the agreement.

Taken together, this combination of historical institutionalist and bargaining theory with a liberal peacebuilding approach leads to a holistic analytical framework for the peacebuilding-success analysis that is highly compatible with the set-theoretic approach presented in the next chapter. The framework also has some disadvantages when it comes to certain aspects of explaining peacebuilding success. It clearly favours a top-down institutionalist approach towards peacebuilding, which is problematic from a critical perspective. Peace agreements and the institutions they aim to establish are usually the result of elite negotiations between warring factions, where civil society often only has an observer position, if it is recognized and heard at all. A macrostudy that focuses on the successful implementation of peace agreements is thus unable to provide any insights into the microrealities of peace processes and what the establishment of these peacebuilding institutions means for the local population in conflict-affected societies. Except for the aspect of TJ, which aims to address some kind of civil society support, the framework is silent when it comes to local conflict resolution mechanisms or alternative ways of building peace. However, I consider the macro-analysis of configurational peacebuilding processes an important step towards more nuanced peacebuilding models that go beyond the inferential correlations between individual peace agreement provisions and the duration of sustaining peace. With the emergence of alternative and bottom-up indicators and data, it will become possible to adapt this analytical framework in the future to also include local aspects of the peacebuilding process in a comparative research design.[11]

4

# A Set-Theoretic, Multi-Method Approach to Peacebuilding

Revealing the (configurational) conditions through which peacebuilding institutions enable the establishment of sustaining peace requires a comparison of varying institutional settings in post-conflict countries that have experienced successful and failed interventions. This requires research designs and methods that enable the systematic assessment of peacebuilding success from an institutionalist perspective and a focus on the cross-case interactions between various institutional factors and the within-case analysis of underlying mechanisms that drive a phenomenon of interest. As there are many social science methods, there are also many possibilities for multi-method designs, which runs the risk of irreconcilable ontological assumptions (Seawright 2016; Goertz 2017; Beach and Kaas 2020). To overcome this incompatibility problem, this book adopts a set-theoretic multi-method (SMMR) approach that applies set theoretic tools and notions at both cross-case and within-case level of analysis in a unifying framework to 'formulate integrated, set-relational descriptive or causal inferences about a phenomenon of interest' (Schneider 2024: 3). I follow the cross-case first SMMR design, which first identifies patterns on the cross-case level, based on which different types of cases are established and selected for within-case analysis (Beach and Rohlfing 2018).

At the cross-case level, I introduce the set theoretic method of QCA as a unique approach to the systematic analysis of successful peacebuilding and argue that it is well suited to capture the complexity of peacebuilding interventions. QCA is deep-seated in set-theoretic reasoning and offers an original perspective on the study of peacebuilding through its core analytical features, such as its innate case orientation, configurational thinking, the focus on equifinality and asymmetric relations (Ragin 1987, 2000, 2008a; Rihoux and Ragin 2009; Schneider and Wagemann 2012; Mello 2021). In cross-case first SMMR designs, QCA begins with the truth table analysis to discern sufficient conditions for the outcome. The result – the QCA

**Figure 4.1:** Analytical level of the SMMR design

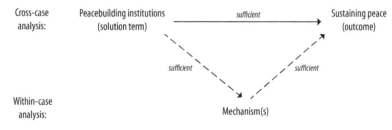

Source: Based on Schneider (2024: 6)

solution formula – is then used to identify appropriate typical cases for within-case level analysis, with the goal of improving the QCA model or probing the mechanism(s) and causal explanation(s) that connect the sufficient configurations to the outcome at the cross-case level (Beach and Pedersen 2013). Set relations alone can indicate but do not prove causality and require the combination with other case-based methods (Haesebrouck and Thomann 2022).

QCA can be combined with different methods and data analysis techniques for the within-case analysis (Meuer and Rupietta 2017; Schneider 2024). Because I focus on probing the mechanism(s) between the sufficient patterns and the outcome, process tracing has been chosen as the method for within-case analysis, which is also the most commonly used combination in the context of set-theoretic methods (Mello 2021). As QCA and process tracing are based on set-theoretic logic and share the same deterministic ontology of causality (Mahoney 2021), they can be meaningfully combined in a SMMR approach: they view causation in deterministic and asymmetric terms at the case level and understand mechanisms as more than intervening variables, but as 'a system of interacting parts that transfer causal forces from causes to outcomes' (Beach and Pedersen 2018: 3). In SMMR designs, the within-case analysis can be based on any form of empirically manifested mechanisms, which, however, need to be perceived as sets in which cases hold membership (Mikkelsen 2017; Mahoney 2021).[1] Figure 4.1 summarizes the chosen cross-case first SMMR design: a uniquely covered *pathway case* (Gerring 2007: 122) will be selected for each of the sufficient solution paths connecting peacebuilding institutions with sustaining peace and the causal mechanism(s) connecting the sufficient configurations to the outcome will be identified.

## How a set-theoretic approach provides new insights for peacebuilding studies

I have argued in the preceding chapters that the previous research focus on single peacebuilding institutions is fundamentally misguided, as sustaining peace is more likely the result of complex interactions of individual institutional options. As there is little generalized knowledge about these interactions, a set-theoretic MMR approach provides a unique tool to: (1) identify peacebuilding patterns that are sufficient for sustaining peace; and (2) substantiate causal inference for the mechanisms linking these patterns to sustaining peace. As a method, QCA is applicable to middle-range theories and statements, and, in combination with mechanism-centred process tracing, the resulting framework will have some degree of generalizability to a particular population of cases. QCA's focus on three aspects of causal complexity offers possibilities for peacebuilding research that can be problematic in regression-based designs: (a) equifinality; (b) conjunctural causality, which allows for the integration and interaction of various theoretical approaches; and (c) asymmetric causal relations. To allow for different membership degrees of cases in sets, I apply fuzzy-set QCA (fsQCA; Ragin 2000) to identify necessary and sufficient conditions for sustaining peace, which will subsequently be called configurations, patterns, scenarios, recipes or paths (Ragin 2008a).

The use of QCA has increased rapidly in the field of IR and is experiencing considerable popularity in peace and conflict studies (Ide and Mello 2022). So far, the method has been used to study war-to-peace transitions (Fontana et al 2021; Mross et al 2022), regional conflict systems (Ansorg 2014), the inclusion of human rights or transitional justice provisions in peace agreements (Caspersen 2019; Leib 2022), violent ethnic conflicts (Bara 2014; Lindemann and Wimmer 2018), UNSC interventions in humanitarian crises (Binder 2015), unintended consequences of UN sanctions (Meissner and Mello 2022), environmental peacemaking (Ide 2018), and EU Member State participation in military interventions (Haesebrouck 2017). Previous studies applying QCA showed the advantages of implementing a disaggregated approach to post-conflict peacebuilding and peace processes, and demonstrated the method's unique benefits to the study of peace and conflict. So far, however, empirical multi-method research combining QCA and process tracing is still the major exception in IR (Ide and Mello 2022). This book thus also contributes to the advancement of research frontiers by demonstrating the applicability of a SMMR designs with an empirical example.

## *The distinctiveness of set-theoretic research*

Set-theoretic approaches differ from other social science methods because of their reliance on sets in contrast to variables. Sets constitute the core analytical blocks of QCA and can be characterized in terms of 'boundaries that define zones of inclusion and exclusion', in which cases are 'measured according to their fit within the boundaries of a set' (Mahoney, as cited in Schneider and Wagemann 2012: 24). Sets adhere to Sartori's idea of concepts as 'data containers' (Sartori 1970: 1039) by defining cases as fully in the set, fully out of a set or partially in between. Within set-theoretic approaches, there are two major types of sets: (1) crisp sets; and (2) fuzzy sets. While crisp sets follow a dichotomous logic by allowing only full membership (1) and full nonmembership (0) in a set, fuzzy sets encompass differences in degree among qualitatively similar cases, thus making it possible to assign partial membership scores to cases in any given set.

Sets differ from variables in many important ways. First, unlike conventional variables, sets must be calibrated. The process of calibration should reflect theoretical knowledge, empirical evidence and the meaning of the concepts the sets stand for (Ragin 2000: 150; Schneider and Wagemann 2012: 32). In the end, the assigned set membership scores represent a numerical link between an empirical case and a theoretical concept. Second, fuzzy sets simultaneously establish qualitative differences in kind between cases (similar to nominal scales) and quantitative differences in degree (similar to ordinal scales), allowing for degrees of membership in the set. The set value of 0.5 is of particular importance, as this crossover point delineates the threshold between being (more) in the set and being (more) out of the set. Third, while ordinal or metric variables are usually based on the full range of their indicators, sets 'distinguish between relevant and irrelevant variation' (Ragin 2008a: 83). For example, we would call a person 'very old', no matter if she is 98 or 102, for both of these individuals are fully in the set of a very old person.

In set-theoretic approaches, connections between two or more social phenomena are analysed in two types of set relations: superset and subset relations (which are interpreted in terms of necessary and sufficient conditions). The statement of necessity describes a situation in which the condition must be present for an outcome to occur. In set relations, a condition can be considered sufficient if, whenever it is present, the outcome is present as well. It is possible that the outcome is present with the condition being absent. As social science research is, to a large extent, based on noisy observational data, set-theoretic approaches like QCA allow for certain inconsistencies and have developed descriptive parameters of fit, such as consistency, coverage and relevance, which measure the degree of how (in)consistent set relations between conditions and outcome are.

Overall, set-theoretic approaches, which are based on Boolean algebra, differentiate themselves from conventional statistical methods, which are based on linear algebra, by the mathematical foundation used[2] and by offering a unique perspective on social realities (Grofman and Schneider 2009; Goertz and Mahoney 2013; Thiem et al 2016). While traditional correlational techniques are good at analysing symmetric patterns in the data, set-theoretic methods are well suited to uncover asymmetric patterns. They are appropriate for alternative research purposes and are developed to achieve contrasting research goals (Goertz and Mahoney 2013). Within peacebuilding research, set-theoretic approaches enable the systematic investigation of patterns across cases that either have a common outcome with the goal of identifying necessary conditions or, by examining shared configurations of conditions with regard to whether they share the same outcome.

## Model development: the analytical components of Qualitative Comparative Analysis

QCA was developed by Charles Ragin in the 1980s and has been substantially refined (Ragin 1987, 2000, 2008a; Schneider and Wagemann 2012; Mello 2021; Oana et al 2021). There are multiple understandings of QCA, but it is generally agreed that 'the application of an algorithm to a truth table is at the core of QCA (truth table analysis)' (Beach and Rohlfing 2018: 10). One of the often-proclaimed benefits of QCA is that it allows for simultaneously drawing cross-case inference and making sense of individual cases at the same time. Set-theoretic research designs usually apply causes-of-effects (or Y-centred) approaches and are interested in explaining specific outcomes. This means that even as QCA usually involves some generalization across cases, there is often also a strong concern for explaining individual cases and making inferences about them. Due to this Y-centred approach, QCA scholars usually start from cases which exhibit positive outcomes and build their universe of cases from there.

This case-orientation enables QCA to uncover different types of cases and measure how well they fit into the overall set-relational configuration. Besides typical cases that exhibit the determined link between (configurational) conditions and the outcome, QCA also reveals deviant or nonconforming cases that are either inconsistent with the cross-case pattern (that is, they should show a certain outcome but do not) or they are not explained by any of the results (Ragin 2004: 135–138). This characteristic of QCA offers singular opportunities for the analysis of peacebuilding success: (1) the approach clusters typical cases that show the same configurations of conditions and are linked to peacebuilding success in a set-theoretic relationship; (2) it identifies deviant cases that entail the packages of conditions but did not experience peacebuilding success, indicating the presence of important confounding or missing conditions; and (3) it uncovers cases in which peacebuilding success cannot be explained based on the conditions included in the analysis, pointing to the need for further research in this area. In comparison to other case-oriented methods, QCA is rather ill-equipped to analyse temporal processes (Ragin and Strand 2008), to detect potential structures within configurations of conditions or to uncover the actual causal mechanism between the (configurations of) conditions and the outcome; however, set-theoretic multi-method designs combining QCA with follow-up case studies offer a solution to the last concern by strengthening causal inference at the cross-case level and adding within-case evidence.

The second key feature distinguishing QCA from other analytical approaches is the specific kind of causal complexity which is inherent to set-theoretic methods and is defined by three distinct characteristics: configurational patterns, equifinality and asymmetry (Schneider and Wagemann 2012: 76–83). First, QCA assumes causes in configurational patterns, which means that the effect of single conditions will unfold only in combination with other conditions. Second, equifinality refers to the fact that there are usually different, mutually non-exclusive alternatives and configurations of conditions explaining social phenomena. Finally, the assumption of asymmetry has two components: (1) the same condition can contribute both to the presence and the absence of an outcome; and (2) we cannot draw any inferences from the explanation of the occurrence of an outcome for the explanation of its absence. Instead, successful peacebuilding (defined as sustaining peace) can be the result of very different combinations of configurations than its opposite – that is, unsuccessful peacebuilding (the absence of sustaining peace). As a result, separate analyses have to be conducted in order to explain the outcome as well as the nonoutcome.

In Chapter 5, I apply fuzzy-set QCA to identify the necessary conditions and sufficient combinations of conditions for sustaining peace (Ragin 2008a). QCA is based on Boolean algebra and it has become standard to use the tilde sign ($\sim$) to indicate the absence of a condition. QCA uses the multiplication sign ($\star$) for the logical AND operator and the addition sign (+) for the logical OR operator. The analysis of necessity (superset relation) focuses on the investigation of set relations between single conditions and the outcome (sustaining peace).[3] I only define a condition as necessary if it passes the consistency threshold, is not empirically trivial, and can be considered conceptually and theoretically meaningful (Ragin 2006; Schneider and Wagemann 2012: 139–147).

The analysis of sufficiency starts with an assumption of maximum complexity and transfers the calibrated empirical data into a truth table. The rows of the truth table represent all logically possible combinations of the selected conditions, illustrating for each row how many and which cases belong to this row. This allows me to identify and treat empirically unobserved configurations (so-called logical remainders). If the fuzzy-set membership of (nearly) all cases in a truth table row is smaller than or equal to its membership in the outcome, then the row is considered as a sufficient path for the outcome. When an outcome value has been assign to all truth table rows, the QCA package for $R$ runs the consistency cubes algorithm on the data to determine redundant conditions and simplify the information contained in the truth table, arriving at the combinations of conditions that imply (→) the outcome, called the solution term (Schneider and Wagemann 2012: 104).[4] This logical – or Boolean – minimization process is at the core of the QCA method. The result is a logically minimized solution 'or in other words, causal complexity reduced to its most simple, valid expression' (Bara 2014: 699).

In QCA, three different types of solution terms can be derived which differ in terms of their treatment of logical remainders: the conservative solution, the parsimonious solution and the intermediate solution (Mello 2021: 133ff). The *conservative solution* does not make assumptions about empty rows in the truth table and treats all logical remainders as not being subsets for the outcome, resulting in the most complex solution term. For the *parsimonious solution*, all logical remainder rows are included in pairwise Boolean minimization to derive a less complex solution; however, it accepts theoretically difficult counterfactuals and may be based on unrealistic assumptions about hypothetical data. The *intermediate solution* is based on a theory-driven evaluation of all logical remainders and only includes those that 'are consistent with theoretical and substantive knowledge' as defined by the researcher (Ragin 2009: 118). As a result, all difficult counterfactuals that conflict with theory and substantive knowledge are banned from being simplifying assumptions.

As a research approach, QCA emphasizes the use of theoretical and conceptual arguments, case knowledge and good explanation (Thomann and Maggetti 2020). I employ a case-oriented approach that includes contextual knowledge and theory for the interpretation of the results and to arrive at cross-case inference. Consequently, I derive and examine all three solution types, but focus my substantive interpretation on the intermediate solution (Schneider and Wagemann 2012, 2013). The choice of solution type has been an ongoing debate among QCA scholars (Baumgartner and Thiem 2020; Duşa 2022; Haesebrouck and Thomann 2022). I interpret the intermediate solution 'because it allows researchers to determine the treatment of logical remainders based on their theoretical expectations and substantive knowledge of the research area' (Mello 2021: 141). This means that I make theory-guided assumptions about empirically unobserved truth table rows to identify easy counterfactuals. These so-called directional expectations (Ragin 2008b) about the presence of absence of a condition and its relationship to the outcome have been specified in the previous chapter.[5] I also avoid making contradictory assumptions, ensuring that the same truth table row cannot be considered sufficient for both the occurrence of the outcome and the nonoccurrence.

To evaluate the results, I apply consistency and coverage measures (Ragin 2006). The values of these parameters of fit range from 0 (low) to 1 (high). Consistency provides a numerical expression for the extent to which the empirical evidence is in line with the statements of necessity and sufficiency.

Consistency should generally not be below 0.9 for necessary conditions and not below 0.75 for sufficient conditions. The measure of coverage has different implications for necessary and sufficient conditions. For sufficient conditions, coverage depicts the empirical importance of the model for explaining the outcome (or how much of the outcome is covered by the configurations). For necessary conditions, coverage expresses their relevance with regard to the condition set not being much larger than the outcome set (Ragin 2006), while the relevance of necessity (RoN) measure takes into account whether the necessary condition is (close to) a constant (Schneider and Wagemann 2012): low RoN values indicate trivialness and high values relevance.

## Model testing: process tracing and the analysis of causal mechanisms

Since set-theoretic methods, including QCA, are essentially case-based methods, they provide good entry points for the integration of case studies. QCA and process tracing are causal case study methods and share the same ontology of causality, which means that they can be meaningfully combined in a multi-method approach (Beach and Pedersen 2016), but where QCA focuses on explicit connections between causal conditions, process tracing is applied to open the black box and take a close look at the underlying mechanism. Process tracing – 'or the use of evidence from within a case to make inferences about causal explanations of that case' (Bennett and Checkel 2015: 4) – is a distinct within-case method that makes it possible to trace a process that links a cause (or conjunction of causes) with an outcome to generate an inference about causal mechanisms (George and Bennett 2005; Gerring 2008; Beach and Pedersen 2013). It shifts the analytical focus from conditions and outcomes to the hypothesized causal process in between them.

In set-theoretic MMR, causal mechanisms are expected to be present in a predefined population of cases, when the conditions that trigger them are also present (Machamer et al 2000; Falleti and Lynch 2009). In this book, process tracing is used to provide an understanding of how peacebuilding institutions produce sustaining peace and of the steps of the causal process in between the cause and the outcome. Because of how process tracing can be employed, there is still some disagreement about what process tracing actually is (Waldner 2012). I follow Beach and Rohlfing in defining process tracing as a 'within-case method that allows one to trace a process that links a cause (or conjunction of causes) [X] with an outcome [Y] in order to generate an inference about the causal mechanism' (Beach and Rohlfing 2018: 7).

## What is process tracing and how does it work?

Process tracing is commonly defined as an in-depth within-case method that involves tracing causal mechanisms that link causes with their effects or outcome (George and Bennett 2005; Hall 2008; Rohlfing 2012; Beach and Pedersen 2013, 2016; Bennett and Checkel 2015); however, the methodological literature on process tracing includes considerable ambiguity and discord about what causal mechanisms actually are (Hedström and Ylikoski 2010). In a variance-based understanding of mechanisms, they are intervening variables between causes and outcomes (King et al 1994; Gerring 2007; Weller and Barnes 2015); yet, this understanding is considered to be incompatible with process tracing, and there is 'a developing consensus that we should use within-case evidence in the form of *mechanistic evidence*, defined as the observable manifestations of the operation of a process in an actual case' (Beach 2018a: 4). I apply a systems understanding of mechanisms to unpack the explicit causal process that occurs in between a cause (or set of causes) and an outcome, tracing each of its constituent parts empirically using mechanistic evidence: empirical fingerprints left by the activities of actors (Beach and Pedersen 2013). Following Machamer (2004), the single parts of a mechanism are conceptualized as entities that engage in activities: 'entities are the factors (actors, organizations or structures) engaging in activities, whereas the activities are the producers of change or what transmits causal forces or powers through a mechanism' (Beach 2018a: 5). In the following analyses, I speak of *actors* and their *behaviours*, instead of entities and their activities, to link the conception of mechanisms with common social science methods (Rohlfing and Schneider 2018).

In process tracing, mechanistic evidence can be any empirical material left by the performance of a causal mechanism that increases or decreases our confidence in the existence of this specific causal mechanism (Beach 2016). Bayesian logic allows for evaluation of this evidence to make inferences about the presence or absence of causal processes in a case (Bennett 2008, 2015; Beach and Pedersen 2013, 2016; Humphreys and Jacobs 2015; Fairfield and Charman 2017). With respect to process tracing, this logic means that mechanistic evidence has to be evaluated with regard to whether we are certain to find this evidence (the theoretical certainty of evidence) and, if found, whether there are any other plausible alternatives for finding that particular evidence in this specific case (the theoretical uniqueness of evidence) (van Evera 1997; Rohlfing 2012; Bennett 2015). With the systems understanding of mechanisms, 'we ask ourselves about what observables would be left in a case by the data-generating process for the activities of entities for each part of the mechanism' (Beach 2018a: 11).

Process tracing can be used for building, testing and refining theories of processes linking causes and outcomes or to simply gain a better understanding of the causal dynamics that produced the outcome of a particular historical case. Beach and Pedersen (2013, 2016) differentiate four variants of process tracing methods within social sciences: theory-testing; theory-building; theoretical revision; and explaining outcome (or case-centric) process tracing. This book includes theory-testing process tracing as one part of the multi-method approach, which 'conceptualizes a theory based on existing literature and then tests whether there is evidence that a hypothesized causal mechanism is actually present in the selected case' (Beach and Pedersen 2016: 305). The results of the QCA suggest a certain causal relationship between the peacebuilding conditions and sustaining peace, but the actual mechanism is unclear. The analytical attention focuses on the most plausible causal mechanism that explains how the conditions are causally linked to sustaining peace (Beach 2018b: 75). By providing empirical evidence of a disaggregated mechanism linking the (configuration of) conditions and the outcome, I will be able to make stronger claims of causation within the individual case.

## Combining process tracing with Qualitative Comparative Analysis

A particular focus in SMMR literature is the general compatibility of single-case process tracing with QCA (Blatter and Haverland 2012; Beach and Pedersen 2013) and the specific logic of selecting cases for follow-up case studies based on QCA results (Ragin and Schneider 2011; Rohlfing and Schneider 2013; Schneider and Rohlfing 2013, 2016). Because the focus of this book is to uncover the mechanisms linking (configurations of) peacebuilding institutions to sustaining peace, I focus on the formalized treatment of SMMR in QCA on sufficiency or, more precisely, the integration of a sufficiency analysis with case studies using process tracing.[6] With fsQCA results, each case can be assigned to one of five types of cases that are discernible in SMMR: typical cases, deviant cases in degree or in kind, unaccounted cases, and individually irrelevant (IIR) cases. These types of cases can be graphically represented in an enhanced XY plot (Figure 4.2; see also Schneider and Rohlfing 2013: 585ff; Mello 2021: 194). The dotted vertical and horizontal lines are anchored at the 0.5 crossover point and indicate the qualitatively different membership of cases in the solution formula (X) and the outcome (Y) (Ragin 2000). Additionally, the secondary diagonal separates cases that are in line with the statement of sufficiency (above the diagonal) from those that are not (below the diagonal).

*Typical cases* hold membership in one or more solution terms (configurations) and the outcome, and are located in the upper-right corner. I follow Schneider and Rohlfing (2016: 532) in further differentiating typical cases into unique members and joint members of solution terms. A typical or pathway case (Gerring 2007: 122) is uniquely covered by only one of the solution paths. In contrast, a typical case is a joint member if it has a membership of > 0.5 in at least two terms of the solution. *Deviant cases* have a membership of > 0.5 in at least one sufficient solution term and should have a higher membership in the

**Figure 4.2:** Ideal types for within-case studies after fsQCA

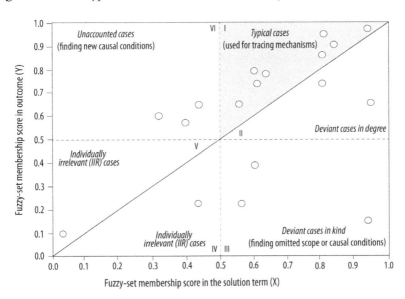

Source: Based on Schneider and Rohlfing (2016: 549); Beach and Pedersen (2018: 849); Mello (2021: 194)

outcome than in the configuration, but do not. We can then further distinguish the type of inconsistency. Deviant cases in degree are inconsistent with the statement of sufficiency, but share qualitatively identical memberships in the solution term(s) and the outcome with typical cases (Schneider and Rohlfing 2013: 587). In contrast, deviant cases in kind are members of X, but not good empirical instances of Y. Cases in the upper-left corner are also consistent with the statement of sufficiency and show the outcome; however, they are outside of all solution terms identified by the QCA analysis and are thus labelled *unaccounted cases* (Mello 2021). Cases in the lower-left quadrant are more out than in both X and Y and are analytically irrelevant when analysing asymmetric causal claims. In the following analyses, I focus on typical cases, deviant cases in kind and unaccounted cases because they are the only ones relevant for causal inference in single-case studies (Schneider and Rohlfing 2016).

The present SMMR design follows the recommendations by Schneider and Rohlfing, starting 'with the analysis of typical cases in order to lend credence to the claim that the QCA solution reflects causation in the first place and is not simply an association' (Schneider and Rohlfing 2016: 546). The (potentially) ensuing analyses of deviant and unaccounted cases would both seek to improve an existing model, in which we already have much confidence. The fsQCA for sufficiency is followed by process tracing case studies for both sufficient conjunctions. Process tracing is used in a theory-testing manner, 'with the emphasis being a structured empirical test of whether there is evidence suggesting that a hypothesized causal mechanism exists between the found conjunction and the outcome' (Beach 2018b: 74).

## Summary: the added value of the set-theoretic multi-method approach

SMMR combines QCA as a cross-case method with process tracing, focusing on the within-case analysis of causal mechanisms. The function that each method has in SMMR designs is conditional on the sequence in which they are implemented (Beach and Rohlfing 2018). Within the *QCA-first design* presented earlier, process tracing is done on the basis of QCA results to confirm the causal mechanism that is triggered by the sufficient term(s). The methods compensate for each other's weaknesses, as process tracing 'provides a helpful tool for making theoretical sense of the conjunctions produced in QCA of sufficiency' and QCA allows for a certain degree of cross-case inference (Beach 2018b: 66).

The previous sections have provided an overview of the distinct analytical perspective that set-theoretic approaches, including QCA and process tracing, offer for the analysis of post-conflict settings, and especially the investigation of peacebuilding success. In summary, the following four characteristics make a set-theoretic multi-method approach especially suitable for the study of peacebuilding processes. First, set relations look at the explicit connections between peacebuilding conditions and sustaining peace, and can detect patterns of superset and subset relations that can be interpreted in terms of necessity and/or sufficiency. Second, the case and complexity orientation of QCA enables the identification of different configurations of peacebuilding conditions, reveals patterns of equifinality (that is, multiple alternative but equally reasonable recipes for peacebuilding success) and highlights several aspects of asymmetric relationships between institutional arrangements and peacebuilding success. Third, process tracing provides the ability to move towards causal inference about why (and how) outcomes are produced in post-conflict settings (Lyall 2015). It allows for the uncovering of the contextual support factors, through which the mechanism can produce the peacebuilding success (Cartwright and Hardie 2012). As a result, the understanding of actual causal processes will help to advance theories of peacebuilding and contribute to more adequate policies in post-conflict settings. Fourth, the results of this SMMR approach allow for the formulation of middle-range peacebuilding theories that are expected to be present when the scope conditions or context that trigger them to operate are also present.

Overall, the SMMR approach provides new empirical insights into the investigation of peacebuilding success based on a unique analytical approach. The analytical value added by combining process tracing with QCA consists of a greater confidence in a causal relationship actually existing between the peacebuilding conditions and sustaining peace, and a greater understanding of how the conditions are causally related to the outcome via a specific mechanism. The goal of the multi-method approach is to formulate a middle-range theory of successful peacebuilding that is valid within a bounded population of post-conflict cases. Further generalization beyond the defined population is problematic for QCA and process tracing because in order for a mechanism to operate correctly in a case, the required and predefined scope conditions need to be present (Falleti and Lynch 2009).

## Calibrating sustaining peace as the outcome set

The outcome of interest is peacebuilding success – or, rather, the degree of peace established in post-conflict transitions after peace agreements in the post-Cold War period (1989–2016). The discussion in Chapter 2 shows that peacebuilding success is a concept that is not easy to define or measure. What counts as peacebuilding success is inherently fuzzy and always disputable, at least to some degree. As a result of its conceptual vagueness, it is hard to define clear-cut thresholds of different degrees of the resulting peace. The idea of fuzzy sets addresses this ambiguity in conceptualizing peacebuilding success by formalizing its fuzziness. As discussed previously, with fuzzy sets, cases can either represent a perfect fit (1), a perfect nonfit (0) or anything in between. Defining peacebuilding success in terms of fuzzy sets thus requires answering a question of the degree to which a post-conflict episode matches the underlying concept of success. Based on empirical information, set membership values can then be assigned to individual cases, aligning the cases with the underlying concept.

The operationalization of the outcome set is based on the sustaining peace (SP) scale, which was introduced in Chapter 2. Based on the definition and conceptualization of sustaining peace, the comprehensive outcome concentrates on the characteristics of post-conflict societies that can range from renewed warfare to sustaining peace. Because the concept structure is formalized by means of set-theoretic reasoning, the consecutive nature of the sustaining peace continuum can be expressed by six degrees of peacefulness, which are assigned fuzzy-set membership scores (see Table 4.1): missing peace (0), armed conflict (0.2), negative peace (0.4), autocratic stability (0.6), functional governance (0.8) and sustaining peace (1). In this way, sustaining peace is calibrated along a continuum rather than as an all-or-nothing state (Regan 2014; Goertz et al 2016), leading to two conceptual points that distinguish this calibration: (a) peace is defined as much more than the absence of war; and (b) peace is understood as a relationship, not an event.

Following set-theoretic reasoning, the levels are assigned a fuzzy-set membership score. Each level of the scale is distinguished by specific characteristics which are measured by six indicators assigned to three dimensions: residual violence; physical integrity; type of governance;

**Table 4.1:** Calibration and fuzzy values for the outcome set sustaining peace (SP)

| Indicator | 0 Fully out of the set | 0.2 Mostly out of the set | 0.4 More out of than in the set | 0.6 More in than out of the set | 0.8 Mostly in the set | 1 Fully in the set |
|---|---|---|---|---|---|---|
| **Security dimension** | | | | | | |
| 1. Residual violence | ≥ 1,000 battle-related deaths a year | 25–999 battle-related deaths a year | 1–24 battle-related deaths or incidences of one-sided violence | No battle-related deaths or one-sided violence | No battle-related deaths or one-sided violence | No battle-related deaths or one-sided violence |
| 2. Physical integrity | | | Level 0 ordinal physical violence index | Level 1–2 ordinal physical violence index | Level 3 ordinal physical violence index | Level 4–5 ordinal physical violence index |
| **Political dimension** | | | | | | |
| 3. Type of governance | | | | -10 to -1 on Polity IV score | 0 to +5 on Polity IV score | +6 to +10 on Polity IV score |
| 4. Civil liberties | | | | Score 6–7 in Freedom rating | Score 4–5.5 in Freedom rating | Score 1–3.5 in Freedom rating |
| **Socioeconomic dimension** | | | | | | |
| 5. Human development | | | | ≤ 0.399 HDI | ≤ 0.399 HDI | ≥ 0.400 HDI |
| 6. Gender equality | | | | | Level 1–2 ordinal women political empowerment index | Level 3–5 ordinal women political empowerment index |

Note: The coding is based on information from the UCDP/PRIO Armed Conflict Dataset v.23.1, UCDP One-Sided Violence Dataset v.23.1, Varieties of Democracy, the Polity IV Project, the Freedom House Index and the HDI.

political and civil liberties; human development; and gender equality. In the following sections, each of the six indicators is calibrated as a fuzzy set, before they are combined in the final outcome set. To do justice to the realities on the ground, the specific characteristics of post-conflict societies are taken into account for the assignment of fuzzy-set values. Accordingly, different implementation expectations are associated with each dimension.

*Indicators of the security dimension*

The two indicators associated with the security dimension evaluate whether a state can provide security for its citizens and guarantee that they can live without personal violence or the fear of violence. The absence of *residual violence* is an indication of a state's ability to maintain peace within its borders and to provide basic physical and human security to its citizens. To determine the level of post-conflict violence, information is sourced from the UCDP Battle-Related Deaths Dataset and the UCDP One-Sided Violence Dataset. The score for this indicator is determined by the number of deaths within the first five post-conflict years. A full membership of 1 is assigned to cases exhibiting no residual violence during the peace process. Peacebuilding episodes, on the other hand, that result in a recurring large-scale conflict or civil war, are treated as full nonmembers and receive a set-value of 0. Between these main anchor points, gradations of partial nonsuccess are assigned: peacebuilding episodes receive a set-membership of 0.2 if they experience a renewed minor armed conflict. Cases not encountering a setback to armed conflict but still experiencing insecurity due to sporadic violent incidents are assigned the set value of 0.4.

The source for the *physical integrity* indicator is the ordinal physical violence index (v2x-clphy_5C), created by the Varieties of Democracy (V-Dem) Project, which measures the extent to which a country's government adheres to physical integrity rights and does not rely on widespread oppression and terror to maintain its power. Physical integrity is understood here as freedom from political killings and torture by the government and is measured in five categories on an ordinal scale ranging from 0 (not respected) to 1 (fully respected). The fuzzy values are determined in accordance with the V-Dem ordinal categories.

*Indicators of the political dimension*

The political dimension comprises two focal points: one regarding the legitimacy of the post-conflict regime and the other regarding the protection of political and civil liberties. Because strong and capable state institutions are essential for the provision of public goods, the *type of governance* operates from the assumption that sustaining peace is best achieved in democratic societies. The indicator is based on the Polity IV data, which measures the level of institutionalized democracy or autocracy using scores in the range of -10 to +10. The calibration of the fuzzy set follows the conversion of polity scores into regime categories suggested by the Polity IV project: autocracy (-10 to 0), minimally democratic (+1 to +5) and democratic (+6 to +10). To account for a potential process of democratization, the highest polity score within the first five postwar years is considered for the calibration.

The measure of *civil liberties* employs the Freedom House Index, which assesses rights and freedoms enjoyed by individuals, based on ten political rights indicators and 15 civil liberties indicators. The index takes the average of a country's or territory's rating for both liberties, which can range between 1 and 7, with 1 representing the greatest and 7 the smallest degree of freedom. The (at least) moderate protection of political rights and civil liberties can be considered a success for a post-conflict country and is thus assigned the full membership value of 1. A score above 6 indicates very restricted civil liberties or even government oppression. These cases are thus assigned a set membership value just above the crossover point (0.6). For the cases in between, governments might protect some political rights and liberties while neglecting others.

### Indicators of the socioeconomic dimension

The socioeconomic indicators assess how well a state guarantees the basic equality of its citizens and provides for a reasonable development. The calibration of the indicator for *human development* is based on data from the Human Development Index (HDI), which focuses on three basic dimensions: the ability to lead a long and healthy life; the ability to acquire knowledge; and the ability to achieve a decent standard of living (UNDP 2015). The fuzzy values are determined in correspondence with the categories used for the HDI groupings. A medium level of human development is considered to be a respectable achievement for post-conflict states and these cases are assigned the fuzzy value 1. In contrast, a low level of human development cannot reach the conceptual threshold for full membership in sustaining peace and these cases are assigned lower set values.

*Gender equality* measures the increasing capacity for women, including greater agency and participation in societal decision making, and is based on the ordinal women political empowerment index (v2x_gender_5C) by the V-Dem Project. The index incorporates three equally weighted dimensions: women's fundamental civil liberties, women's participation in civil society organizations, and descriptive representation of women in political positions. The set-membership values are determined in accordance with the V-Dem ordinal categories, whereby a low level of women empowerment is associated with levels 1 and 2 on the index, and a moderate/high level of women empowerment is assigned to levels 3–5.

Taken together, these six indicator sets depict a balanced picture of how well post-conflict countries perform or fail to perform with regard to the three dimensions of sustaining peace. Because the six indictors are all necessary for sustaining peace and thus completely nonsubstitutable, the set intersection (logical AND) is used to determine the sustaining peace membership value for each case. This means that the minimal values across the individual dimensions dictate the overall membership value of a peacebuilding episode in the set of sustaining peace.

## Calibrating the institutional peacebuilding conditions

Several potential peacebuilding factors could be included in an analysis of the institutional structures enhancing and restricting the consolidation of sustaining peace; however, to keep the model from becoming overly complex and theoretically uninterpretable, I have selected only a moderate number of explanatory conditions for further analysis. The choice of conditions draws from the findings of the literature review on institutional peacebuilding factors and their influence on civil war and peacebuilding processes, and is guided by the three selection principles of theoretical, empirical and configurational relevance (Amenta and Poulsen 1994; Berg-Schlosser and de Meur 2009). The following sections present the fuzzy-set calibration of the four selected peacebuilding conditions, based on qualitative and categorial data.

### Extensive international commitment

International commitment to peace processes can take various forms, ranging from sanctions and mediations to military interventions. The calibration of the condition *extensive international commitment* (INT) represents types of involvement and assesses the degree to which the international community is engaged in the peace process (see Table 4.2). The coding of the condition is based on a combination of data: for information on sanctions, I rely on observation variables from the Targeted Sanctions Consortium (TSC) Database and the Threat and Imposition of Sanctions (TIES) dataset (Morgan et al 2014). Diplomatic interventions and mediation are coded based on the 'Medyes_no' variable from the Civil Wars Mediation (CWM) Dataset (DeRouen et al 2011) and the diplomatic variable from the Diplomatic Interventions and Civil War Dataset (Regan et al 2009). Information on types of peace operations is premised on the 'ThirdParty' variable from the Third Party Peacekeeping Missions Dataset (Mullenbach 2013) and the replication datasets by Doyle and Sambanis

**Table 4.2:** Calibration and fuzzy values for the condition extensive international commitment (INT)

| Conceptual meaning | Coding | Set value and description | Case distribution |
|---|---|---|---|
| **Extensive commitment** International organizations or individual states deploy a multidimensional or enforcement mission | If international interventions include peace operations mandated beyond the provision of protection and/or authorized under Chapter VII | **1** *Fully in the set* | 15 cases (28%) |
| **Strong commitment** International organizations or individual states deploy a traditional peacekeeping mission | If international interventions include peace operations with a mandate to provide security through interposition or monitoring (Chapter VI) | **0.8** *Mostly in the set* | 13 cases (24%) |
| **Moderate commitment** International organizations or individual states deploy a political and/or observer mission | If international interventions include peace operations with a mandate to monitor, report or observe | **0.6** *More in than out of the set* | 8 cases (15%) |
| **Weak commitment** International organization or individual states engage in diplomatic intervention | If international interventions include mediation, international forums or the recall of an ambassador. | **0.4** *More out than in of the set* | 5 cases (9%) |
| **Minimal commitment** Sanctions and/or sieges are imposed by international organizations or individual states | If international interventions include travel bans, asset freezes, arms embargoes, commodity bans, air or naval blockades, or no-fly zones | **0.2** *Mostly out of the set* | 4 cases (7%) |
| **Missing** None of the above | If the international community does not engage in any kind of intervention | **0** *Fully out of the set* | 9 cases (17%) |

(2006) and Fortna (2008). Missing data for all three types of involvement were hand coded by the author.

Multidimensional and enforcement missions represent the most extensive type of international involvement in peace processes, which is why peacebuilding episodes including either one of these missions are coded as full members in the set (1). The 0.5 crossover point delineating the border of being more in and out of the set is placed at the shift from sanctions and diplomatic engagements, representing a weak form of international commitment, towards peacekeeping and enforcement missions, which represent a qualitative change in the type of engagement as they require a stronger (military) engagement and usually include long-term commitments towards the peace process. Peacebuilding episodes obtain a full nonmembership score of 0 if they did not experience any kind of engagement by the international community.

A partial membership of 0.8 is assigned to peacebuilding episodes that exhibit strong but not overwhelming international support in the form of traditional peacekeeping missions. Peacebuilding episodes receive a partial set membership of 0.6 if they include an observer or political mission. Observer or monitoring missions are unarmed missions, mandated to watch and report what they see. Political missions usually consist only of a special representative or a handful of observers (such as the Organization for Security and Co-operation in Europe (OSCE) mission in Nagorno-Karabakh).

In the lower part of the set, cases are coded with a partial nonmembership of 0.4 if international organizations or individual states engage only in diplomatic interventions defined as 'attempts by outside parties to transform a conflict by enhancing communication between warring parties' (Regan et al 2009: 138). In the dataset, three specific efforts are coded as diplomatic intervention: mediation; international forums; and the recall of ambassadors. Finally, the lowest partial nonmembership of 0.2 is assigned to those peacebuilding episodes in which only sanctions and sieges have been imposed by international organizations or individual states before and/or during the peace process.

*Inclusive power sharing*

For the calibration of the condition *inclusive power sharing* (SHARE), I collect data on the type of governance implemented during the peacebuilding episode (see Table 4.3). With regard to data sources, I rely on the Ethnic Power Relations (EPR) Dataset Family (Wimmer et al 2009; Vogt et al 2015) and the Power-Sharing Event Dataset (PSED; Ottmann and Vüllers 2015). The EPR Core Dataset identifies all politically relevant ethnic groups and their access to executive-level state power, which ranges from monopoly power to political discrimination. The PSED provides information on the implementation of political and territorial power-sharing provisions. I rely on both datasets to distinguish different degrees of group access to executive power.

Full membership (1) is given to peacebuilding episodes that include political power sharing at the national level – that is, where executive power is divided among leaders representing particular groups. The 0.5 crossover point marks the shift towards some access to (national or subnational) power for opposition groups, as opposed to the monopoly control of state power through one group. Peacebuilding episodes are coded as complete

**Table 4.3:** Calibration and fuzzy values for the condition inclusive power sharing (SHARE)

| Conceptual meaning | Coding | Set value and description | Case distribution |
|---|---|---|---|
| **Power-sharing government** Executive power is divided among leaders representing particular groups | If members of opposition groups are given positions in the post-conflict cabinet or a specific quota in the main branches of government | **1** *Fully in the set* | 29 cases (54%) |
| **Regional autonomy** Opposition groups are granted political, financial or administrative powers at the regional level | If opposition groups have no access to central power, but gain some influence at subnational level (province or district) or territorial autonomy | **0.75** *Mostly in the set* | 7 cases (13%) |
| **Inclusive dominant government** Leaders of one group hold dominant executive power with limited inclusion | If the government does not significantly share power with other political groups, but offers limited inclusion – that is, token cabinet positions | **0.25** *Mostly out of the set* | 14 cases (26%) |
| **Exclusive monopoly power** Leaders of one group hold monopoly power at the exclusion of other groups | If the government holds monopoly power in the executive-level while intentionally targeting and discriminating other groups | **0** *Fully out of the set* | 4 cases (7%) |

nonmembers (0) if one group holds the monopoly of government power, while intentionally targeting and discriminating other groups with the aim to exclude them from political power. Partial membership (0.75) is assigned to peacebuilding episodes in which opposition groups have no access to central power but gain some influence at the subnational level (province or district). Cases receive partial nonmembership (0.25) if leaders of one group hold dominant executive power, but the government offers limited inclusion of other groups through special cabinet positions.

## Comprehensive security sector reform

As there is not yet comprehensive data available on successful transformation of the security sector, I approximate this condition by looking at the degree to which peace agreement provisions for security sector reform have been implemented in the peacebuilding episode. For the calibration of the condition *comprehensive security sector reform* (SSR), I collect data on the presence of SSR-related provisions in peace agreements and on the degree of their

A SET-THEORETIC, MULTI-METHOD APPROACH

**Table 4.4:** Calibration and fuzzy values for the condition comprehensive security sector reform (SSR)

| Conceptual meaning | Coding | Set value and description | Case distribution |
|---|---|---|---|
| **Comprehensive SSR process** SSR process includes various provisions with (nearly) full implementation | If the SSR process includes different provisions, most of which have been fully implemented | **1** *Fully in the set* | 12 cases (22%) |
| **Strong SSR process** SSR process includes various provisions with intermediate implementation | If the SSR process includes different provisions, but the majority have only reached intermediate implementation | **0.8** *Mostly in the set* | 7 cases (13%) |
| **Partial SSR process** SSR process deals with only a few provisions or shows mixed implementation | If the SSR process includes only few (1–2) provisions with intermediate implementation or different provisions with partly minimal implementation | **0.6** *More in than out of the set* | 13 cases (24%) |
| **Weak SSR process** Initialization of SSR process, but weak implementation | If the provisions for SSR have only been minimally implemented | **0.4** *More out than in of the set* | 5 cases (9%) |
| **SSR provisions** Pledges or provisions for SSR have been made | If the peace agreement includes provisions for SSR, but they are not implemented | **0.2** *Mostly out of the set* | 5 cases (9%) |
| **Missing** None of the above | If peace agreement did not include any SSR provisions and if none has been implemented after the conflict | **0** *Fully out of the set* | 12 cases (22%) |

implementation based on the Matrix Implementation Dataset, the PAM-ID (Joshi et al 2015) and the PSED (Ottmann and Vüllers 2015).[7] I rely on these datasets to distinguish different degrees of SSR implementation: minimal, intermediate and full implementation (see Table 4.4).

Full membership (1) in the set is assigned to peacebuilding episodes in which the SSR process included multiple provisions, of which most have also been fully implemented. The 0.5 crossover point distinguishes nonviable SSR processes – processes initiated but not on track for completion – from those considered viable or nearly completed. Peacebuilding episodes obtain a full nonmembership score of 0 if the peace agreement did not include any SSR provisions and if none has been implemented after the conflict.

Partial membership in the upper half of the fuzzy set represents viable but uncompleted security sector reform. Strong SSR processes are coded with a partial membership score of 0.8 if the peace agreement included different provisions, but most of them had only reached intermediate implementation. Cases are slightly more in than out of the set (0.6) if SSR includes few provisions with intermediate implementation, or several provisions of which most only reach minimal implementation. In the lower part of the set, cases receive a partial nonmembership (0.4) if provisions for SSR have only been minimally implemented. These peacebuilding episodes in which the peace agreement included provisions for SSR, but where they were never implemented, are coded with a partial nonmembership of 0.2.

### The holistic transitional justice approach

The condition of *holistic transitional justice* (TJ) is based on data from the Post-conflict Justice Dataset (Binningsbø et al 2012) and the Transitional Justice Database (Olsen et al 2010). Data were collected on seven types of TJ measures, which were included as provisions in the peace agreement and implemented in the five-year peacebuilding period: truth commissions, trials, reparation programmes, amnesties, purges and vetting, exile, and judiciary reforms (see Table 4.5). The TJ approach needed to include more than one type of TJ measure and some form of restorative justice to be more in the set than out of the set. A full membership score of 1 is assigned to cases in which the post-conflict justice approach consists of at least three TJ measures that must include truth commissions or trials and can thus be considered holistic and comprehensive (Olsen et al 2010).

The 0.5 crossover point delineating the border of being more in or out of the set is placed at the shift from one-sided and security-oriented TJ approaches towards comprehensive measures focused on collective actions and restorative TJ. Cases receive a full nonmembership value of 0 if no TJ measures had been implemented after the termination of the conflict. A partial membership score of 0.75 is assigned to cases in which victim-oriented and restorative TJ measures, such as reparations, represent a move towards a holistic TJ approach if they are combined with a second measure. In the lower part of the set, the sole use of security-centred TJ measures represents a weak and one-sided approach to reconciliation that might even damage the peace process and cases are coded with a partial nonmembership of 0.25.

## Concluding remarks

This chapter has shown that investigating peacebuilding success with a set-theoretic multi-method approach entails some innovative potential

**Table 4.5:** Calibration and fuzzy values for the condition holistic transitional justice approach (TJ)

| Conceptual meaning | Coding | Set value and description | Case distribution |
|---|---|---|---|
| **Holistic transitional justice** Comprehensive TJ process aiming to produce truth about the past and ensure accountability for past crimes | If the TJ process combines at least three TJ elements that must include truth commission and/or trial | 1 *Fully in the set* | 13 cases (24%) |
| **Restorative transitional justice** Victim-oriented TJ process, focusing on repairing harm caused by crimes and some form of accountability | If the TJ process includes at least reparations, a trial or a truth commission (combined with another measure) | **0.75** *Mostly in the set* | 11 cases (20%) |
| **One-sided transitional justice** Biased TJ process, focusing on amnesty and removing those responsible for human rights violations from office | If the TJ process includes only amnesties, purges, exile and vetting of the former leadership | **0.25** *Mostly out of the set* | 20 cases (37%) |
| **Missing** None of the above | If no TJ measures have been implemented after the conflict | **0** *Fully out of the set* | 10 cases (19%) |

based on the specific causal logic inherent in QCA and process tracing. The next chapter shows how the QCA analysis addresses patterns of set relations between degrees of peacebuilding success (according to the sustaining peace scale) and institutional peacebuilding conditions. Table 4.6 provides additional information about the sets' calibration, distribution and directional expectations. The second column summarizes the central calibration thresholds and their theoretical rationales. The third column provides an overview of the data distribution within each calibrated set. Skewed set membership occurs when a large majority of cases has a high or low membership in either the conditions or the outcome (or both). This unequal distribution can affect the subsequent analysis by causing flawed inference, exacerbating limited diversity or producing simultaneous subset relations (Schneider and Wagemann 2012: 232–249; Cooper and Glaesser 2016; Thomann and Maggetti 2020). It is thus advisable to diagnose potential skewedness prior to the actual analysis to adjust the measurement or calibration strategy, if necessary. The information in Table 4.6 shows some (but not troubling) skewed distribution within the calibrated sets. The

**Table 4.6:** Measurement and calibration of peacebuilding conditions

| Set (acronym) | Operationalization and main set thresholds | Set skewedness | Directional expectations |
|---|---|---|---|
| Sustaining peace (SP) | Index of different characteristics of post-conflict societies ranging from renewed warfare to sustaining peace<br>1.0 – fully in: absence of violence, political and socioeconomic development<br>0.5 – crossover: distinguishes negative from more positive forms of peace<br>0.0 – fully out: recurrence of civil war | 59% > 0.5 < 41%<br>56% ≥ 0.75 < 44%<br>74% > 0.25 ≤ 26% | – |
| Extensive international commitment (INT) | Index of different types of international interventions ranging from sanctions and diplomatic engagement to different mandates of peace operations<br>1.0 – fully in: deployment of multidimensional or enforcement mission<br>0.5 – crossover: shift from mediation to military interventions and peacekeeping<br>0.0 – fully out: no international engagement | 65% > 0.5 < 35%<br>52% ≥ 0.75 < 48%<br>76% > 0.25 ≤ 24% | +<br>If present, it contributes positively to sustaining peace |
| Inclusive power sharing (SHARE) | Set membership scores denoting the form of power sharing that has been implemented during the peacebuilding episode<br>1.0 – fully in: divided executive power<br>0.5 – crossover: shift to access to power (local or national) for opposition groups<br>0.0 – fully out: one group holds monopoly power | 67% > 0.5 < 33%<br>67% ≥ 0.75 < 33%<br>67% > 0.25 ≤ 33% | +<br>If present, it contributes positively to sustaining peace |
| Comprehensive security sector reform (SSR) | Presence of SSR provisions in peace agreements and the degree of their implementation during the peace process<br>1.0 – fully in: different SSR provisions are (mostly) implemented<br>0.5 – crossover: distinguishes nonviable SSR processes from viable ones<br>0.0 – fully out: no inclusion of SSR provisions | 59% > 0.5 < 41%<br>35% ≥ 0.75 < 65%<br>68% > 0.25 ≤ 32% | +<br>If present, it contributes positively to sustaining peace |
| Holistic transitional justice approach (TJ) | Index of different types of TJ measures implemented during the peace process<br>1.0 – fully in: three TJ measures including truth commissions and/or trials<br>0.5 – crossover: shift towards more comprehensive TJ measures<br>0.0 – fully out: no inclusion of TJ provisions | 44% > 0.5 < 56%<br>44% ≥ 0.75 < 56%<br>44% > 0.25 ≤ 56% | +/–<br>ambiguous theoretical expectations |

outcome itself is slightly skewed towards values above the 0.5 threshold. Except for TJ, which represents a balanced distribution, all peacebuilding conditions are slightly skewed towards higher set membership values, in particular INT. The following analysis will thus pay special attention to those issues. Finally, the last column entails information on the directional expectations regarding the theoretically predicted effects of the explanatory conditions on peacebuilding success. They are based on the theoretical assumptions discussed in Chapter 3 and guide the handling of logical remainders when it comes to the interpretation of the truth table.

5

# Institutional Patterns
# of Peacebuilding Success

There is no easy answer to the question of which peacebuilding strategy should be applied in post-conflict settings, as international actors use a wide variety of approaches and instruments to support post-conflict societies in their transition towards sustaining peace (Barnett et al 2007). Sectoral approaches, such as humanitarian assistance, development aid, security stabilization, the rule of law, good governance, and truth and reconciliation, are generally assumed to increase the likelihood that conflict will not resume and to enhance the consolidation of sustaining peace (Binningsbø et al 2012: 732). However, effective peacebuilding strategies must be designed to fit the unique post-conflict case if they are going to constitute pathways to sustaining peace (World Bank and United Nations 2018). A one-size-fits-all approach is rather misplaced, and peacebuilding success is more likely the result of different mutually non-exclusive configurations of peacebuilding strategies, depending on the post-conflict episode.

This chapter takes a closer look at four previously identified peacebuilding institutions – INT, SHARE, SSR and TJ – and addresses the question of which institutional configurations lead to varying degrees of peacefulness in peacebuilding episodes. Based on the underlying set-theoretic perspective of this book, this chapter introduces a new perspective for the inquiry of successful peacebuilding: instead of focusing on the effects of single peacebuilding factors, the subsequent analyses investigate how institutional conditions interact in peacebuilding episodes, facilitating or impeding their success. The objective of this chapter is twofold: first, it aims to uncover necessary institutional conditions and sufficient configurations that represent consistent peacebuilding patterns for sustaining peace; and, second, it introduces a configurational model for peacebuilding success and discusses potential clusters in the data that might skew the results.

Following the agreed-upon standards of best practices in QCA, necessary and sufficient conditions will be analysed separately to avoid inferring false statements about necessity from the results of a sufficiency analysis or to make contradictory assumptions regarding logical remainders (Schneider and Wagemann 2012; Mello 2021; Oana et al 2021). While the first analysis of superset relations aims to identify the shared antecedent (or necessary) conditions of an outcome, the second analysis of subset relations checks for sufficient configurations of conditions that share the same outcome. In the following sections, I conduct several separate analyses for the influence of institutional peacebuilding conditions in post-conflict episodes, the first of which deals with the complete sample and the presence of sustaining peace. Then, I take a closer look at the variations in peacebuilding patterns and conduct a comparative cluster analysis and separate examinations of set relations across conflict types and regions.

## Patterns of sustaining peace

In this chapter, I use fsQCA to analyse the interplay between the four previously identified and calibrated peacebuilding institutions – INT, SHARE, SSR and TJ – and assess patterns of necessity and sufficiency regarding the establishment of sustaining peace.[1] The analysis of set relations between peacebuilding institutions and sustaining peace starts with an examination of necessary conditions or 'shared antecedents' (Ragin 2013: 174), which are defined in terms of superset relations between any condition and an outcome, meaning that whenever the outcome is present, the condition has to be present as well.

Table 5.1 shows the results of the analysis of necessity. I use the tilde sign (~) to indicate the absence of a condition or the outcome. With regard to the interpretation of these results, the parameter of consistency indicates the degree to which a given condition represents a superset of the outcome with high values indicating strong superset patterns. The measures for coverage and relevance only have to be consulted for those conditions that pass the consistency threshold in the first place. The consistency values in Table 5.1 indicate that none of the institutional conditions is able to individually display a strong superset relationship with the presence or absence of sustaining peace when the consistency threshold is set at the generally recommended value of 0.9 (Ragin 2006, 2009; Schneider and Wagemann 2012).

Without any theoretically well-grounded higher-order concepts or functional equivalents, it is not advisable to search for additional necessary macroconditions of logical alternatives (Berg-Schlosser et al 2009; Schneider and Wagemann 2012; Schneider 2019). In sum, the analysis of superset relations for the occurrence of sustaining peace has demonstrated that there is no single peacebuilding institution that is shared by (nearly) all cases featuring sustaining peace. This finding is theoretically reasonable and in line with previous studies on civil wars and peacebuilding success: a necessity

**Table 5.1:** Necessary conditions for the presence (SP) and absence (~SP) of sustaining peace

| Condition | Presence of sustaining peace (SP) | | | Absence of sustaining peace (~SP) | | |
|---|---|---|---|---|---|---|
| | Consistency | Coverage | Relevance | Consistency | Coverage | Relevance |
| INT | 0.747 | 0.770 | 0.734 | 0.650 | 0.394 | 0.512 |
| ~INT | 0.412 | 0.667 | 0.825 | 0.620 | 0.590 | 0.793 |
| SHARE | 0.722 | 0.650 | 0.552 | 0.818 | 0.433 | 0.432 |
| ~SHARE | 0.371 | 0.775 | 0.912 | 0.340 | 0.418 | 0.800 |
| SSR | 0.641 | 0.768 | 0.795 | 0.620 | 0.437 | 0.615 |
| ~SSR | 0.529 | 0.703 | 0.789 | 0.670 | 0.523 | 0.700 |
| TJ | 0.643 | 0.832 | 0.863 | 0.463 | 0.352 | 0.620 |
| ~TJ | 0.500 | 0.613 | 0.709 | 0.780 | 0.562 | 0.684 |

claim would mean that sustaining peace can only occur with extensive international commitment, inclusive power sharing, comprehensive SSR or a holistic transitional justice approach as shared antecedents. Thus, without any necessary condition being found, (un)successful peacebuilding is (in general) possible in all institutional settings.

### Sufficient institutional conditions for sustaining peace and its absence

The second part of the analysis of set relations between peacebuilding institutions and sustaining peace moves away from looking at single conditions and instead aims to identify quasi-sufficient configurations of conditions defined in terms of subset relations. This definition means that whenever the condition is present across cases, the outcome has to be present as well or, with regard to fuzzy sets, the set values in the condition have to be consistently smaller than or equal to those in the outcome. For the analysis of sufficiency, the calibrated data are converted into a truth table that includes all logically possible AND combinations between the explanatory conditions included in the analysis. Table 5.2 represents an enhanced truth table for the analysis of peacebuilding conditions and sustaining peace that provides information on the parameters of fit (consistency, PRI)[2] for each row and indicates how many and which cases show a certain combination of conditions. Truth table rows not containing empirical evidence (cases) represent logical remainders (Ragin 2008: 124–130; Schneider and Wagemann 2012). The parameters of fit are reported for the subset relations between each configuration and sustaining peace as well as its absence in order to detect contradictory statements of sufficiency stemming from simultaneous subset relations (in other words, that a configuration is a subset

**Table 5.2:** Enhanced truth table for the analysis of sustaining peace (SP) and its absence (~SP)

| Row | INT | SHARE | SSR | TJ | SP | | ~SP | | Cases | Case names (membership in configuration/membership in SP) |
|---|---|---|---|---|---|---|---|---|---|---|
| | | | | | Cons. | PRI | Cons. | PRI | | |
| 14 | 1 | 1 | 0 | 1 | 0.965 | 0.925 | 0.565 | 0.075 | 3 | GRG1 (0.75/0.8), MLI2 (0.75/0.8), SRB2 (0.75/1) |
| 10 | 1 | 0 | 0 | 1 | 0.923 | 0.889 | 0.385 | 0.111 | 2 | MLD1 (0.6/1), NIC1 (0.6/0.8) |
| 8 | 0 | 1 | 1 | 1 | 0.902 | 0.721 | 0.748 | 0.279 | 3 | **CON1 (0.6/0.2)**, SAF2 (0.6/1), UKG1 (0.6/1) |
| 7 | 0 | 1 | 1 | 0 | 0.891 | 0.641 | 0.805 | 0.359 | 2 | DJI2 (0.75/0.8), **NIR1 (0.6/0.2)** |
| 16 | 1 | 1 | 1 | 1 | 0.885 | 0.800 | 0.538 | 0.200 | 10 | **BOS1 (0.6/0.4)**, BOS2 (0.6/0.8), **BUI1 (0.6/0.2)**, **CHA1 (0.6/0.4)**, DRC1 (0.6/0.8), INS1 (0.6/1), **INS2 (0.6/0.4)**, LBR2 (1/1), MOZ1 (0.75/0.8), MAC1 (0.75/1) |
| 12 | 1 | 0 | 1 | 1 | 0.873 | 0.840 | 0.333 | 0.160 | 5 | **COL1 (0.6/0.2)**, CRO1 (0.6/1), SAL1 (1/1), GUA1 (0.75/1), SIE1 (0.75/1) |
| 15 | 1 | 1 | 1 | 0 | 0.872 | 0.733 | 0.633 | 0.233 | 7 | BUI2 (0.8/0.8), **DJI1 (0.75/0.2)**, CDI1 (0.75/0.8), NEP1 (0.6/0.8), PNG2 (0.6/0.8), SAF1 (0.75/1), **SUD1 (0.75/0.4)** |
| 4 | 0 | 0 | 1 | 1 | 0.836 | 0.710 | 0.600 | 0.290 | 1 | BNG1 (0.75/1) |
| 13 | 1 | 1 | 0 | 0 | 0.836 | 0.569 | 0.766 | 0.385 | 5 | **CAR1 (0.6/0.2)**, **CHA2 (0.6/0.4)**, COM1 (0.6/0.8), DRC2 (0.6/0.6), **LBR1 (0.75/0.4)** |
| 1 | 0 | 0 | 0 | 0 | 0.827 | 0.690 | 0.614 | 0.310 | 4 | MEX1 (0.75/0.8), **MYA1 (0.75/0.2)**, NIR2 (0.6/0.8), NIR3 (0.75/0.8) |
| 9 | 1 | 0 | 0 | 0 | 0.809 | 0.639 | 0.662 | 0.361 | 2 | **LIB1 (0.6/0.4)**, SRB1 (0.6/1) |
| 3 | 0 | 0 | 1 | 0 | 0.746 | 0.484 | 0.762 | 0.516 | 2 | **ANG1 (0.6/0.2)**, **CON2 (0.6/0.4)** |
| 5 | 0 | 1 | 0 | 0 | 0.744 | 0.441 | 0.798 | 0.559 | 6 | **IND1 (0.75/0.2)**, **IND2 (0.75/0.2)**, **MLI1 (0.6/0.2)**, **MOZ2 (0.6/0.2)**, **PNG1 (0.6/0.2)**, SEN1 (0.75/1) |
| 11 | 1 | 0 | 1 | 0 | 0.694 | 0.400 | 0.735 | 0.480 | 2 | **ANG2 (0.6/0)**, *ANG3 (0.75/0.6)* |
| 2 | 0 | 0 | 0 | 1 | – | – | – | – | 0 | |
| 6 | 0 | 1 | 0 | 1 | – | – | – | – | 0 | |

Note: The truth table was created via the 'truth table command' in the *QCA* package (Duşa 2019). Additional information based on own calculations. Grey-shaded cells indicate truth table rows considered sufficient for the outcome. – indicates logical remainders. Italic letters imply contradictory cases in degree, bold letter contradictory cases in kind.

of the outcome and the nonoutcome), which can be a result of skewed data distribution (Cooper and Glaesser 2011).

The truth table is the starting point for the systematic analysis of configurations that are consistently linked to sustaining peace in a statement of sufficiency. In order to refrain from automatically considering a predefined consistency value in line with a statement of sufficiency and to avoid making contradictory or untenable assumptions about perceived subset relations, the truth table will be subjected to an in-depth inspection. The following discussion of the truth table is based on two analytical criteria: (a) a level of consistency of 0.85 or higher is required to determine a strong degree of subset relation between the combinations of conditions (truth table rows) and the outcome of sustaining peace and its negation (Ragin and Fiss 2017: 127ff); and (b) in this medium-sized $N$ design, the frequency threshold is set at a minimum of one case per row (representing 2 per cent of the sample) or the truth table row is otherwise treated as a logical remainder (Schneider and Wagemann 2012: 153).

The truth table displays high consistency values across all rows, for the analysis of sustaining peace (SP), ranging from 0.694 to 0.965. The following analysis could apply three different consistency thresholds of $\geq 0.9$, $\geq 0.85$ or $\geq 0.75$ for the inclusion of truth table rows into the minimization process, following established cut-off points and expressing moderate to almost perfect subset relations between the configurations and the outcome (Ragin and Fiss 2017: 127ff). The inspection of the truth table also reveals that the last two rows do not include any empirical evidence needed to assess whether they are sufficient for the outcome. This finding means that the configurations in rows 2 and 6 are not empirically observed in the data and are therefore treated as logical remainders in the subsequent analysis. As part of the enhanced standard analysis (ESA) procedure, it was ascertained that they do not represent implausible counterfactuals or that they contradict previously made statements of necessity (Schneider and Wagemann 2012: 198–211). All difficult counterfactuals are excluded from being simplifying assumptions, and only logical remainders that are in line with directional expectations and represent easy counterfactuals are included in the minimization process for the intermediate solution term. I choose to interpret the intermediate solution because it is based on a theory-driven evaluation of all logical remainders, as well as those rows that are both consistent subsets of the outcome and represent the most similar combination to the unobserved truth table rows, using theoretical expectations as a guide. But as none of the two logical remainders could be identified as relevant for the intermediate solution, all three solution types (conservative, most parsimonious and intermediate) are identical.

The results of the enhanced intermediate solutions with three consistency thresholds are shown in Table 5.3. The first analysis with a very high

**Table 5.3:** Enhanced intermediate solutions for the analysis of sustaining peace (SP) based on three consistency thresholds

| | Enhanced intermediate solutions | | Cons | PRI | RawCov | UniCov |
|---|---|---|---|---|---|---|
| **Subset cons. ≥0.90** | (1) INT*~SSR *TJ + | | 0.946 | 0.903 | 0.282 | 0.204 |
| | (2) ~INT*SHARE*SSR*TJ | | 0.902 | 0.721 | 0.163 | 0.085 |
| | *Solution consistency: 0.916* | *Solution coverage: 0.368* | | | | |
| **Subset cons. ≥0.85** | (1) INT*TJ + | | 0.867 | 0.818 | 0.554 | 0.250 |
| | (2) SHARE*SSR | | 0.800 | 0.701 | 0.506 | 0.201 |
| | *Solution consistency: 0.815* | *Solution coverage: 0.756* | | | | |
| **Subset consistency ≥0.75** | (1) INT*~SSR + | | 0.842 | 0.727 | 0.376 | 0.126 |
| | (2) SHARE*SSR + | *(based on inclusion of two* | 0.800 | 0.701 | 0.506 | 0.097 |
| | (3) SSR*TJ + | *difficult counterfactuals)* | 0.830 | 0.760 | 0.466 | 0.096 |
| | (4) ~SHARE*~SSR*~TJ | | 0.772 | 0.629 | 0.165 | 0.069 |
| | *Solution consistency: 0.785* | *Solution coverage: 0.859* | | | | |

consistency of ≥ 0.90 reveals two solution terms that share the outcome of sustaining peace. While the overall solution consistency is very high, the too low solution coverage means that the solution derived from the first threshold is not explaining much of the outcome. Lowering the consistency threshold to ≥ 0.85 further minimizes these two explanatory patterns, while increasing the coverage of the overall solution. Lastly, by using a moderate consistency threshold of ≥ 0.75, only the second solution term remains, while three more explanatory paths are added to the intermediate solution, making it overly complex. In addition, the intermediate solution for the moderate threshold is based on the inclusion of two difficult counterfactuals, which has to be avoided. Comparing the different solutions exemplifies that the results at a high consistency level of ≥ 0.85 present a good trade-off between explaining consistent enough with a solution consistency of 0.815 and simultaneously explaining much of the outcome with an overall coverage of 0.756. The solution resulting from the high consistency threshold is thus selected for further in-depth examination and interpretation, expressing good subset relations between the peacebuilding configurations and sustaining peace (Ragin and Fiss 2017: 127ff).

For ease of comparison across the two sufficient patterns, the results of the enhanced intermediate solution are presented in the form of a configurational chart (Table 5.4) that uses filled circles to indicate the presence of a condition while crossed circles indicate their absence. Empty cells indicate a 'don't care' situation, in which the condition is not part of the solution term and can be either present or absent (Ragin and Fiss 2008; Fiss 2011). The chart

**Table 5.4:** Configurations of peacebuilding institutions sufficient for sustaining peace (SP)

| | Enhanced intermediate solution | |
|---|---|---|
| | (1) | (2) |
| Configuration | INT★TJ | SHARE★SSR |
| International commitment (INT) | ● | |
| Power sharing (SHARE) | | ● |
| Security sector reform (SSR) | | ● |
| Transitional justice (TJ) | ● | |
| Consistency | 0.867 | 0.800 |
| PRI | 0.818 | 0.701 |
| Raw coverage | 0.554 | 0.506 |
| Unique coverage | 0.250 | 0.201 |
| Covered cases | **MLD1**, **NIC**, COL1, **CRO1**, **SAL1**, **GUA1**, **SIE1**, **GRG1**, **MLI2**, **SRB2**, BOS1, BOS2, BUI1, CHA1, DRC1, INS1, INS2, LBR2, MOZ1, MAC1 | **DJI2**, NIR1, CON1, **SAF2**, **UKG1**, **BUI2**, DJI1, **CDI1**, **NEP1**, **PNG2**, **SAF1**, SUD1, BOS1, BOS2, BUI1, CHA1, DRC1, INS1, INS2, LBR2, MOZ1, MAC1 |
| Solution | INT★JUST + SHARE★SSR → SP | |
| Solution consistency | 0.815 | |
| Solution PRI | 0.752 | |
| Solution coverage | 0.756 | |

Note: Black circles indicate the presence of a condition. Blank spaces indicate 'don't care'. Covered cases are cases with membership in pathways > 0.5. Cases in bold are uniquely covered cases, explained by one path only.

also provides a visual representation of the empirical relevance of patterns by distinguishing between 'core' (large circles) and 'contributory' (small circles) conditions.[3] The configurational chart presents the two patterns that imply the establishment of sustaining peace. The asterisk (★) signifies AND, which means that several institutional factors occur in conjunction. The individual paths are combined with the logical OR (+). The single cases that are explained by each pattern and the consistency and coverage scores for the single paths and the overall solution are listed beneath the patterns. Cases can be members of several paths.

In the first pattern, peacebuilding episodes see extensive international commitment (INT) alongside the implementation of a holistic transitional justice approach (TJ). The combined focus on security and justice is sufficient for the establishment of sustaining peace. Most peacebuilding interventions require some form of justice measure to effectively support reconciliation, and thus many UN peace missions have either had a rule of law and justice component (for example, the UN Mission in Liberia and the UN Stabilization Mission in Haiti) or were even mandated to directly address transitional justice (for example, the UN Interim Administration Mission in Kosovo and the UN Transitional Administration in East Timor). Meaningfully combined, international commitment in the form of peacekeeping and transitional justice can positively reinforce each other and contribute to achieving the broader objectives of peacebuilding and reconciliation. For example, in Sierra Leone, the peacebuilding framework included a comprehensive transitional justice component that was implemented alongside the peacekeeping mission and supported by international actors. The UN acknowledged the need for comprehensive approaches, including justice and security, in fragile post-conflict settings, highlighting that the consolidation and maintenance of peace 'cannot be achieved unless the population is confident that redress for grievances can be obtained through legitimate structures for the peaceful settlement of disputes and the fair administration of justice' (UNSG 2004).

In the second path, inclusive power sharing (SHARE) occurs in combination with comprehensive SSR. This scenario highlights the relevance of addressing commitment problems by 'rewarding' former rebels and government forces for maintaining a peace agreement, through political or military incentives and power (Walter 1997, 2002; Spear 2002; Hartzell and Hoddie 2003, 2007; Mattes and Savun 2009). Inclusive power sharing and comprehensive SSR aim to incorporate the main warring factions into the political system by offering incentives to maintain a peace agreement. This approach was implemented after the peace agreements in South Africa and Nepal, where the integration of these two peacebuilding institutions led to the establishment of sustaining peace.

The overall solution has high consistency (0.815) and coverage (0.756) scores, demonstrating its empirical relevance. The results also partly validate previous findings about the impact of peacebuilding institutions on durable peace. With regard to empirical relevance, the first configuration covers the most cases and exhibits the highest values for unique and raw coverage, which makes it especially relevant for closer inspections; however, none of the detected patterns can explain why peacebuilding interventions were successful in nine out of 54 cases, situated in the upper-left quadrant of the scatterplot in Figure 5.1.

The preceding analysis has shown that the identified institutional pathways offer a consistent and comprehensive picture in which the two configurations are consistently linked to the presence of sustaining peace; however, the explanatory power varies across the two solution terms with regard to how consistently they assess patterns of peacebuilding success, as well as to how

**Figure 5.1:** Scatterplot for the enhanced intermediate solution for sustaining peace (SP)

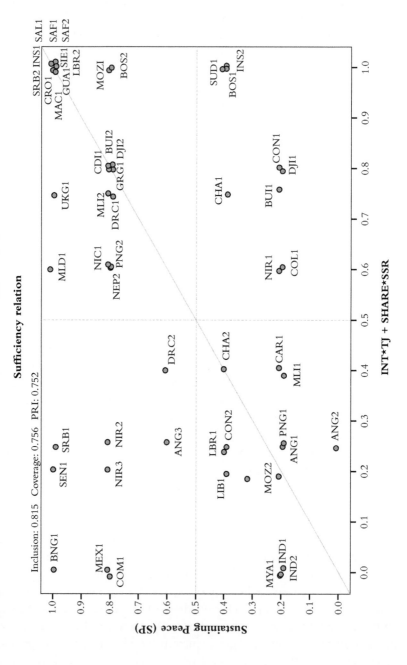

broadly they describe the occurrence of sustaining peace. I take a closer look at case distributions to better interpret the QCA results and provide some answers for the varying explanatory power across the peacebuilding patterns. The focus is first put on the identification of cross-case institutional patterns that enable the establishment of sustaining peace in post-conflict societies, before the next two sections focus on detailed discussions of typical and deviant cases for each sufficient solution term.

Based on the scatterplot presented in Figure 5.1, the overall solution provides a mixed account of peacebuilding patterns associated with sustaining peace, with regard to the accuracy of the captured patterns of peacebuilding success and the breadth of the explanation. Many typical cases cluster in the upper-right quadrant of the plot, indicating a good fit between the sufficient configurations and the outcome. Ten of these typical cases even represent ideal typical cases (CRO1, SAL1, GUA, SRB1, SIE1, INS1, LBR2, SAF1, SAF2 and MAC1), which have a unique membership of 1 in both the solution term and the outcome. These cases represent the best empirical instances for explaining how the peacebuilding institutions are linked to the outcome. On the downside, nine cases (BOS1, BUI1, CHA1, COL1, INS2, SUD1, CON1, DJI1 and NIR1) located in the lower-right quadrant have relatively high membership in the solution, but low membership in the outcome set, which makes them deviant cases for consistency, undermining the subset relation. Additionally, there is a cluster of peacebuilding episodes located in the upper-left quadrant of the scatterplot, including cases that result in sustaining peace, yet these cases are only minimally represented by the two sufficient patterns. Among those unaccounted cases, the peacebuilding episode in Bangladesh (BNG) is even a full member of sustaining peace, while displaying no coverage through the sufficient solution terms. This is left unexplained by the cross-case model and would represent an ideal case for the identification of additional explanations lying outside of the chosen explanatory framework.

Besides case distribution in the overall solution term, it is also meaningful to check for differences between the two sufficient terms of the enhanced intermediate solution. Figure 5.2 includes two scatterplots, one for each sufficient term of the intermediate solution. The case distribution in these plots is relatively even across both sufficient pathways, concerning both consistency and coverage, which supports the empirical relevance and explanatory power of the sufficient configurations for sustaining peace. The first scatterplot illustrates the case distribution for the subset relation between the combination of extensive international commitment and holistic transitional justice (INT*TJ) and the presence of sustaining peace. This configuration includes the peacebuilding episodes in Serbia (SRB2), Croatia (CRO1), North Macedonia (MAC1), Guatemala (GUA1), Indonesia (INS1), El Salvador (SAL1), Sierra Leone (SIE1) and Liberia (LBR2) as ideal typical cases with full membership in both the sufficient pattern and

# PATTERNS OF SUSTAINING PEACE

**Figure 5.2:** Scatterplots for the two terms of the enhanced intermediate solution for sustaining peace (SP)

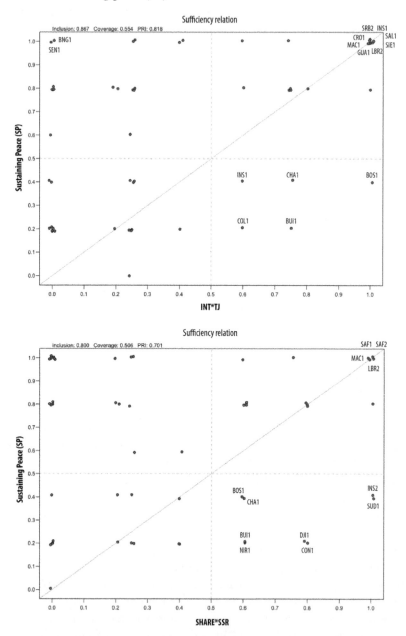

the outcome. Of these cases, the successful peacebuilding episode in Sierra Leone represents a pathway case for this first configuration and has been chosen for an in-depth case study to trace the actual mechanism underlying this subset relationship. The detailed process is outlined in the following chapter. The plot also shows five deviant cases in the lower-right quadrant and several unaccounted cases in the upper-left quadrant, of which the successful peacebuilding episodes in Senegal (SEN1) and Bangladesh (BNG) are completely unexplained by the pathway. Overall, no severe skewedness or clustering of the data are visible in the scatterplot, supporting the empirical relevance of the first pathway.

The second scatterplot illustrating the subset relation between the combined presence of inclusive power sharing and comprehensive security sector reform (SHARE*SSR) shows a similar case distribution pattern and no severe skewedness or clustering of the data. The peacebuilding episodes in South Africa (SAF1, SAF2), Liberia (LBR2) and North Macedonia (MAC1) represent ideal typical cases, while eight deviant cases are in the lower-right quadrant. The successful peacebuilding episode in South Africa (SAF1) represents a pathway case for this second sufficient pattern and is later studied in depth to trace the actual mechanism underlying this subset relationship. There is also a small cluster of unaccounted cases, which includes many cases that are typical cases in the first solution term, increasing the breadth of the explanation for the overall solution, but also meaning that the different patterns explain very different types of successful peacebuilding settings.

Lastly, as set relations are asymmetric, the outcome and its negation should always be studies in two separate analyses. We can learn from revisiting the enhanced truth table (Table 5.2) that the configurations in rows 7, 13, 3 and 5 are consistently linked to the absence of sustaining peace if we apply a moderate consistency threshold of $\geq 0.75$; however, truth table row 7 has already been included as a sufficient configuration in the minimization process for the outcome of sustaining peace. According to the ESA procedure, it thus represents a contradictory assumption for the nonoccurrence of the outcome and has to be excluded prior to the logical minimization procedure (Schneider and Wagemann 2012: 209). Using Boolean algebra, the three remaining truth table rows 13, 3 and 5 can be minimized to two sufficient configurations that are moderately associated with peacebuilding episodes resulting in renewed violence or civil war and are able to cover roughly half of the cases experiencing the absence of sustaining peace:

$$SHARE*\sim SSR*\sim TJ + \sim INT*\sim SHARE*SSR*\sim TJ \rightarrow \sim SP$$

The first sufficient pattern includes the presence of inclusive power sharing (SHARE) combined with the absence of comprehensive security sector

**Table 5.5:** Enhanced intermediate solutions for the analysis of the absence of sustaining peace (~SP)

| | Enhanced intermediate solution | Cons | PRI | RawCov | UniCov | Covered cases |
|---|---|---|---|---|---|---|
| Subset consistency ≥0.75 | (1) SHARE*~SSR*~TJ + | 0.762 | 0.535 | 0.527 | 0.462 | IND1, IND2, MLI1, MOZ2, PNG1, SEN1, CAR1, CHA2, COM1, DRC2, LBR1 |
| | (2) ~INT*~SHARE*SSR*~TJ | 0.762 | 0.516 | 0.120 | 0.055 | ANG1, CON2 |
| | *Solution consistency: 0.756* | | | | | |
| | *Solution coverage: 0.582* | | | | | |

reform (~SSR) and holistic transitional justice (~TJ). This configuration has a high unique coverage and empirical relevance, as it explains nearly half of all peacebuilding episodes resulting in renewed armed conflict or civil war (Table 5.5). The second sufficient configuration for the nonoccurrence of sustaining peace includes the presence of comprehensive security sector reform (SSR) with the simultaneous absence of international commitment (~INT), power sharing (~SHARE) and transitional justice (~TJ).

Taken together, these two configurations underline the ambiguous role of political power sharing and SSR, which, in their combined presence, are sufficient for peacebuilding success, while, implemented on their own, they lead to peacebuilding failure. Without additional security guarantees from international actors and accountability for previously committed human rights violations, peacebuilding approaches that focus only on single measures rewarding former belligerents might trigger resentments in the general public or from other armed groups, especially if they are combined with amnesties for previous crimes (the nonholistic transitional justice approach). The results show that if peacebuilding episodes face the absence of international support and meaningful transitional justice, they cannot overcome this institutional lack by comprehensively reforming the security sector or the political system but must instead experience a relapse to armed conflict.

Overall, the only moderate consistency (0.756) for the enhanced intermediate solution combined with the mediocre coverage (0.582) indicates an inferior fit of the model for those peacebuilding cases resulting in the absence of sustaining peace. The scatterplot in Figure 5.3, showing the set-theoretic fit of all peacebuilding episodes with regard to their membership in the intermediate solution and the absence of sustaining peace, supports this finding. While the data is not skewed in any discernible way, we cannot identify an ideal typical case exhibiting full membership in both the sufficient configurations and the negative outcome. The peacebuilding episode in Mozambique (MOZ2) represents

**Figure 5.3:** Scatterplot for the enhanced intermediate solution for the absence of sustaining peace (~SP)

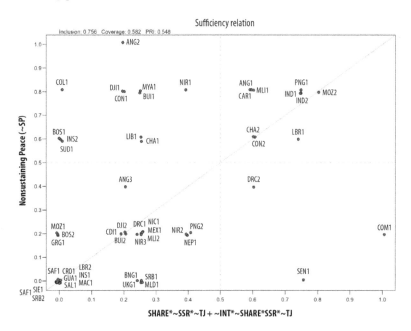

the best typical case, but is far from being ideally typical, with only a set membership of 0.8 in the solution term and the negative outcome. Additionally, for the unaccounted cases in the upper-left quadrant, the selected peacebuilding institutions cannot explain the failure of these peace processes. Because it is highly relevant to also learn from peacebuilding mistakes, future research should focus on identifying alternative factors and configurations that are highly consistent with the absence of sustaining peace. A good starting point would be the detailed analysis of one of the unaccounted cases to identify sufficient factors for peacebuilding failure. Even if the results of the examination for the absence of sustaining peace are not very satisfactory, this analysis has shown that the causal relations between peacebuilding institutions and the presence/absence of sustaining peace are very asymmetrical and that the selected conditions are much better suited to explain the success of peacebuilding episodes than their failure.

## A configurational model of peacebuilding success

The two quasi-sufficient paths to sustaining peace can be labelled based on theoretical concepts identified by peacebuilding research: the *assisted accountability approach* for the conjunction of extensive international commitment and a holistic transitional justice approach (Hannum 2006; Rodman 2011), and the *spoils-of-peace approach* for the combination of inclusive power sharing and comprehensive SSR (Clark 2001; Pugh 2002). The following paragraphs explain and discuss these two patterns in more detail, with Figure 5.4 presenting the complete configurational model of peacebuilding institutions and sustaining peace. The model is valid for the predefined universe of cases, but also any future case that complies with the scope conditions (previous conflict ended by a peace agreement, post-conflict peacebuilding occurring).[4]

## *The assisted accountability approach*

The first path to sustaining peace is via the assisted accountability for previous war crimes and violations of human rights, and includes the combined presence of INT and TJ. The combined focus on security guarantees and justice is sufficient for the establishment of sustaining peace. This approach also provides the most accurate picture describing a peacebuilding pattern associated with sustaining peace by explaining a large number of cases and partly validating previous findings regarding the impact of peacebuilding institutions on lasting peace. Transitional justice has been incorporated into the mandates of many recent UN peace missions, and efforts to achieve justice, peace and democracy are treated by the UN as 'mutually reinforcing imperatives' (UNSG 2004b). Peace operations have an effective role in coordinating and implementing transitional justice processes, as successful initiatives require the continued support and active engagement of all relevant actors. Ultimately, a combination of security-restoring measures with restorative and retributive justice elements – ensuring principles of security provision, accountability, the rule of law and a victim-centred approach that focuses on reconciliation and the establishment of truth – leads to sustaining peace as one of two sufficient patterns.

The logic behind this argument is that in post-conflict situations, peace can only be sustained if the country receives assistance for addressing national reconciliation through accountability and justice measures (Hannum 2006; Rodman 2011). The focus on security without justice would only support underlying animosities and grievances within societies, as victims do not feel acknowledged and perpetrators are 'politically rewarded' for the atrocities they have committed (Hannum 2006: 585). The UN thus acknowledged the need for comprehensive peacebuilding approaches including justice and security in fragile post-conflict settings, highlighting that the consolidation and maintenance of peace 'cannot be achieved unless the population is confident that redress for grievances can be obtained through legitimate structures for the peaceful settlement of disputes and the fair administration of justice' (UNSG 2004b: para 2). According to this pattern, if they are to

**Figure 5.4:** Configurational model of peacebuilding institutions and sustaining peace (SP), 1989–2016

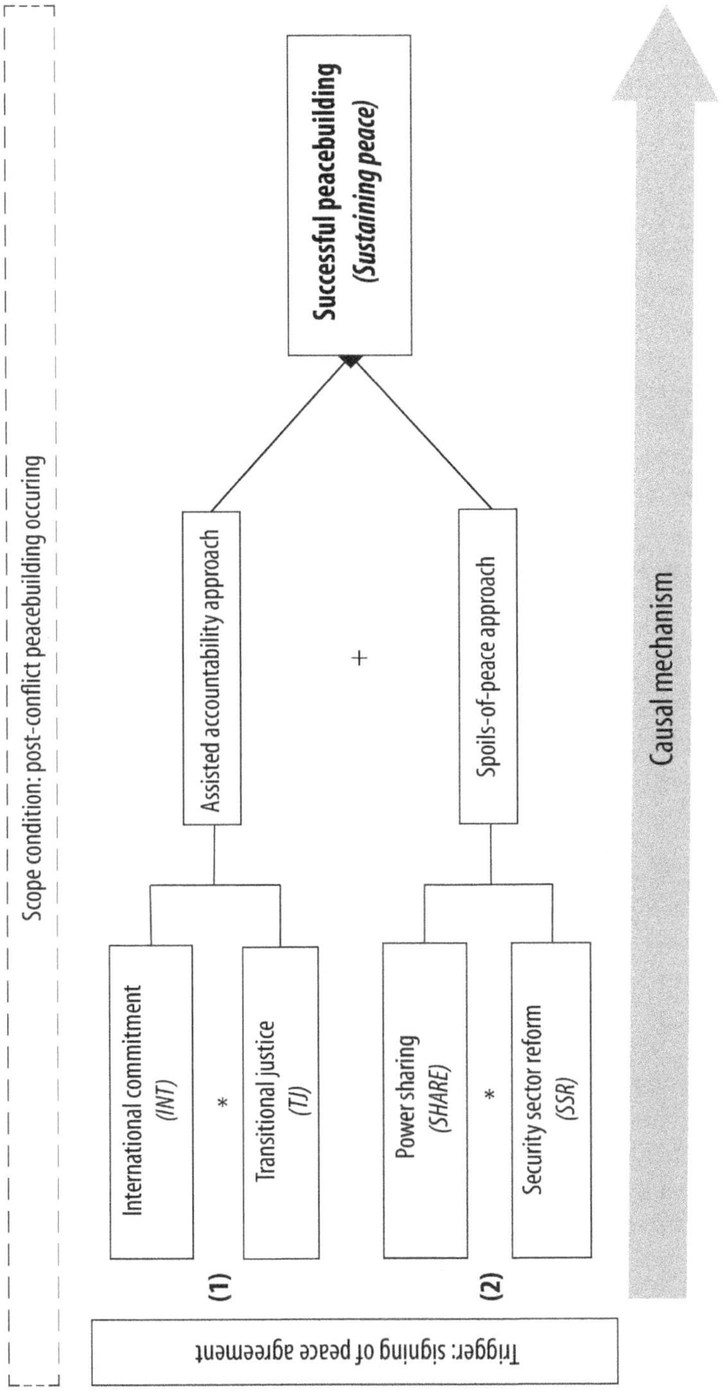

Scope condition: post-conflict peacebuilding occuring

Trigger: signing of peace agreement

**(1)**
International commitment
*(INT)*

\*

Transitional justice
*(TJ)*

Assisted accountability approach

**(2)**
Power sharing
*(SHARE)*

\*

Security sector reform
*(SSR)*

Spoils-of-peace approach

+

**Successful peacebuilding**
*(Sustaining peace)*

Causal mechanism

be successful, peacebuilding operations need to provide both security for the societies emerging from armed conflicts and justice for the atrocities committed in the past.

The conjunction between these two conditions becomes especially apparent when UN peacekeeping operations are mandated to carry out certain TJ tasks, like delivering reparations, facilitating truth-seeking processes and prosecution initiatives, or reforming public institutions. Most current peacebuilding interventions require some form of justice measure to effectively support reconciliation, and many UN peace operations have had rule of law and justice components or were even mandated to directly address transitional justice. The commitments made towards accountability and justice in peace agreements have to be implemented and guaranteed by third-party actors: 'the success of efforts for justice and accountability may depend not only on their incorporation into peace agreements, but also on the actors responsible for negotiation and implementation' (Vinjamuri and Boesenecker 2007: 31). An ideal typical and uniquely covered pathway case for this pattern can be found in the peacebuilding approach after the civil war in Sierra Leone, in which a comprehensive transitional justice component (including a Truth and Reconciliation Commission, a Special Court and a reparations programme) was implemented alongside security-centred initiatives and the presence of a UN peace operation. Meaningfully combined, security-centred approaches and TJ can positively reinforce each other and contribute to achieving the broader objectives of peacebuilding and reconciliation.

### The spoils-of-peace approach

The second pathway can be characterized as a spoils-of-peace approach that connects power sharing and SSR with sustaining peace by providing the warring factions with some political or monetary gains from the peace agreement (Clark 2001; Pugh 2002). Inclusive power sharing and comprehensive SSR both aim at incorporating the main warring factions into the political system by offering them some incentives to maintain a peace agreement (Spear 2002; Walter 2002; Hartzell and Hoddie 2007; Mattes and Savun 2009). Taken together, these two institutions focus on resolving the security dilemma and building or restoring key state functions 'that have the capacity to generate basic public goods and possess a modicum of legitimacy' (Barnett et al 2007: 49). The guaranteed access for former combatants to executive power is of the utmost importance for peacebuilding initiatives, as the representation by all factions in government prevents former enemies from capturing the state (Walter 2002). In this regard, power sharing facilitates the transition from civil war to sustaining peace by reassuring opposition and minority groups that their interests will be taken into account through the participation of their representatives in governmental decision-making processes. It also enables faction leaders to make some personal gains with their new positions in transitional governments, while still facilitating the transition to democratic governance and their participation as political parties in general elections.

In addition to restoring key political functions, a functioning security system that ensures the security of civilians and discourages combatants from returning to war is also a prerequisite for the establishment of sustaining peace. The remnants of a wartime security apparatus pose great risks for any peace process, as they continue to jeopardize internal security in societies already devastated by conflict (Schnabel and Ehrhart 2005). The goal of SSR is to consolidate peace through comprehensive disarmament, demobilization and tenable reintegration of all ex-combatants into civil society, preventing them from becoming a threat to peace and stability. The demobilization of former combatants and their inclusion in national security institutions form the cornerstone for successful peacebuilding. If carried out successfully, this offers former combatants and faction leaders an alternative to a life with the gun and a stable means of income, reducing the risk of conflict recurrence. This pattern is best represented by the ideal typical and uniquely covered pathway case of the peacebuilding episode following South Africa's civil war and the end of the apartheid regime, which saw the implementation of a spoils-of-peace approach containing power sharing and SSR.

## Variations in successful peacebuilding patterns

The two previously identified patterns of peacebuilding success seem to explain the selected peacebuilding episodes well; however, the results might cluster around certain geographical or conflict structures that are analytically relevant but not captured by the underlying model (Oana and Schneider 2018). To keep the issue of limited diversity at bay, the QCA model does not capture any geographical or other substantive differences between the cases and thus assumes that any potential analytical differences do not matter; however, it is advisable to check for possible analytical differences and to empirically test whether it is OK to pool cases across the different types of conflicts that preceded the peacebuilding episodes and across different conflict regions. Those two types of clusters also represent common control variables for robustness checks and were coded according to selected variables from the UCDP/ PRIO Armed Conflict Dataset: region (including Europe, Asia, Africa and the Americas) and incompatibility (regarding territory or government).

The results of a cluster analysis[5] for the intermediate solution do indeed reveal some minor structures around conflicts regions and two types of conflicts (see Table 5.6). For example, the overall pooled solution has a slightly higher consistency for peacebuilding episodes in Europe and

**Table 5.6:** Results for the cluster analysis of the enhanced intermediate solution

| | Solution | INT★TJ | SHARE★SSR |
|---|---|---|---|
| **Consistencies** | | | |
| Pooled | 0.815 | 0.867 | 0.800 |
| Africa | 0.823 | 0.973 | 0.826 |
| Americas | 0.875 | 0.875 | 0.900 |
| Asia | 0.826 | 0.915 | 0.929 |
| Europe | 0.892 | 0.882 | 1.000 |
| Conflict over government | 0.851 | 0.947 | 0.851 |
| Conflict over territory | 0.832 | 0.896 | 0.886 |
| **Coverage** | | | |
| Pooled | 0.756 | 0.554 | 0.506 |
| Africa | 0.828 | 0.526 | 0.724 |
| Americas | 0.737 | 0.737 | 0.118 |
| Asia | 0.594 | 0.448 | 0.542 |
| Europe | 0.825 | 0.750 | 0.369 |
| Conflict over government | 0.882 | 0.646 | 0.671 |
| Conflict over territory | 0.673 | 0.531 | 0.407 |
| **Distances** | | | |
| Between 'region' and pooled | 0.018 | 0.021 | 0.034 |
| Between 'type' and pooled | 0.008 | 0.019 | 0.014 |

the Americas, which becomes even more pronounced for the second configuration (SHARE★SSR), where cases in Europe exhibit a perfect consistency. In contrast, peacebuilding episodes in Africa and Asia show higher consistency values for the first configuration (INT★TJ) compared to other regions. Similar results can be found for coverage, where more cases are covered for the European and African samples. A similar picture emerges for the cluster analysis of different types of conflicts. Here, the complete solution has a slightly higher consistency and coverage for peacebuilding episodes after conflicts that were fought over government control, which is even more pronounced for the first configuration. In general, the underlying model has a higher explanatory power for peacebuilding after conflicts over government. While the cluster analysis can validate the general robustness of the underlying peacebuilding model, it also highlighted some small variations across regions and two types of conflict, pointing towards the need of further analysis.

INSTITUTIONAL PATTERNS OF PEACEBUILDING SUCCESS

**Figure 5.5:** Venn diagrams showing peacebuilding patterns for sustaining peace (SP) across types of conflict

(a) Conflict over government

(b) Conflict over territory

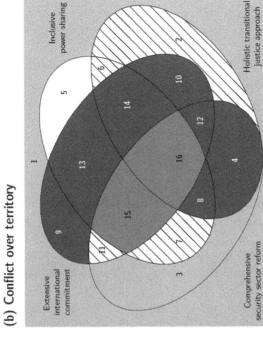
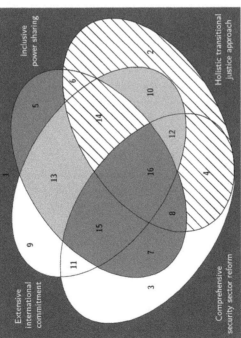

Note: ■ Subset consistency > 0.90; ■ Subset consistency > 0.85 and < 0.90; ■ Subset consistency > 0.75 and < 0.85; □ Subset consistency < 0.75; ☒ logical remainder

Source: Own illustration based on Ragin and Fiss (2017)

121

## Patterns of sustaining peace according to the type of conflict

According to the cluster analysis, multiple dynamics should be at work in peacebuilding patterns, depending on the type of the previous conflict. If we split the sample of peacebuilding episodes into conflicts over government and conflicts over territory, no individual peacebuilding condition exhibits a consistent superset relationship with the outcome set irrespective of the conflict type.[6] Therefore, patterns of sustaining peace across types of conflict do not share any meaningful antecedent peacebuilding conditions. The second step of the analysis aims at identifying sufficient configurations for sustaining peace across the two types of conflict. Figure 5.5 graphically represents the truth tables for the two subsamples in the form of Venn diagrams, which illustrate variations between different intersections of peacebuilding conditions that are consistently linked to sustaining peace across the two conflict types (Rubinson 2019). They show the four intersecting peacebuilding conditions and the 16 set intersections generated by them, labelled according to their corresponding truth table row numbers.[7] The Venn diagrams include the three consistency thresholds of very high ($\geq 0.90$, dark grey), good ($\geq 0.85$, medium grey) and moderate ($\geq 0.75$, light grey) to show the differences in consistency for the intersections. Rows with subset consistency $< 0.75$ are left blank (white) and rows that represent logical remainders are represented by a striped pattern (Ragin and Fiss 2017).

The Venn diagrams show the pronounced variation among the observed configurations displaying consistent subset relations. The subsample of peacebuilding episodes after territorial conflicts exhibits the greatest range of sufficient institutional configurations, with a total of 11 combinations consistently linked to sustaining peace, whereas patterns of peacebuilding success after conflicts over government can be consistently described by nine configurations, which also show lower consistency values. Additionally, seven consistent configurations from the governmental conflict subsample (#1, #8, #10, #12, #13, #15 and #16) are also shared by the sample of peacebuilding episodes after territorial conflicts, which mean that both types experience some similar patterns when it comes to the impact of peacebuilding institutions on sustaining peace and that they do not follow completely different causal logics. In the case of peacebuilding after conflicts over territory, seven truth table rows exhibit very high consistency values above 0.9, compared to only one row for conflicts over government, demonstrating a very good model fit. Overall, the QCA model seems better suited to explain the impact of peacebuilding institutions on the establishment of sustaining peace after conflicts over territory, which slightly contrasts with the findings from the cluster analysis for the overall intermediate solution.

Additionally, the consistent intersections in both Venn diagrams include the presence of more than one peacebuilding condition connected to sustaining peace in both samples. This is in line with the theoretical expectations that peacebuilding institutions are more relevant for sustaining peace in their presence than in their absence. Most consistent intersections in the second sample also include the presence of extensive international commitment, which makes the intervention of IOs and individual states in territorial conflicts highly relevant for the establishment of sustaining peace. Overall, the observable similarities in the Venn diagrams of these two subsamples point towards shared causal logics when it comes to the impact of peacebuilding institutions and the explanation of successful peacebuilding.

Additional similarities are apparent in Table 5.7, which presents the enhanced intermediate solution terms based on the respective truth table analyses across both types of conflict. The overall consistency ranges between 0.795 for the conflict-over-government solution and 0.847 for the conflict-over-territory sample, substantiating the previous claim that the QCA model is well suited to explain the impact of peacebuilding institutions on the establishment of sustaining peace after conflicts over territory. Similarly, the coverage parameters assessing the explanatory power of the results vary between 0.750 for peacebuilding episodes after conflicts over government control and 0.787 for those after territorial conflicts. For both samples, the underlying model is empirically relevant as it can cover a large part of the cases that experience the occurrence of sustaining peace.

Regarding peacebuilding episodes after conflicts over government, one institutional recipe for the establishment of sustaining peace was already sufficient in the complete sample: the presence of inclusive power sharing and comprehensive SSR (1a). The second sufficient pattern is characterized by the rather surprising finding that the combined absence of international commitment, SSR and TJ leads to sustaining peace for some of the peacebuilding episodes after conflicts over government (1b); however, due to its much higher unique coverage of 0.458, the first pattern can reliably explain more cases and is thus more relevant empirically.

For peacebuilding after territorial conflicts, two enabling paths for sustaining peace are very consistent and broadly explain most of the success patterns in territorial post-conflict settings. The first recipe includes only the presence of extensive international commitment as a single sufficient condition (2a). The second pattern includes the combined presence of comprehensive SSR and a holistic transitional justice approach (2b). The two patterns represent diverse institutional settings that are mostly in line with the theoretical expectations. For peacebuilding after separatist conflicts, there are two potential combinations of peacebuilding institutions that lead to sustaining peace, wherein the sole presence of international commitment has the bigger empirical relevance due to the pattern's higher PRI and unique coverage values. After territorial conflicts, credible international support makes a significant difference for a successful peacebuilding approach. Overall, a comparison with the solution terms for the complete sample

## PATTERNS OF SUSTAINING PEACE

**Table 5.7:** Solution terms for the intermediate solution for sustaining peace (SP) across types of conflict

| | Conflict over government | | Conflict over territory | |
|---|---|---|---|---|
| Configuration | (1a) | (1b) | (2a) | (2b) |
| International commitment (INT) | | ⊗ | ● | |
| Power sharing (SHARE) | ● | | | |
| Security sector reform (SSR) | ● | ⊗ | | ● |
| Transitional justice (TJ) | | ⊗ | | ● |
| Consistency | 0.811 | 0.839 | 0.859 | 0.868 |
| PRI | 0.717 | 0.545 | 0.820 | 0.802 |
| Raw coverage | 0.640 | 0.292 | 0.679 | 0.364 |
| Unique coverage | 0.458 | 0.110 | 0.423 | 0.108 |
| Covered cases | DJI2, NIR1, CON1, SAF2, BUI2, DJI1, CDI1, NEP1, BUI1, CHA1, DRC1, LBR2, MOZ1, MAC1 | MEX1, NIR3, MOZ2 | SRB1, MLD1, CRO1, COM1, GRG1, MLI2, SRB2, PNG2, SAF1, SUD1, BOS1, BOS2, INS1, INS2 | BNG1, UKG1, CRO1, BOS1, BOS2, INS1, INS2 |
| Solution | SHARE*SSR + ~INT*~SSR*~TJ → SP | | INT + SSR*TJ → SP | |
| Solution consistency | 0.795 | | 0.847 | |
| Solution PRI | 0.696 | | 0.806 | |
| Solution coverage | 0.750 | | 0.787 | |

Note: Black circles indicate the presence of a condition, and circles with 'X' indicate its absence. Blank spaces indicate 'don't care'. Large circles represent core conditions; small ones contributing conditions. Covered cases are cases with membership in pathway > 0.5.

Source: Based on Fiss (2011)

(see Table 5.4) shows patterns of many similarities irrespective of the preceding conflict, which makes the overall results more robust.

Overall, the four peacebuilding factors included in the QCA model seem to possess more explanatory power when it comes to successful peacebuilding episodes after territorial conflicts than after conflicts over government. This finding is also supported by the scatterplots in Figure 5.6, which show the

**Figure 5.6:** Scatterplots for enhanced intermediate solutions for sustaining peace (SP) according to type of conflict

**(a) Conflict over government**

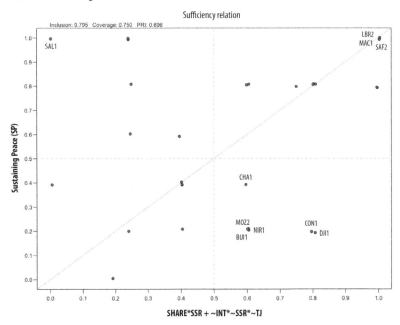

**(b) Conflict over territory**

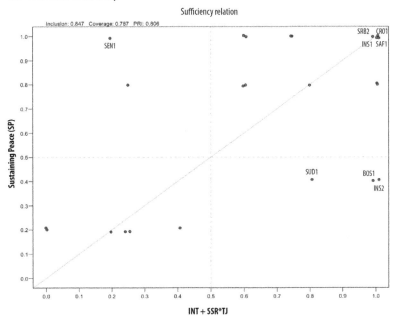

distribution of cases with regard to their membership in the solution terms and the outcome according to the type of conflict. These two plots exhibit only minor differences in case distribution: while the sufficient configurations for peacebuilding episodes after territorial conflicts (Figure 5.6b) include more typical cases in the upper-right corner and three deviant cases for consistency, the sufficient institutional paths for peacebuilding after conflicts over government (Figure 5.6a) cover less typical cases and also include six deviant cases for consistency. In both subsamples, the data are not skewed to any side of the scatterplot and the overall distribution patterns are rather similar, indicating that the overall model and results are rather robust in relation to the different types of conflict preceding a peacebuilding episode.

The corresponding analysis of sufficient subset relations for the absence of sustaining peace yields three consistent paths[8] for peacebuilding failure after conflicts over government and is not feasible for the conflicts-over-territory subsample, as none of the combinations of conditions displays a consistent enough subset relation for a meaningful analysis. While the institutional model can partly explain unsuccessful peacebuilding after conflicts over government, it is not applicable for analysis of nonpeace after territorial conflicts.

## Patterns of sustaining peace according to regions

Based on the cluster analysis results, multiple dynamics should also be at work in peacebuilding patterns according to the region in which the peacebuilding episode takes place. If we split the sample of peacebuilding episodes into regional subsamples, no individual peacebuilding condition exhibits a consistent superset relationship with the outcome set irrespective of the region in which the peacebuilding episode takes place.[9] Therefore, patterns of sustaining peace across conflict regions do not share any meaningful antecedent peacebuilding conditions. The second step of the analysis aims at identifying sufficient configurations for sustaining peace across conflict regions. The Venn diagrams in Figure 5.7 graphically represent the individual truth tables and illustrate variations between different intersections of peacebuilding conditions that are consistently linked to sustaining peace across the four conflict regions. They also support the discussion of commonalities and differences between peacebuilding patterns across regions and exemplify the variations among those configurations that display consistent subset relations.

For instance, the sample of peacebuilding episodes in Europe exhibits by far the highest range of sufficient configurations, with a total of six combinations each being very consistently connected to sustaining peace. All combinations that are empirically observed in this sample have (nearly) perfect consistency scores for the subset relation, which makes the underlying model very relevant for European peacebuilding episodes. In contrast, the sample for peacebuilding episodes in Asia includes only three consistent configurations,

**Figure 5.7:** Venn diagrams showing peacebuilding patterns for sustaining peace (SP) across conflict regions

(a) Africa

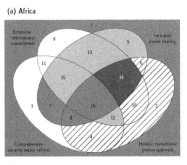

(b) Americas

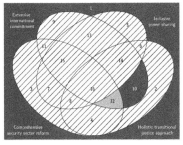

(c) Asia

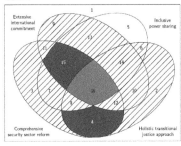

(d) Europe

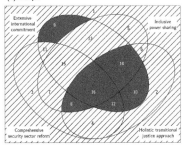

Note: ■ Subset consistency > 0.90; ■ Subset consistency > 0.85 and < 0.90;
▒ Subset consistency > 0.75 and < 0.85; ☐ Subset consistency > 0.75 and < 0.85;
▨ Subset consistency > 0.75 and < 0.85

Source: Own illustration based on Ragin and Fiss (2017)

while other rows are not consistent enough to be linked to peacebuilding success. A similar picture is discernible for peacebuilding episodes in the Americas, where we have only three configurations that are represented by empirical cases; however, these three patterns are highly consistent and completely cover all empirically observed cases in this subsample. Lastly, the sample of peacebuilding episodes in Africa displays the most empirical diversity, with nine truth table configurations that are consistently linked to sustaining peace. Only one configuration shows a very high consistency, while the remainder display moderate to good consistency values. Overall, the Venn diagrams substantiate the claim that the regional peacebuilding samples follow partly different dynamics when it comes to the impact of peacebuilding institutions on sustaining peace.

Table 5.8 presents the enhanced intermediate solution terms based on the respective truth table analyses across the four conflict regions.[10] The overall high consistency ranges between 0.823 and 0.893 for the four solutions, substantiating the general coherence of the findings, especially in light of the particularities of post-conflict settings; however, the coverage parameter, assessing the explanatory power of the results, varies considerably, between 0.421 for peacebuilding episodes in the Americas and 0.837 for those in Europe. While the identified patterns are thus rather concise across the four regions, a considerable proportion of successful peacebuilding cases is not covered by the QCA model in the American and Asian samples.

For peacebuilding after conflicts in Africa, we can identify three institutional settings for the establishment of sustaining peace, which have the lowest consistency (0.823) of all the subsamples, and a moderate coverage of 0.641. The first pattern includes the presence of power sharing and SSR in the absence of international commitment (1a). The second path consists of the three-way combination of international commitment, power sharing and TJ (1b), and is empirically the most relevant with the highest consistency and coverage values of all three configurations. And the last configuration is empirically intriguing as it includes the combined absence of all four peacebuilding institutions (1c), which cannot be explained by theoretical approaches. Because this pattern only covers two peacebuilding episodes in Niger, it is empirically less relevant, but the actual causal process could be uncovered through a case study on these two typical cases.

Regarding peacebuilding episodes in the Americas, the table shows two enabling paths for sustaining peace, which have high solution consistency (0.889) but low coverage (0.421), as they only reliably explain one case each. The first highly consistent recipe includes a focus on international commitment in the absence of SSR (2a) and covers the peacebuilding episode in Nicaragua. The second sufficient configuration is characterized by the conjoined absence of SSR and transitional justice (2b) and explains the case of Mexico. The regional sample for Asia also includes two sufficient

**Table 5.8:** Solution terms for the enhanced intermediate solution for peacebuilding conditions and sustaining peace (SP) across conflict regions

| | Africa | | | Americas | | Asia | | Europe* | | |
|---|---|---|---|---|---|---|---|---|---|---|
| Configuration | (1a) | (1b) | (1c) | (2a) | (2b) | (3a) | (3b) | (4a) | (4b) | (4c) |
| International commitment (INT) | ⊗ | ● | ⊗ | ● | | | ● | ● | ● | |
| Power sharing (SHARE) | ● | ● | ⊗ | | | | ● | | ⊗ | ● |
| Security sector reform (SSR) | ● | | ⊗ | ⊗ | ⊗ | ● | ● | | ⊗ | ● |
| Transitional justice (TJ) | | ● | ⊗ | | ⊗ | ● | | ● | | ● |
| | | | | | | | | | | |
| Consistency | 0.840 | 0.857 | 0.855 | 1.000 | 0.840 | 0.789 | 0.917 | 0.882 | 1.000 | 0.926 |
| PRI | 0.580 | 0.750 | 0.704 | 1.000 | 0.765 | 0.707 | 0.875 | 0.867 | 1.000 | 0.905 |
| Raw coverage | 0.316 | 0.414 | 0.135 | 0.211 | 0.276 | 0.469 | 0.458 | 0.750 | 0.287 | 0.312 |
| Unique coverage | 0.115 | 0.253 | 0.072 | 0.145 | 0.211 | 0.156 | 0.146 | 0.263 | 0.044 | 0.044 |
| Covered cases | 4 | 6 | 2 | 1 | 1 | 3 | 4 | 7 | 2 | 4 |
| Solution consistency | 0.823 | | | 0.889 | | 0.831 | | 0.893 | | |
| Solution PRI | 0.698 | | | 0.857 | | 0.782 | | 0.881 | | |
| Solution coverage | 0.641 | | | 0.421 | | 0.615 | | 0.837 | | |

Note: Black circles indicate the presence of a condition, and circles with 'X' indicate its absence. Blank spaces indicate 'don't care'. Large circles represent core conditions; small ones contributing conditions. Covered cases are cases with membership in pathway > 0.5. * indicates conservative solutions, where no further minimization is possible.

Source: Based on Fiss (2011)

institutional settings for sustaining peace that exhibit a high coverage (0.831) and moderate consistency (0.615). In the first pattern, the combined presence of SSR and transitional justice is sufficient for sustaining peace (3a). And the second setting includes the combined presence of international commitment, power sharing and SSR (3b), which exhibits a high consistency.

Finally, there are three paths for sustaining peace observable for European peacebuilding episodes, which have the highest consistency of all four regional samples (0.893) and broadly explain success patterns in post-conflict settings with a high solution coverage of 0.837.[11] The first path consists of the combined presence of extensive international commitment and holistic transitional justice (4a), and is identical to the first sufficient pattern of the overall solution for the complete sample. With the highest unique coverage, it is also the empirically most relevant pattern for successful European peacebuilding episodes. The second configuration comprises the presence of extensive international commitment together with the combined absence of inclusive power sharing and comprehensive SSR (4b). The last pattern for European peacebuilding episodes sufficient for sustaining peace shows the three-way combination of inclusive power sharing, comprehensive SSR and holistic transitional justice (4c).

A comparison of the solution terms highlights some differences and uniqueness of the configurations sharing the presence of sustaining peace for each of the four regional clusters, which makes comparisons and the disclosure of commonalities rather difficult. Peacebuilding success seems to be based on diverse institutional settings across these regions, which complicates the formulation of general recommendations and findings and also explains some of the deviant cases for coverage in the complete sample. A comparison with the solution terms for the complete sample (see Table 5.4) points to some shared patterns, as both recipes are also (partly) included in the solution terms for the European sample (4b, 4c). The peacebuilding patterns for sustaining peace thus differ with regard to the region in which the initiatives take place and also share some common ground, supporting a substantive analysis across regions.

Overall, the four peacebuilding factors seem to possess less explanatory power for successful peacebuilding episodes in the Americas and Africa, while peacebuilding processes in Europe are almost entirely explained by the model. This finding is also supported by the scatterplots in Figure 5.8, which show the distribution of cases with regard to their membership in the solution terms and the outcome according to the conflict regions. These plots clearly show differences in regional case distributions:

(a) The African subsample includes the typical case of Liberia (LBR2), with the rest of the cases being relatively even distributed. The plot does not reveal any ideal unaccounted cases, but three cases (SEN1, SIE1 and SAF1) are mostly left unexplained by the overall solution. However, two of these cases are ideal typical cases for the complete model. Lastly, four peacebuilding episodes (CHA1, CON1, NIR1 and BUI1) represent deviant cases for consistency in kind, which contradict the statement of sufficiency.

(b) The scatterplot for peacebuilding episodes in the Americas displays no ideal typical cases, but the two peacebuilding episodes in El Salvador (SAL1) and Guatemala (GUA1) as unaccounted cases. This case distribution explains the low coverage values and makes the overall model less relevant for the American sample.

(c) The sufficient institutional pattern for peacebuilding episodes in Asia includes four peacebuilding episodes as typical cases, most of which are,

**Figure 5.8:** Scatterplots for enhanced intermediate/conservative solutions for sustaining peace (SP) across regions

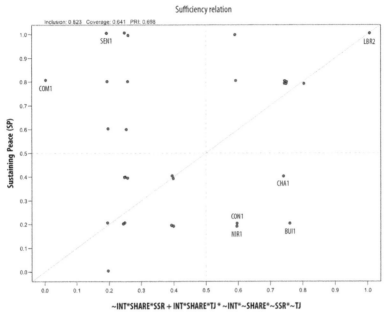

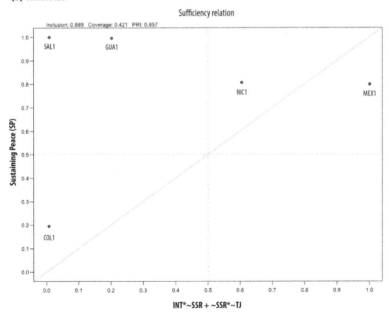

**Figure 5.8:** Scatterplots for enhanced intermediate/conservative solutions for sustaining peace (SP) across regions (contiued)

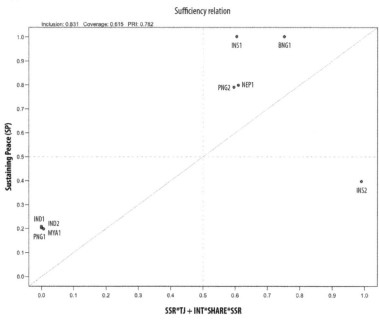

(c) Asia

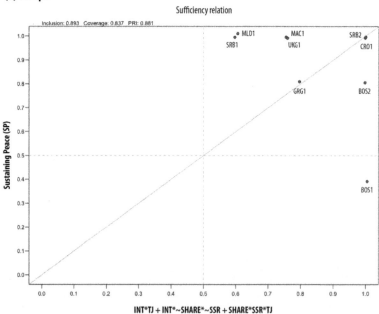

(d) Europe

however, located just over the 0.5 threshold. The peacebuilding episode in Indonesia (INS2) represents a clear deviant case for consistency, located in the lower-right corner.

(d) The final scatterplot for peacebuilding episodes in Europe shows the best distribution pattern, with most episodes representing typical cases and just two deviant cases consistency in degree (BOS2) and kind (BOS1). Furthermore, CRO1 and SRB2 describe ideal typical cases which have a unique membership of 1 in the solution terms and the outcome.

Overall, the cluster analysis has revealed variations in institutional patterns of peacebuilding success. The four peacebuilding conditions included in the QCA model seem to possess more explanatory power when it comes to successful peacebuilding episodes after territorial conflicts than after conflicts over government; however, the results for both subsamples share similarities that point towards shared causal logics when it comes to explaining successful peacebuilding. Pooling them together in one analysis does not greatly distort the results and makes the configurational model presented in Figure 5.4 robust towards different types of previous conflicts. Concerning regional clusters, the four peacebuilding factors seem to possess less explanatory power for successful peacebuilding episodes in the Americas, while peacebuilding processes in Europe are almost entirely explained by the model.[12] This represents a discernible weakness of the configurational peacebuilding model, which will be discussed in more detail in the final chapter of this book.

## Summary

This chapter has presented the empirical analysis studying the influence of peacebuilding institutions on sustaining peace by looking at various configurations of peacebuilding conditions that are jointly linked to the establishment of sustaining peace in post-conflict settings. The main goal of the analyses was to find answers to four questions: which peacebuilding factors serve as shared antecedent (or necessary) conditions of sustaining peace and its absence? What configurations of peacebuilding conditions enable the establishment of sustaining peace in post-conflict situations? Conversely, which combinations are consistently linked with the absence of sustaining peace in peacebuilding episodes? Do these peacebuilding patterns of sustaining peace vary with regard to certain clusters in the data?

The findings of this chapter provide some valuable insights with regard to all four questions and lead to new questions that were not addressed satisfactorily and therefore remain tasks for future research. The first superset analysis of cases sharing the same antecedent conditions have shown that there are no institutional conditions that need to be present all the time for peacebuilding episodes to successfully result in sustaining peace, so peacebuilding success is (in general) possible with various institutional settings. This lack of necessary conditions is theoretically reasonable and comes as no surprise, since a necessity claim would have meant that peacebuilding can only be (un)successful with one of the peacebuilding institutions always being present or absent.

Regarding the second and third questions, the findings have underscored the added value of the set-theoretic perspective for peacebuilding studies, as none of the included peacebuilding conditions was solely and consistently linked to sustaining peace or its absence, and as the results for the outcome and its negation diverged, indicating an asymmetrical relationship. Only the combined presence of several peacebuilding institutions, made up by two-way configurations, led to sustaining peace. The configurational model also supports the notion that there is no single recipe for peacebuilding success, but there are rather two equifinal paths: (1) the assisted accountability approach, including the presence of international commitment and TJ; and (2) the spoils-of-peace approach, combining the presence of power sharing and SSR. The first approach is the empirically more relevant one, as it explains the largest share of successful peacebuilding episodes. In contrast, the selected institutional framework was less suitable for the explanation of unsuccessful peacebuilding episodes, which indicates that different causal patterns are relevant for the absence of sustaining peace than for its presence.

Regarding the final question, the cluster analysis of variations in peacebuilding patterns for sustaining peace has shown several commonalities, but also differences across conflict types and regions. While the four peacebuilding factors included in the QCA model seem to possess more explanatory power, when it comes to successful peacebuilding episodes after territorial conflicts than after conflicts over government, a comparison with the solution terms for the complete sample also points to the fact that the patterns show many similarities irrespective of the preceding conflict, which makes the overall results more robust. The results for the regional samples are less robust as the QCA model possesses less explanatory power for successful peacebuilding episodes in the Americas, while peacebuilding processes in Europe are almost entirely explained by the model. Overall, peacebuilding processes in the Americas, and partly in Africa, seem to be subject to a distinct causal logic, which could not be uncovered within this configurational analysis and warrants a different analytic perspective in future research. One should thus exercise caution when making generalizing statements about effective peacebuilding strategies, as the results show regional differences regarding their explanatory power. To gain first insights into the different causal logics underlying successful peacebuilding interventions, the next two chapters trace the mechanisms that connect the two sufficient peacebuilding patterns to the establishment of sustaining peace in the pathway cases of post-conflict Sierra Leone and South Africa.

6

# Assisted Accountability in Sierra Leone

The previous comparative study has identified the peacebuilding episode after the civil war in Sierra Leone (1991–2001) as a pathway case for the assisted accountability approach, leading to sustaining peace. According to this configurational pattern, the combined presence of extensive international commitment and holistic transitional justice is sufficient for the establishment of sustaining peace. The successful peace process after Sierra Leone's experience with a horrendous civil war has generally been portrayed as *the* example for national reconciliation and international efforts in supporting post-conflict societies with their transitions towards sustaining peace. Whereas the previous comparative analysis focused on explicit connections between explanatory peacebuilding conditions, I now look at the peacebuilding process in Sierra Leone to test the causal mechanism that links the assisted accountability configuration to the outcome of sustaining peace.

The main argument of the analysis is that international commitment and TJ are necessary and fundamental components of the assisted accountability approach, which must both be addressed. Ultimately, the combination of a multidimensional international peacekeeping mission with restorative and retributive justice elements, which ensures principles of security provision, accountability and a victim-centred approach, leads to sustaining peace in post-conflict societies. In typical post-conflict situations, one way to sustain peace is by providing security in combination with accountability and justice measures that address national reconciliation. The focus on peace without justice would only support underlying animosities and grievances in societies, when victims do not feel acknowledged and perpetrators are 'politically rewarded' for the atrocities they committed.

To test the assisted accountability approach as an explanation for the successful peace process in Sierra Leone, I apply the method of process tracing to uncover the causal mechanism linking the peacebuilding configuration to sustaining peace. Data for this analysis were mainly gathered during two months of fieldwork in Sierra Leone and expert interviews in Sierra Leone and New York. This chapter begins by providing the background to the civil war in Sierra Leone. Then I go on to outline the methodological approach and data collection. The third section constitutes the core of this chapter and conceptualizes the assisted accountability mechanism on the theoretical level, before I present empirical evidence on the case-specific level to trace the implementation of the mechanism in post-conflict Sierra Leone.

## Patterns of peace and conflict in Sierra Leone

Sierra Leone is a small West African coastline country with roughly 7.5 million people (in 2021) and is still recovering from ten years of civil war that resulted in around 50,000 fatalities, mass amputations and mutilations, and the displacement of two thirds of the population (ICG 2001b; Gberie 2005). The burden was particularly heavy for women and children (SLTRC 2004). Sierra Leone is home to about 16 ethnic groups, of which the Mende in the south and east and the Temne in the north are the most dominant groups; each making up around 30 per cent of the population. Sierra Leone shares borders with Guinea and Liberia, and its landscape is characterized by mostly flat coastal plains and high mountains in the east close to the Guinean border (see Figure 6.1). The civil war lasted from March 1991 to January 2001 and owes its notorious fame to the phenomena of 'blood diamonds' and 'child soldiers' (Cubitt 2012: 27).

In 1787, the British Crown founded the first settlement in Sierra Leone and in 1792 established the capital of Freetown as a settler community of 'repatriated' emancipated slaves and 'free persons of color' from Britain and the Americas. These communities became known as Krios and represented an elite, educated group, appointed to high-ranking positions in the colonial administration (Harris 2013: 10). It was not until 1896 that the British also annexed the wider hinterland, declaring it to be the Sierra Leone Protectorate. Tensions soon emerged around this colony/protectorate fault line between the privileged Krios of Freetown and the Indigenous African elite in the hinterland.

In the 1930s, the mining of two extremely important minerals – iron ore and diamonds – began in the south and railway lines were built to connect Freetown to the main towns in areas of production, with only a small line going to the town of Makeni in the north (Gberie 2005). This uneven development increased resentment and a sense of relative deprivation among the northerners in the Protectorate and encouraged the politicization of ethnicity. The British ruled the Protectorate through indirect rule, relying on traditional chiefs as intermediaries of hegemony and a patronage system among rural elites and their subordinates: 'chieftaincy became a direct route to acquisition for rural elites, a practice which was to persist after the war,

**Figure 6.1:** Political map of Sierra Leone

causing serious concerns for the prospects of effective decentralisation of state resources' (Cubitt 2012: 12).

On 27 April 1961, Sierra Leone became independent from Great Britain and held its first general elections in May 1962. These elections were won by the Sierra Leone People's Party (SLPP), a Mende-dominated party, and their leader Sir Milton Margai. The frustration of the relative impoverished northern elite led to the emergence of the opposition All People's Congress

(APC), which consisted mainly of Limba and Temne representatives and took over the country after a marginal victory in the 1967 elections. The APC restricted political opposition and used the revenues from diamond and other mineral mining to 'consolidate political alliances instead of investing them into the development of the country' (Ottendörfer 2014: 17). These developments culminated in 1978 with the adoption of a new constitution establishing a one-party state under APC rule.

In the subsequent years, the economic situation in the country deteriorated, leading to inflation, increased inequality and unemployment, especially among young people. In addition, 'the exclusion of multiple social groups, caused by decades of misrule under an autocratic and patrimonial one-party system, led to collapse and start of the war in 1991' (Ainley et al 2015, 9).

The civil war in Sierra Leone lasted from April 1991 to January 2001 and resulted in 'a decade of tension, political quagmire, societal dislocations, and military contests that not only psychologically destabilized, but equally put terror on the faces of the war victims' (Badmus and Ogunmola 2009: 721). As ample literature has already explored the origin, dynamics and dimensions of the civil war in Sierra Leone, this review will focus on the core developments to provide the backdrop for the subsequent assessment of the assisted accountability peacebuilding process (Conteh-Morgan and Dixon-Fyle 1999; Hirsch 2001; Gberie 2005; Keen 2005). The civil war began on 23 March 1991, when a rebel movement, the Revolutionary United Front (RUF) led by Foday Sankoh, took up arms against the APC government of President Joseph Momoh (see Figure 6.2). While the demands of the movement changed over the years, the RUF originally fought for the liberation of Sierra Leone from its corrupt one-party dictatorship and patrimonial system that marginalized the country's poor; however, the RUF soon started to terrorize the population and expanded its rule by plundering diamond mines and villages, and conscripting children into its forces (Keen 2005; Mitton 2013).[1] The conflict soon spiralled out of control and a number of armed groups and militias committed various atrocities throughout the country (Millar 2013).

Overall, the civil war in Sierra Leone has become 'famous' for the following three characteristic features that ultimately also resulted in increased global attention. First, all warring factions – including rebels, members of the Sierra Leone army (SLA) and militias on both sides – engaged in plundering and committed extreme atrocities against the civilian population, including widespread executions, mutilations and amputations, gang rapes and sexual assaults, and the use of civilians as human shields. There are no accurate statistics of the casualties, but conservative estimates suggest that between 50,000 and 70,000 were killed, two thirds of the population were displaced from their homes, and thousands were mutilated (Human Rights Watch 1999; Kaldor and Vincent 2006). Children were abducted by all conflict

**Figure 6.2:** Timeline of conflict events and fatalities in Sierra Leone, 1991–2001

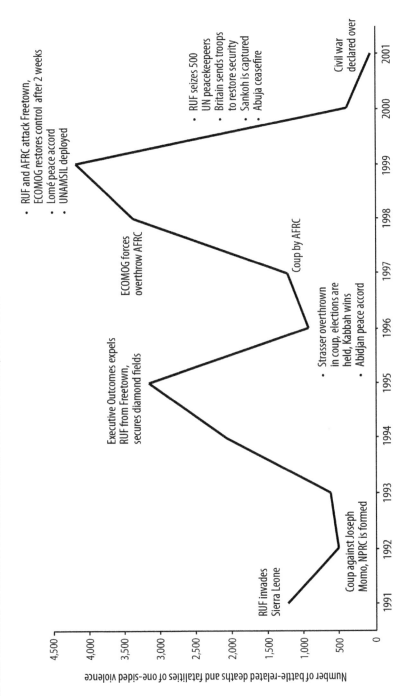

parties and injected with drugs or given alcohol to make them compliant. Second, a countless number of armed forces and indigenous militias have fought in the Sierra Leone conflict. These include the RUF; the SLA; dissident soldiers of the Armed Forces Revolutionary Council (AFRC); various civil defence forces (CDF), including the Kamajors; the Economic Community of West African States' Monitoring Group (ECOMOG); the UN; and unemployed youths, child soldiers, mercenaries, traders and diamond miners (Ero 2000). Third, the revenues from the massive and illegal exploitation of the country's natural resources, especially diamonds, were used to fund the war.

The national army response to the RUF was weak and ineffective, allowing the rebel group to take control of much of the diamond-rich southern and eastern regions of Sierra Leone. In April 1992, the authoritarian government of Joseph Momo was overthrown in a military coup organized by government soldiers who installed the National Provisional Ruling Council (NPRC) under the leadership of Captain Valentine Strasser (Gberie 2005).

A second military coup, led by Brigadier Julius Maada Bio, removed Strasser from power and paved the way for peaceful democratic elections in March 1996, which resulted in the instalment of a new civilian government under the leadership of former UN employee Ahmad Tejan Kabbah, representing the SLPP. Kabbah secured the support of the local pro-government CDF composed of ethnic militias (the largest of which were the Kamajors led by Chief Norman), which had been active since the early days of the war (Binningsbø and Dupuy 2009). Under international pressure, Kabbah signed the Abidjan peace accord in November 1996, which included amnesty for the RUF and its transformation into a political party, and the disarmament and demobilization of combatants (UNSC 1996).

The agreement was soon terminated, as the RUF rejected the presidential election outcome, refused to recognize the new civilian administration and intensified its armed campaign (Badmus and Ogunmola 2009). In May 1997, a military coup, led by disgruntled junior SLA soldiers, overthrew the Kabbah government and made their leader Major Johnny Paul Koroma head of the new military junta, the AFRC. The AFRC collaborated with the RUF and gave its leader, Foday Sankoh, the position of vice president (Alao and Ero 2001). An intervention by ECOMOG with the help of the CDF was eventually successful in ousting the AFRC and restoring the Kabbah government, but they were unable to defeat the RUF.

In January 1999, RUF and AFRC rebels launched the horrendous attack labelled 'Operation No Living Thing' on Freetown, killing, mutilating and abducting thousands of people (Olonisakin 2008). This massive offensive by the RUF represented the 'most brutal and vicious operation ever undertaken by the revels with untold human and material losses' (Badmus and Ogunmola 2009, 726): Had it not been for the ECOMOG peacekeepers and the

Kamajors, the RUF would have taken power again in the capital (Hirsch 2001; Keen 2005).

These massive killings of civilians finally prompted the international community to act. International negotiation efforts led by the UN finally pressured the government of Sierra Leone and the RUF, which held the upper hand militarily, to sign the Lomé peace agreement in July 1999, which granted RUF leader Sankoh the vice presidency and control of Sierra Leone's strategic minerals, including diamonds, in return for a cessation in the fighting (UNSC 1999b). The RUF was amnestied for its crimes, and the United Nations Mission in Sierra Leone (UNAMSIL) was deployed as an intervention force to disarm the rebels and enforce the peace accord (UNSC 1999a).

Despite international efforts, fighting continued between the RUF, the AFRC, ECOMOG, the CDF and UNAMSIL. In the security vacuum left by the departure of ECOMOG forces in May 2000, the RUF attacked Freetown and captured 500 UNAMSIL peacekeepers and their equipment (Nilsson and Söderberg Kovacs 2013). As the UN mission was failing, the UK declared its intention to intervene in the former colony to support the weak government of President Kabbah. The ensuing British military intervention, codenamed Operation Palliser, moved in to support UNAMSIL by creating a secure zone in and around Freetown and was finally able to defeat the RUF (Curran and Williams 2016).

In November 2000, a final ceasefire and demobilization agreement was signed in Abuja, Nigeria, and UNAMSIL's strength was expanded to 17,500 troops to assist with the demobilization and the training of the Sierra Leone armed forces. On 8 January 2002, President Kabbah officially declared 'di war don don' – the war is at an end.

## Data collection and method

Whereas the previous comparative analysis focused on the explicit connections between explanatory peacebuilding conditions, process tracing is applied to open the black box and take a closer look at the mechanism between the configurational conditions and the outcome. In this chapter, the goal of process tracing is to analyse how the two peacebuilding institutions of the assisted accountability approach interact with each other and lead to sustaining peace. The mechanism is traced in the individual case of peacebuilding in Sierra Leone to gain a better understanding of the causal relationship between the sufficient configuration and sustaining peace. The process tracing method, which was discussed in detail in Chapter 4, is used to look at the mechanism between the explanatory configuration (the assisted accountability approach) and the outcome (sustaining peace). In the following sections, I discuss data collection and the types of evidence used before I conceptualize an assisted accountability theory based on the existing literature and then test whether there is empirical evidence for the hypothesized mechanism to actually be present in the case of Sierra Leone (theory-testing process tracing).

## Data collection and types of evidence

The analysis here draws on several sources of empirical information and uses multiple types of evidence to identify empirical fingerprints for each part of the theorized mechanism. This triangulation of data and types of evidence was used to view the mechanism from multiple perspectives, using multiple data sources (Yin 2009; Flick 2011; Bennett and Checkel 2015). The data corpus consists of institutional documents, civil society reports, newspaper articles, public opinion surveys, expert interviews and secondary sources. Institutional documents include the UN Secretary-General's quarterly reports on UNAMSIL's activities, other UNAMSIL publications, and reports by intergovernmental organizations and think tanks.[2] Civil society organizations were highly active during the peace process and provided reports that were consulted to find empirical fingerprints of the mechanism. Local actors, such as the Special Court or the Campaign for Good Governance, conducted public opinion surveys in Sierra Leone (CGG 2003; SCSL 2012), and the responses provide additional valuable information about the impact of different peacebuilding institutions.

In addition, large parts of the data used for the analysis were gathered through two months of fieldwork in Sierra Leone and one month of research in UN archives and meetings with staff of the UN Secretariat.[3] To assess the institutional perspective, I conducted expert interviews with UN officials, government agents, NGO representatives, and former or current commissioners of the Truth and Reconciliation Commission (SLTRC) and the Human Rights Commission (HRC). Experts were contacted via email or through snowballing (direct referrals by interviewees). The interviews were not recorded, but were captured by written transcripts, and the experts were promised confidentiality.

To complement this top-level institutionalist approach with some insights about perceptions of the Sierra Leonean people regarding their peace process, I conducted public opinion surveys on local perceptions of (inter) national peacebuilding.[4] The selection of respondents for the survey was based on a randomized sampling procedure, for which I first selected three districts in Sierra Leone (Western, Northern and Southern Areas) and then focused on a major city in each of the districts and the surrounding rural communities.[5] Data collection took place over six weeks, from 24 January to 6 March 2019, and was carried out by local interviewers, who were Sierra Leonean university students and professionals with research experience.

Prior to collecting the data, the interviewers were informed about the objectives and content of the study, and we discussed potential problems during data collection. The interviews were conducted one on one and confidentially, with the interviewers obtaining oral informed consent from each selected participant; neither monetary nor material incentives were offered for participation. While I aimed to formulate the interview questions as clearly as possible, the interviewers also ensured that the respondents understood potentially complex questions about peacebuilding interventions and translated them into local dialects when necessary. In the three survey areas, interviewers randomly selected adult respondents, from all age groups and social backgrounds, who were willing to participate in the survey. The sampling procedure resulted in a total sample of 265 respondents (115 in Western Area, 99 in Northern Area and 51 in Southern Area) and included more respondents from urban areas than from rural communities.

The interviewers collected information using a standardized structured questionnaire including closed questions on the social background of the respondents, their satisfaction with the peace process, as well as their viewpoints on different peacebuilding measures.[6] The questionnaire was designed around measurement models already used and validated in previous studies on perceptions in post-conflict settings (Smith-Höhn 2009). Questions about perceptions of the peace process employed a scaling format and were built around a five-point Likert scale, which allowed an approval or rejection of statements.

*Theorizing the assisted accountability mechanism*

Theory-testing process tracing involves three distinct steps. In the first step, a causal mechanism between the cause and the outcome needs to be conceptualized based on existing theories. In the second step, the theorized causal mechanism is operationalized to define case-specific and clear empirical observables, which each part of the mechanism should have left in the case if the mechanism is operating as theorized. Step three involves a structured empirical test to see whether the predicted evidence can be identified and to evaluate its trustworthiness. This theory-testing process tracing allows the inference that the assisted accountability mechanism was present in the case of Sierra Leone.

Cross-case studies from the field of QCA usually do not establish a temporal or sequential order among the explanatory conditions. In addition, the mechanisms tying a conjunction to the outcome might not be monomechanistic, but composed of different empirically independent mechanisms. From the previous comparative study, we know that the combined presence of two peacebuilding institutions (international commitment and TJ) triggers a mechanism labelled the 'assisted accountability

**Figure 6.3:** Possible mechanistic constellations compatible with conjunction INT★TJ

**(a) Simultaneous operation of conditions**

**(b) Two-way conjunction of mechanisms**

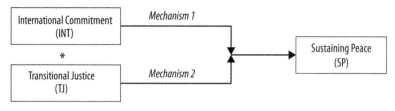

**(c) Triggering conjunction and mediating condition**

approach', which connects the configuration to sustaining peace; however, it is unclear how this mechanism operates and whether it consists of multiple or sequential mechanisms.

In general, different (sequential) constellations are compatible with linking the assisted accountability approach (INT★TJ) to sustaining peace. Figure 6.3 depicts three potential arrangements that are compatible with this two-way conjunction in a mechanism-centred research design.[7] Example (a) illustrates the simplest setting in which both peacebuilding conditions operate simultaneously and trigger a single mechanism. We could theorize that once a peace agreement includes provisions for both institutional approaches, they enable and support each other to be effective. Model (b) illustrates a relationship where each INUS[8] condition triggers 'an empirically independent mechanism which forms a [two-way] conjunction of mechanisms in an aggregated, causal perspective' (Beach and Rohlfing 2018: 22). Extensive international commitment (INT) triggers Mechanism 1, such as supporting the government in the establishment of the state monopoly on the use of force; however, this mechanism alone is not sufficient for producing the outcome because one additional mechanism needs to be present as well. Independently, Mechanism 2 is triggered by the establishment of transitional justice institutions addressing the question of accountability (TJ). The single mechanisms are empirically independent, but the establishment of sustaining peace requires the presence of both, which implies that they form a conjunction and are jointly sufficient.

Model (c) demonstrates that what seems like a conjunction from the cross-case perspective can turn out to be a sequence in process tracing, where a conjunction triggers a mechanism that produces another condition that again triggers a mechanism leading to the outcome. The causal chain for sustaining peace is initiated by the condition INT, and the single condition TJ serves as a mediator. According to this example, the presence of international commitment is sufficient for a holistic TJ approach, for example, because the aspect of justice can only be addressed after the commitment problem has been solved and some basic security has been established (Mechanism 1). Transitional justice would then in turn be sufficient for sustaining peace (Mechanism 2) by addressing the underlying animosity and providing some closure for the victims.

The discussion of these three examples has demonstrated that a single mechanism linking a configuration to an outcome is just one possible constellation out of many. Process tracing allows for the determination of the actual arrangement of the two peacebuilding conditions. Therefore, we need to consider all theoretically plausible constellations that could be hidden by the comparative analysis and 'cast the net widely' to identify the actual sequence of conditions and mechanisms (Bennett and Checkel 2015).[9] To obtain first indications of potential sequences within the configurational arrangement, it is useful to take a closer look at the timeline of peacebuilding activities in postwar Sierra Leone. Figure 6.4 summarizes the assisted accountability approach in Sierra Leone by displaying the duration of the two peacebuilding institutions included in the sufficient configuration and important milestones in their implementation; however, this timeline simply illustrates the sequence and does not explain the mechanisms itself.

In looking at the timeline, it becomes immediately apparent that both peacebuilding initiatives show a temporal overlap instead of being sequenced. Combined with theoretical expectations of the impact of these two peacebuilding institutions, the empirical evidence suggests the following conjunctural assisted accountability peacebuilding mechanism for sustaining peace which focuses on the simultaneous establishment of security and justice.

The UN has acknowledged the need for comprehensive approaches, including justice, peace and democracy, in fragile post-conflict settings, highlighting that 'the maintenance of peace ... cannot be achieved unless the population is confident that redress for grievances can be obtained through ... the fair administration of justice' (UNSG 2004b, para 2). Most

PATTERNS OF SUSTAINING PEACE

**Figure 6.4:** Timeline of the assisted accountability approach in Sierra Leone, 2002–2013

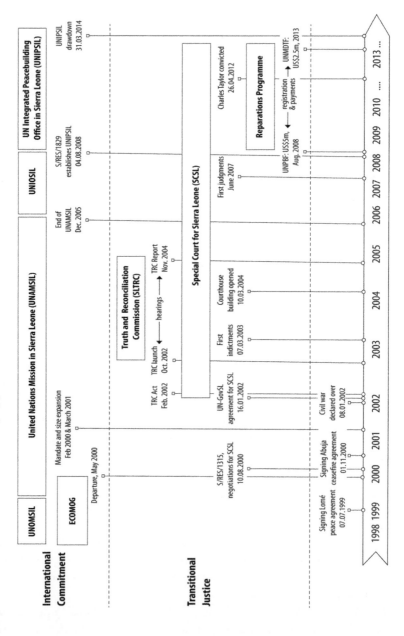

post-conflict peacebuilding interventions thus require some form of justice to effectively support reconciliation, and many UN peace operations have had rule of law or justice components or were even mandated to directly address TJ and rule of law activities; however, peacebuilding interventions usually take place in situations where neither security nor justice exists, leaving the question of whether one of these objectives should take priority. This 'peace versus justice' debate is consulted to explain the constellation of the assisted accountability mechanism (Rodman 2011).

Those supporting the inclusion of justice and accountability argue that there is a moral and legal duty to prosecute perpetrators of the gravest human rights abuses and that sustaining peace is not possible without justice and accountability (Sriram 2009). Critics of a justice-based approach warn of the potentially destabilizing consequences of pursuing justice and accountability for the consolidation of post-conflict peace. For reasons of feasibility and morality of UN peace operations, it might also be advisable to adhere to a policy of peace over justice, at least in the short term: 'the UN needs to concentrate on ensuring the establishment and maintenance of peace. Once that has been accomplished, its energies can then be devoted to meeting its justice goals' (Bratt 1999: 63). Following Mallinder and McEvoy (2011), offering unconditional amnesties to rebel leaders as a shield from prosecution presents a necessary evil in convincing conflict parties to lay down their weapons or enter into peace negotiations. Some scholars also argue in favour of sequencing security and justice measures as a solution to the peace versus justice debate (Mbeki and Mamdani 2014). This approach suggests peace (in its negative form, as the absence of violence) should take precedence, while acknowledging the importance of justice in building a sustaining and positive peace, and suspending it until the underlying political problems have been addressed (Kersten 2016). Others argue that sequencing ignores victims' perspectives, as 'justice delayed is justice denied' (Hannum 2006: 585). Looking at the empirics, warring parties often sign peace agreements that include accountability provisions, signalling that the pursuit of justice might not always be an obstacle to peace and security.

Security and justice are both seen as necessary and fundamental components of sustaining peace: 'justice and peace are not contradictory forces. Rather, properly pursued, they promote and sustain one another' (UNSG 2004b: para 21). Ultimately, a simultaneous combination of security-restoring measures with restorative and retributive justice elements, ensuring principles of security provision, accountability, the rule of law and a victim-centred approach focusing on reconciliation and the establishment of truth should lead to sustaining peace in post-conflict societies. The focus on peace without justice supports underlying animosities and grievances within societies – when victims do not feel acknowledged and perpetrators are 'politically rewarded' for the atrocities they have committed.

## Tracing the assisted accountability mechanism in postwar Sierra Leone

The 1999 Lomé peace agreement and the 2000 Abuja ceasefire agreement, signed by all major conflict parties, acted as a critical juncture for the peace process and specified some of the relevant peacebuilding institutions. After the war ended in 2002, the peacebuilding process in Sierra Leone included four key initiatives: (a) UNAMSIL; (b) the SLTRC; (c) a reparations programme; and (d) the Special Court for Sierra Leone (SCSL). While the first initiative addressed the apparent lack of security, the last three institutions focused on the rehabilitation of victims and ensured justice and accountability. Taken together, these four (inter)national peacebuilding institutions were supposed to lay the foundations for peace and reconciliation in Sierra Leone. Regarding the local perception of their contribution to the peace process, I found some divergence between security-centred and justice-focused institutions (see Table 6.1). While 94 per cent of respondents indicated that UNAMSIL made an 'excellent' or 'good' contribution to the peace process, the positive rating is lower for the TJ institutions: only around 70 per cent have the same perception of the SLTRC and the special court, while only 60 per cent attribute an 'excellent' or 'good' contribution to the reparations programme. While the ratings are positive for all institutions, the apparent discrepancies warrant further investigations of the individual processes. The following sections describe the different steps of the two mechanisms causally connecting the peacebuilding institutions with sustaining peace, as outlined in Figure 6.5.

### The credible commitment mechanism

The 1999 Lomé peace agreement, signed between the government of Sierra Leone and the RUF, provided for the establishment of a UN peacekeeping

**Table 6.1:** Perceptions of (inter)national peacebuilding institutions in Sierra Leone

| | Contribution to the peace process (in %) | | | | | |
|---|---|---|---|---|---|---|
| | Excellent | Good | Neutral | Rather bad | Poor | Don't know/ no answer |
| UNAMSIL peacekeeper | 64.5 | 29.4 | 1.5 | 0.4 | 0.4 | 3.8 |
| SLTRC | 38.1 | 32.5 | 15.5 | 3.4 | 2.3 | 8.3 |
| SCSL | 38.1 | 34.0 | 16.2 | 2.6 | 1.9 | 7.2 |
| Reparations programme | 21.1 | 38.5 | 22.3 | 7.2 | 4.5 | 6.4 |

Note: N = 265; Question: 'In your opinion, how was the contribution of the following actors/ mechanisms to the peace process in Sierra Leone?'

**Figure 6.5:** Constellation of the assisted accountability approach

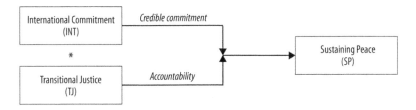

mission with an extended mandate to provide credible international support for the peace process (UNSC 1999b). The credible commitment mechanism connects international commitment to a peace process with sustaining peace by providing a secure environment and supporting the government in the establishment of the state monopoly on the use of force and a peaceful transfer of power. For the mechanism to be present, we would expect empirical evidence of the establishment of a multidimensional peacekeeping mission and, depending on the mission's mandate, proof of protection of civilians, demobilization and reintegration of former opposition troops, and the conducting of free and fair elections. The mechanism concludes with the establishment of a secure environment, the state monopoly on the use for force and the inauguration of a new democratically elected government (Figure 6.6).

*Part I: Peace agreement with provisions for UN peacekeeping mission*

The credible commitment mechanism is initiated when armed groups are militarily defeated or weakened enough to sign a peace agreement, including provisions for a peacekeeping mission. In the case of Sierra Leone, the Lomé peace agreement, signed by the government and the RUF in July 1999, provided for the withdrawal of ECOMOG forces (Article XIII) and requested the UNSC to 'amend the mandate of UNOMSIL [UN Observer Mission in Sierra Leone] to enable it to undertake the various provisions outlined in the present agreement' (Article XIV) to provide the former warring factions with credible international support of the peace process (UNSC 1999b). Before the deployment of an extended UN mission, ECOMOG peacekeepers were stationed in Sierra Leone since 1997, and in 1998, the UNSC established UNOMSIL, consisting of 41 military observers mandated to monitor the military and security situation as well as the disarmament and demobilization of former combatants (UNSC 1998). Shortly after the signing of the Lomé peace agreement, the UNSC authorized an increase in the number of UNOMSIL military observers to 210 as a first measure.

**Figure 6.6:** Application of the credible commitment mechanism in Sierra Leone

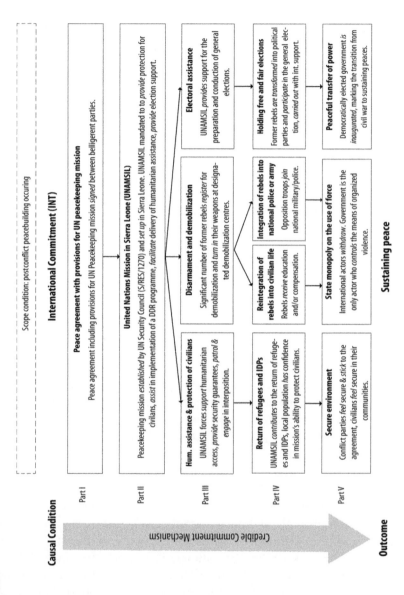

## Part II: Establishment and deployment of UNAMSIL

On 22 October 1999, the UNSC formally established UNAMSIL through its Resolution 1270, as a new and much larger mission with an initial maximum deployment of 6,000 military personnel to assist the government of Sierra Leone and the conflict parties in carrying out the provisions of the Lomé peace agreement.[10] UNAMSIL was mandated to assist in the implementation of the DDR plan, to establish a presence at key locations throughout the territory of Sierra Leone and to monitor adherence to the ceasefire. In addition, UNAMSIL was the first UN peacekeeping mission mandated under Chapter VII of the UN Charter to take the necessary action 'within its capabilities and areas of deployment, to afford protection to civilians under imminent threat of physical violence' (UNSC 1999a). The same resolution also called for close cooperation and coordination with ECOMOG, which, however, proved to be difficult, as 'UNAMSIL and ECOMOG officers were at loggerheads and excelled in buck-passing over alleged involvement in illegal possession of diamonds' and collusion with the RUF (Badmus and Ogunmola 2009: 730). The departure of ECOMOG forces in May 2000 created a security vacuum leading to the RUF attack of Freetown and the capture of 500 UNAMSIL peacekeepers and their equipment (Nilsson and Söderberg Kovacs 2013).

In its first years, UNAMSIL was impaired by financial and logistical constraints and peacekeepers' poor knowledge of the terrain and the guerrilla warfare nature of the conflict: 'The UN leadership felt that all parties to the conflict had accepted the Lomé peace agreement, which the RUF clearly did not' (Bernath and Nyce 2004: 127). To adapt to the military and political situation on the ground, UNAMSIL's mandate and the mission's military structure were revised in 2000 and 2001, leading to a new concept of operations (UNSC 2001c). Faced with apparent constraints in implementing the mandate on the ground, the UNSC expanded the maximum troop size for UNAMSIL three times, to 11,100 military troops in February 2000 (UNSC 2000b), 13,000 in May 2000 (UNSC 2000d) and 17,500 in March 2001 (UNSC 2001d), making UNAMSIL the largest deployed UN peacekeeping mission (between 2001 and 2003). An overview of the number and deployment of UNAMSIL uniformed personnel is provided in Figure 6.7.

With this increased troop size, UNAMSIL was finally able to establish headquarters at key locations throughout Sierra Leone and to build a presence in all regions of the country, making it difficult for anyone to mobilize rebel forces. Due to the UN's rapid reaction in putting UN boots on the ground and to increase the necessary strength in a timely manner, all conflict parties were finally convinced that they could not achieve their goals through further violence. The type of deployment, a strong enough mandate and a strong

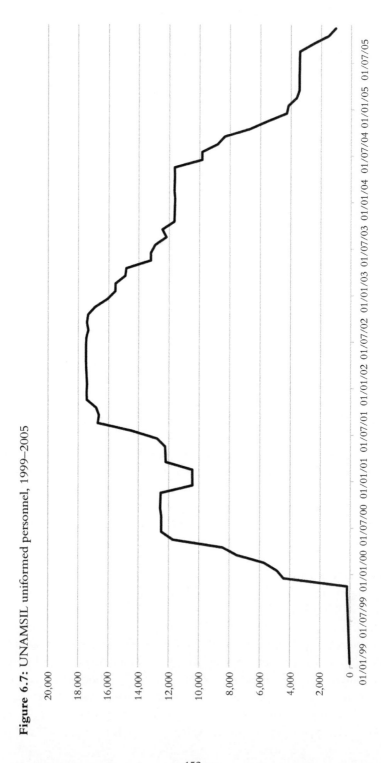

**Figure 6.7:** UNAMSIL uniformed personnel, 1999–2005

enough force to accomplish a mission's goals were also main 'lessons learned' for UN peacekeeping (UN 2000). Despite its initial faltering, UNAMSIL eventually became widely acknowledged as one of the UN's most successful peacekeeping missions and 'has been cited by Sierra Leoneans and the international community as a major factor in the remarkable recovery of Sierra Leone since May 2000' (Bernath and Nyce 2004: 120).

## Part III: Humanitarian assistance, start of disarmament and demobilization, and preparation of elections

Two early disarmament phases were carried out from October to December 1998 and from November 1999 to May 2000, but both were halted due to the RUF attacks. The disarmament and demobilization process was reinstated after the signing of the Abuja ceasefire agreement. Between May 2001 and January 2002, a total of 47,076 combatants (19,183 RUF, 27,695 CDF and 198 AFRC) were disarmed and demobilized in specific DDR camps, and 15,840 assorted weapons and two million rounds of ammunition were collected (UNSC 2002a). UNAMSIL was tasked with providing security at DDR sites: 'receive, screen and process ex-combatants; collect and disable weapons and ammunition, including through mobile destruction facilities; transport ex-combatants from the reception centres to the demobilisation centres', as well as the storage and destruction of collected weapons (UNSC 2001c: para 77). The disarmament of RUF and CDF combatants was declared to have been officially completed on 17 January 2002 by the Joint Committee on DDR, and subsequent ceremonies to mark the end of the war were held in the provincial capitals (UNSC 2002a).

The improved access and deployment of UNAMSIL peacekeepers to multiple regions of Sierra Leone, together with the disarmament of RUF, CDF and AFRC fighters, opened areas of the country up to humanitarian assistance (UNSC 2001b). Refugees and internally displaced persons (IDPs) received assistance and emergency relief from the Office of the UN High Commissioner for Refugees (UNHCR), the World Food Programme and other aid agencies.

With the gradual improvement of the overall security situation in Sierra Leone, refugees made their way back to Sierra Leone; however, at the beginning of May 2001, the number of Sierra Leonean refugees and IDPs in need of assistance was estimated at 513,200 (UNSC 2001a). UNAMSIL peacekeepers also conducted high-profile patrols throughout Sierra Leone to deter violence and to reassure the population and 'also stepped up air and land patrols along the Sierra Leone/Liberia border in view of the escalations of fighting in Liberia' (UNSC 2002a: para 9).

According to the constitutions of Sierra Leone, presidential elections were due in February 2001 and parliamentary elections in May 2001.

Due to the state of emergency, the terms of office of both branches of government were extended and on 5 September 2001, the government announced that parliamentary and presidential elections were to be held in May 2002 (UNSC 2001e). In preparation for the elections, an intensive civic education campaign commenced in July 2001 to inform, educate and raise public awareness of the upcoming elections (UNSC 2001b). This was followed by a nationwide registration of the estimated 2.7 million eligible Sierra Leonean voters between 24 January and 10 February 2002, and returning refuges could register in transit camps (UNSC 2002a). Electoral campaigns by 23 registered parties started at the beginning of April 2002. In support of the elections, UNAMSIL's electoral component provided technical, logistical and public information support to the National Electoral Commission and closely monitored the various stages of the electoral process (UNSC 2002c).

*Part IV: The return of refugees and internally displaced persons, reintegration of former rebels and holding of general elections*

The resettlement of IDPs and repatriation of refugees commenced in all districts of Sierra Leone on a large scale at the beginning of 2002, facilitated by the UNHCR, the International Organization for Migration and other UN agencies. Returnees were assisted with resettlement packages and transportation to districts that had been declared safe (UNSC 2002a). The final phase of the national programme for the resettlement of IDPs was completed in early December 2002, resulting in the resettlement of approximately 220,000 IDPs (UNSC 2002b). The UNHCR officially completed the Sierra Leone voluntary repatriation operation on 21 July 2004, after more than 270,000 Sierra Leonean refugees, mainly from Guinea and Liberia, had been repatriated or returned unassisted (UNSC 2004).

In the DDR camps, all ex-combatants were briefed on the existence of the Military Reintegration Programme, as part of the predischarge orientation and were given the option to seek entry into the armed forces or to participate in a short-term civilian reintegration programme of six months; however, 'messages of DDR were targeted at men and did not include a gender perspective. The women did not come out as fighters and were not formally reintegrated and did not get any reparations'.[11] If ex-combatants aimed for military reintegration, the potential recruits were brought to temporary holding camps, where they underwent a formal screening processes, medical examinations, and physical, educational and military experience tests (Albrecht and Jackson 2009). The screening process was limited to previous discharges from the army and existing criminal records, and paid little attention to human rights abuses committed during the civil war (ICG 2001a; Keen 2005). This approach was pragmatic: 'it was considered preferable to keep these ex-combatants in the army where they could be monitored and controlled than have them causing trouble out in the streets' (Nilsson and Söderberg Kovacs 2013: 9). All potential recruits attended a selection tribunal that was normally chaired by a UNAMSIL colonel and included RUF and CDF liaison officers. Successful applicants were then offered entry to the RSLAF and undertook basic military training. Of the large number of ex-combatants, only about 3,000 former RUF and CDF fighters entered the military reintegration programme and 2,349 passed the basic training, joining the existing army consisting of former SLA and AFRC soldiers, leading to a final size of the expanded RSLAF of about 14,500 (Albrecht and Jackson 2009).

In comparison to the military reintegration, the process of reintegrating the disarmed combatants into civilian life remained slow because of inadequate funding for the government-managed reintegration programme (UNSC 2002a). Disarmed ex-combatants needed to register with a regional reintegration centre to be eligible for the payment of an initial reinsertion payment and the placement in one of various short-term reintegration projects. The reinsertion package had a value of about US $200 and included 'food supplies, some materials and cash to assist with shelter, food and health care' (UNSC 2001b: para 30). While all registered ex-combatants received their initial reinsertion payment, placement in reintegration projects was slow due to a lack of funding and reliable service providers in most areas in the east and north of the country. Even when ex-combatants received a spot in one of these programmes, the short-term reintegration offered through the DDR programme did not guarantee long-term employment or other means of income generation: 'How can you train someone to become a driver, who when he goes back to his village doesn't even have a car to drive? Or a carpenter, who doesn't have the tools in his village to use his new knowledge?'[12]

On 14 May 2002, Sierra Leone had its first peaceful, democratic elections in more than a decade. Nine political parties, including the Revolutionary United Front Party (RUFP) and the ex-AFRC Peace and Liberation Party (PLP), nominated presidential candidates, and 11 parties contested in the parliamentary elections. The incumbent President Kabbah of the ruling SLPP won 70.06 per cent of the presidential votes, while Ernest Koroma of the APC came in second with 22.35 per cent. Former AFRC leader Johnny Paul Koroma ended up in third place with 3 per cent, followed by the RUFP candidate Alimamy Bangura, who received 1.7 per cent. Three political parties managed to win parliamentary seats: the SLPP won 83 of the 124 seats, the APC won 27 seats and the PLP won two seats (see Table 6.2). The RUFP did not win a single seat in Parliament. During the elections, 'UNAMSIL temporarily redeployed 11,000 troops to some 200 high-risk areas throughout the country, and assisted the Sierra Leone police

**Table 6.2:** Results of the 2002 parliamentary elections in Sierra Leone

| Party | Votes | % | Seats |
|---|---|---|---|
| Sierra Leone People's Party (SLPP) | 1,293,401 | 67.67 | 83 |
| All People's Congress (APC) | 409,313 | 21.41 | 27 |
| Peace and Liberation Party (PLP) | 69,765 | 3.65 | 2 |
| Revolutionary United Front Party (RUFP) | 41,997 | 2.20 | 0 |
| Grand Alliance Party (GAP) | 25,436 | 1.33 | 0 |
| United National People's Party (UNPP) | 24,907 | 1.30 | 0 |
| People's Democratic Party (PDP) | 19,941 | 1.04 | 0 |
| Movement for Progress (MOP) | 15,036 | 0.79 | 0 |
| National Democratic Alliance (NDA) | 6,467 | 0.34 | 0 |
| Young People's Party (YPP) | 5,083 | 0.27 | 0 |
| Paramount Chiefs | | | 12 |
| **Total** | **1,911,346** | **100** | **124** |

in deploying 4,400 police personnel as well as mobile armed units to provide security for the elections' (UNSC 2002c: para 8).

## Part V: Establishment of a secure environment and a state monopoly over the use of force

The new democratically elected SLPP government under President Kabbah was inaugurated on 19 May 2002, marking the transition from civil war to sustaining peace. In addition, state authority had been consolidated throughout the country with the deployment of government officials to all districts completed by March 2003 (UNSC 2003). Security was formally handed over from UNAMSIL to the Sierra Leonean government, and after the mission's withdrawal, the government possessed the state monopoly on the use of force necessary for sustaining peace. With no remaining armed nonstate group or international force on its territory, the government of Sierra Leone is the only actor that controls the means of organized violence in the country. While not all threats to the security of the people and the state have been removed, the environment is relatively stable and secure, with personal security being perceived as better than before or during the war. This finding is also supported by results from a survey I conducted in 2019 as part of my fieldwork, where 62 per cent of respondents indicated the general security in Sierra Leone was good or very good, while 89 per cent even stated that their personal security was at least somewhat better than it was during the war (see Table 6.3).

**Table 6.3:** General and personal security in Sierra Leone

| | General security (in %)* | Personal security (in %)** |
|---|---|---|
| Very good/Very much better | 17.7 | 50.9 |
| Good/Somewhat better | 44.5 | 37.7 |
| Neither/No change | 23.0 | 5.3 |
| Bad/Somewhat worse | 8.7 | 2.6 |
| Very bad/Very much worse | 5.7 | 0.0 |

Note: N = 265; *Question: 'How would you describe the general security situation in Sierra Leone?'; **Question: 'Compared to before the end of the war, how is your personal safety today?'

Overall, the credible commitment mechanism for sustaining peace has been realized, and a generally secure environment allowed the actors to pursue the parallel accountability process that is discussed in the next section. In order to also include a local voice in this assessment, survey respondents were asked about their agreement with various statements regarding international commitment during the peacebuilding process in Sierra Leone (see Table 6.4). Some doubts about the long-term sustainability of the peace process remained, with 63 per cent of respondents at least agreeing with the statement that Sierra Leone was a stable and peaceful country, while 23 per cent could not clearly support this statement. One reason for this assessment might be that 'the problems and early-warning signals that led to the conflict are still around. They have to be addressed before Sierra Leone is really peaceful'.[13] Most respondents agreed that peace would not have lasted without international support (91 per cent) and that UNAMSIL was crucial for the success of the peace process (85 per cent). Regarding the security sector, the reform of the police and the armed forces was generally considered successful (78 per cent agreement), as was the reintegration of former combatants into society, albeit to a lesser extent (60 per cent agreement). A civil society representative summarized the effects of the peacekeepers and international commitment towards the peace process quite aptly: 'Without the interventions, Sierra Leone would be hell.'[14]

### The accountability mechanism

The accountability mechanism supports the establishment of sustaining peace through the implementation of various TJ measures. After the peace agreement has already included TJ provisions, we would expect to find evidence for the establishment of the SLTRC and the SCSL. In a subsequent step, the recommendations from the SLTRC report would be implemented, including the establishment of a reparations programme. Taken together,

**Table 6.4:** Local perceptions of the Sierra Leonean peace process regarding international commitment

| | Perceptions of the peace process (in %) | | | | | |
|---|---|---|---|---|---|---|
| | Strongly agree | Agree | Neither agree nor disagree | Disagree | Strongly disagree | Don't know/ no answer |
| Today, Sierra Leone is a stable and peaceful country | 25.7 | 37.7 | 23.4 | 7.9 | 4.5 | 0.8 |
| Without international support, peace would not have lasted | 67.9 | 23.0 | 4.9 | 1.9 | 0.4 | 1.9 |
| UNAMSIL was crucial for the success of the peace process | 57.0 | 27.5 | 4.5 | 9.1 | 0.0 | 1.9 |
| Former combatants have been successfully integrated into society | 29.8 | 30.6 | 23.4 | 9.8 | 4.2 | 2.3 |
| The reform of the police and the army has been successful | 40.8 | 37.0 | 9.8 | 7.2 | 4.5 | 0.8 |

Note: N = 265; Question: 'Now I'm going to read out a number of statements regarding the peace process in Sierra Leone. For each one, could you tell me how much you agree or disagree with it?'

the successful implementation of these measures by the government would combat impunity and lead to national healing and reconciliation (Figure 6.8).

## Part I: Peace agreement with transitional justice provisions and government-induced transitional justice

The accountability mechanism is triggered by the signing of a peace agreement including provisions for TJ measures and the government's decision to establish additional TJ institutions. In the case of Sierra Leone, the Lomé peace agreement included a framework for truth telling, according to which 'a Truth and Reconciliation Commission shall be established to address impunity, break the cycle of violence ... get a clear picture of the past in order to facilitate genuine healing and reconciliation' (UNSC 1999b: Article XXVI). It was agreed that the SLTRC should deal with human rights violations committed in the Sierra Leonean conflict since 1991 and to recommend measures to be taken for the rehabilitation of victims of these atrocities. While other matters were agreed on relatively quickly at Lomé, representatives from the Office of the High Commissioner for Human

**Figure 6.8:** Application of the accountability mechanism in Sierra Leone

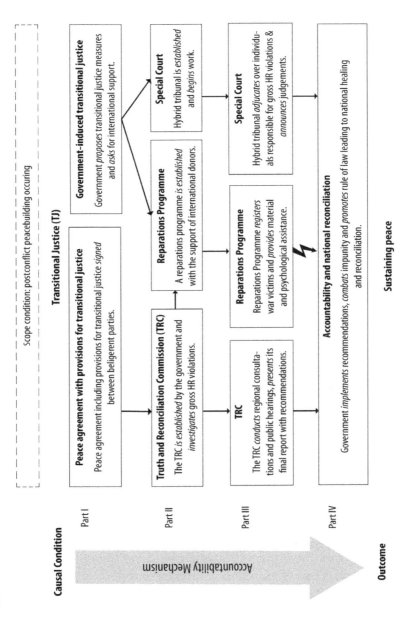

Rights (OHCHR) pressed for the inclusion of a truth commission as a form of accountability (Rashid 2000). The peace agreement did not specify a mandate for the SLTRC and included few details regarding its composition – matters that would later complicate the work of the commission (SLTRC 2004: 23–24).

The peace agreement also included a provision for general amnesty, which was, however, opposed by the UN and led the Special Representative of the Secretary-General to append his signature to the agreement with a last-minute reservation that the UN did not regard the amnesty as applying to genocide, crimes against humanity, war crimes and other serious violations of international humanitarian law (UNSC 1999c). Due to these amnesty provisions, the government of Sierra Leone could not pursue criminal prosecutions in the domestic judicial system in relation to atrocities committed prior to the signing of the Lomé peace agreement (Schabas 2003; Hollis 2015). To address these crimes under international law, President Kabbah wrote to the UN Secretary-General on 12 July 2000, requesting an ad hoc tribunal in Sierra Leone, with the assistance of the UN to try senior members of the RUF for crimes against the people of Sierra Leone (UNSC 2000a). In response, the UNSC requested the UN Secretary-General to negotiate an agreement with the government of Sierra Leone for the creation of an independent special court, with jurisdiction over people who bore the greatest responsibility for the commission of atrocity crimes during the Sierra Leonean civil war (UNSC 2000c). The TJ process in Sierra Leone set precedents as the first case in which an internationalized tribunal and a TRC were established in parallel, working alongside each other (Ainley et al 2015).

## Part II: Establishment of several transitional justice institutions

The Sierra Leonean government was not particularly engaged in the establishment of the SLTRC, and the process was instead led by the OHCHR, which provided the technical support for the design of the SLTRC. On 23 February 2000, the Sierra Leonean Parliament approved the Truth and Reconciliation Commission Act, officially establishing the SLTRC with a broad mandate to 'create an impartial historical record of violations and abuses of human rights and international humanitarian law related to the armed conflict in Sierra Leone'.[15] The commission was supposed to begin its work within two weeks of the signing of the Lomé peace agreement, but the process was held up by RUF attacks and further escalations. As a result, it did not appoint commissioners until July 2001. The president selected four local commissioners in a rather opaque process, while the OHCHR selected the three international commissioners. Due to the alienation of international consultants over political obstacles, budget decisions and the appointment of SLPP loyalists to key SLTRC posts, it took the commission until March 2002 to become fully operational (Mahony and Sooka 2015).

A shift in international policy preferences and funding towards a war crimes court also affected the delay. After negotiations, the government of Sierra Leone and the UN signed a bilateral treaty in January 2002, establishing the SCSL with a mandate to 'prosecute persons who bear the greatest responsibility for serious violations of international humanitarian and Sierra Leonean law committed in the territory of Sierra Leone since 30 November 1996' (UNSC 2000c).[16] In March 2002, the legislature of Sierra Leone ratified this agreement and the Office of the Prosecutor (OTP) began operations in the summer of 2002. Over the course of several months, 'representatives from the OTP visited virtually all the districts in Sierra Leone, gathering evidence, identifying potential witnesses, bringing that evidence back and putting it in the framework of what we had to prove to establish that the crimes within the jurisdiction of the Court had been committed' (Hollis 2015: 24–25). In July 2002, the UN Secretary-General announced the appointment of eight special court judges and two alternates, who took their oaths of office in December 2002 (Schabas 2003). The assessment of the evidence gathered by the OTP, along with a restrictive interpretation of the mandate phrase 'those who bear greatest responsibility' for horrific crimes, led to the 2003 indictment of 13 people from all leading factions.[17]

### Part III: Established transitional justice institutions successfully implement their mandates

A total of 11 of the 13 individuals indicted by the SCSL were arrested and brought before the court: four leaders of the RUF – including Foday Sankoh, who died before his trial began – three AFRC leaders, three leaders of the CDF and former Liberian President Charles Taylor.[18] The indictment of the CDF leaders was seen as controversial, as many Sierra Leoneans viewed the CDF as the saviours who had protected them from the desolation of the RUF (*BBC News* 2007). They were indicted by the SCSL 'because, in pursuing this goal, they were responsible for war crimes and crimes against humanity' (Hollis 2015: 26).

During a survey conducted in November 2003, 60 per cent of the respondents believed the SCSL to be necessary and for the benefit of the people of Sierra Leone (CGG 2003). Only a minority fully understood the purpose of the court (10 per cent) or could tell the difference between the special court and national courts (24 per cent). In a 2012 survey, general understanding of the SCSL's work had improved. When asked 'What was the SCSL established to achieve?', 53 per cent of respondents said that it was established to prosecute perpetrators of crimes committed during the war, while 29 per cent said that it was established to bring justice and 23 per cent stated that its aim was to bring peace (SCSL 2012: 27).

The trials began in 2004 and were completed in 2012, with the conviction of Charles Taylor for planning, aiding and abetting all 11 crimes he was charged with. The final sentences of all indictees ranged from 15 to 52 years, which they serve in prisons in Rwanda and the UK. With the judgment against Taylor, the work of the SCSL was completed. It has been replaced by the Residual Special Court for Sierra Leone (RSCSL), which is responsible for managing the archives of the court, the enforcement of sentences and the continued protection of witnesses.

The SLTRC operated from November 2002 to October 2004 and attempted to catalyse reconciliation through public education, mass media sensitization, and nationwide public hearings, collecting over 8,000 statements. The public hearings were carried out between April and August 2003, in each of the country's district headquarter towns and in Freetown, and were 'public performances of victim, witness, and perpetrator stories, in front of audiences of local people, key stakeholders, and the media in town halls and community centres' (Millar 2013: 191). Poster, leaflets, and radio and television broadcasts translated the goals of the SLTRC into Sierra Leone's lingua franca, Krio, and urged survivors and perpetrators to 'come blow your main [mind]' (Shaw 2005: 184). The hearings, in which more than 450 people testified, were also broadcast live on the radio, and the highlights of each day were edited into a 45-minute television show (Kelsall 2005).

As relatively few ex-combatants testified, the SLTRC had to rely on cooperation with the war victims to collect information about human rights violations. In return for their statements, victims and survivors expected to receive economic assistance and threatened to boycott the SLTRC if the government did not meet their demands (*IPS News* 2002). In most public hearings, audience numbers were lower than expected, consisting overwhelmingly of adult men, and 'the surprising indifference shown by much of the population to the TRC' raised 'doubts whether they served one of their main purposes: to develop understanding of what happened and so lead to healing' (ICG 2003: i and 12; Shaw 2007). While it has been stated that evidence gathered by the SLTRC would be inadmissible in the procedures of the special court, many Sierra Leoneans held the misconception that the SLTRC acted as an investigative arm of the court (ICG 2002; Schabas 2003). This troubled relationship between the SLTRC and the court deterred many witnesses from speaking openly in the public hearings, if they agreed to give a statement at all (Kelsall 2005).

The final report was released at the end of 2004 and identified bad governance, endemic corruption and the denial of basic human rights as the causes for thousands of young people joining the war (SLTRC 2004). It also included the names of individual perpetrators and recommendations for the government as it moved forward in the peace process. Overall, the SLTRC proved to be responsive to the views of victims and 'placed a focus on people's entitlement to economic and social rights and the state's obligation to take care of those most in need' (Ottendörfer 2014: 13). This responsiveness was expressed in the recommendations focusing on enhancing accountability, transparency and responsiveness of the Sierra Leone state to its citizens – that is, the introduction of a peace tax from mining revenues to finance the reparations programme (SLTRC 2004: vol II, Chapter 4, Article 227(c)).

The victims of the civil war were represented by the Sierra Leone Amputees and War Wounded Association (AWWA), which demanded the payment of pensions and government services, such as housing and scholarships for the children of amputees and other persons affected by the war (*IPS News* 2002). The SLTRC took up some of these demands and recommended the establishment of a reparations programme for the victims, which should include housing, free access to physical and mental healthcare, scholarships for education and vocational training and the payment of pensions for individuals severely affected by human rights violations (SLTRC 2004: vol II, Chapter 4). It also formulated guidelines for assessing the eligibility of victims for reparations and categorized them into five groups according to their vulnerability: amputees; other war-wounded persons; children affected by the war; war-wounded children; and sexually abused women and widows.[19]

The government of Sierra Leone accepted the recommendations for a reparations programme and agreed to 'use its best endeavours to ensure [a] full and timely implementation', while also pointing out that it expected international donor organizations to provide the necessary resources since state funds were unavailable (GoSL 2005: 16). Together with national and international human rights organizations, the AWWA kept drawing attention to the reparations issue until the government agreed in 2007 to apply for funding through the UN Peacebuilding Fund (UNPBF). After the application was approved, the UNPBF provided US$3 million in August 2008 for a reparations programme in Sierra Leone.[20] As part of the official regulations, the funds had to be used within one year and 75 per cent had to be spent directly as a benefit for victims (Suma and Correa 2009). Due to this urgency, an interim relief payment of 300,000 Leones (at that time roughly US$100) was agreed upon, combined with operations for victims who were still suffering from injuries and symbolic reparations in the form of memorials or spiritual cleansing (Ottendörfer 2014: 14).

Registration was scheduled to take place from December 2008 to March 2009, in every district capital, and people were informed via sensitization campaigns over the radio. Victims had to travel on their own funds and provide a registration officer with a detailed account of what had happened to them during the war. Their name was then cross-referenced with an official list of victims or verified by a letter from an official person, such as a chief. Due to insufficient outreach, registration was very low, had to be extended to the end of June 2009, and was moved to chiefdom headquarter towns and locations where massacres had been committed (Suma and Correa 2009). In total, 29,733 people registered for the reparations programme, roughly half of the estimated number, and 20,107 of them received the relief payment of 300,000 Leones (Suma and Correa 2009). Over the course of the next four years, additional funds were provided by the UNPBF, the UN agency for women (UNWOMEN) and the UN Multi-partner Trust Fund for reparations in Sierra Leone for relief payments of remaining beneficiaries, skills training for women, and start-up grants for amputees and war-wounded persons (Sierra Leone MDTF 2015). At the end of 2013, the total international funding accounted for nearly US$8.5 million of reparations for war victims in Sierra Leone.

### Part IV: Accountability and national reconciliation

The response of the Sierra Leone government to the final report of the SLTRC was released as a White Paper in June 2005. The government accepted the report's findings and more than 220 recommendations (GoSL 2005). In response to these recommendations, the government established several institutions, including the Human Rights Commission, the National Electoral Commission and the Political Party Registration Commission, to protect and promote human rights and good governance (UNGA 2011b). The government has also adopted codes of conduct for judicial officials, enacted laws on corruption, prosecutions and disclosures of state officials, legislation for the protection of women and children, and established institutions to support vulnerable groups, including conflict victims, youths and those affected by HIV/AIDS (Mahony and Sooka 2015; Oosterveld 2015).[21] The government also conducted symbolic memorialization events (that is, erecting memorials, reburials, or religious and traditional rites) in 40 of Sierra Leone's 149 chiefdoms, and in March 2010, President Koroma issued a public apology to all women for the violations they suffered during the conflict (UNGA 2011a).

One of the most eagerly awaited recommendations by the Sierra Leone population was the reparations programme, which was launched five years after the SLTRC issued its report and has already been discussed in detail. By the end of 2014, a lack of funds brought the implementation to a standstill and illustrates the government's inability and unwillingness to provide victims of human rights violations an effective remedy (ICTJ 2010). In addition, the registration process and the implementation and allocation of resources were criticized by national and international civil society organizations (Suma and Correa 2009). Even as reparations were finally paid to registered victims, seven years after the war had ended, the distribution of these reparations became politicized: 'Reparations are about acknowledging that something wrong was done to people. However, most of the reparations' money went to the North, due to political affiliations with the government, while most victims were in the South. Reparations became political.'[22]

According to official assessments,[23] the people in Sierra Leone understood what the SLTRC and the special court were doing, and were well informed about the proceedings by outreach programmes;[24] however, while many non-elite locals had knowledge of the existence of different TJ bodies, they could not distinguish between the different procedures. For example, some believed that the SLTRC would provide 'packages' to victims who testified, 'as had been received by the ex-combatants who participated in DDR' (Millar 2013: 195). One core shortcoming of the SLTRC can thus be found in victims' disappointment that they did not receive significant help from the government in exchange for their statements, such as monetary support or medical services (Millar 2015). A problem that also led to immense frustration and doubts among SLTRC staff members, who had to repeatedly tell witnesses that nothing could be done for them (Menzel 2020). While the SLTRC was at least created as a victim-oriented platform for national reconciliation, the court had relatively little to do with the demands of average Sierra Leoneans for justice (Sriram 2012).

Even after the official conclusion of the TJ process, many victims were compelled to live side by side with the perpetrators, without true justice, and adopted a coping strategy of 'forgiving and forgetting' to deal with the past (Shaw 2007). While Sierra Leone can thus be seen as a successful case of TJ, as the implementation of different TJ institutions has reduced the likelihood of human rights atrocities in the country, many Sierra Leoneans 'from marginalized groups have been required to "cope" in a society in which hope for social and economic advance remains scare, constraining localized efforts at authentic reconciliation' (Mahony and Sooka 2015: 51). This mixed opinion is evident in the results for the 2019 survey, in which I asked about the general agreement with three statements regarding the TJ process in Sierra Leone (see Table 6.5). In the public opinion, the SCSL could deliver justice to the people in Sierra Leone, with only 9 per cent disagreeing with this statement. Over 60 per cent believed the SLTRC created an accurate account of what happened during the war, but nearly 30 per cent did not believe reparations were made to the right people, reiterating the civil society critique of the reparations programme, which did not reach many victims in the communities: 'What do we get out of it [the peace process], even if we had been victims of the war?'[25]

## A look ahead: Sierra Leone today

Peace is not just when the guns are silent.[26]

The guns have been silent for nearly 20 years and Sierra Leone has made a lot of progress, leading some analysts to even call it the 'most peaceful

**Table 6.5:** Local perceptions of the Sierra Leonean peace process regarding transitional justice

| | Perceptions of the peace process (in %) | | | | | |
|---|---|---|---|---|---|---|
| | Strongly agree | Agree | Neither agree nor disagree | Disagree | Strongly disagree | Don't know/no answer |
| The Special Court delivered justice to Sierra Leone people | 32.5 | 32.1 | 21.5 | 4.9 | 3.8 | 5.3 |
| The SLTRC created an accurate account of what happened during the war | 28.7 | 33.6 | 24.5 | 8.3 | 0.0 | 4.9 |
| Reparations have been made to the right people/victims of the war | 12.8 | 22.3 | 34.3 | 22.6 | 4.5 | 3.4 |

Note: N = 265; Question: 'Now I'm going to read out a number of statements regarding the peace process in Sierra Leone. For each one, could you tell me how much you agree or disagree with it?'

country in West Africa'.[27] In December 2005, the UN peacekeeping mission completed its withdrawal from Sierra Leone and was replaced by a peacebuilding presence, first the UN Integrated Office in Sierra Leone (UNIOSIL) and then the UN Integrated Peacebuilding Office in Sierra Leone (UNIPSIL). At the final mission-closing ceremony in Freetown on 5 March 2014, UN Secretary-General Ban Ki-moon praised what he called 'the great strides towards peace, stability and long-term development in Sierra Leone and called it "one of the world's most successful cases of post-conflict recovery, peacekeeping and peacebuilding"' (UNIPSIL 2014). With no remaining armed nonstate groups or international forces on its territory, the government of Sierra Leone is the only actor that controls the means on the use of force in the country. The environment is relatively stable and secure, and personal security is perceived as better than before or during the war. Refugees and IDPs were able to return to their places of origin and former combatants have been demobilized and either trained in civilian professions or integrated into the RSLAF. In 2018, Sierra Leone saw the first peaceful transfer of power after the civil war from former President Ernest Bai Koroma (APC) to the current President Julius Maada Bio (SLPP).

Regarding accountability, the peacebuilding mechanism has also been quite successful and represents one of the most comprehensive TJ approaches with its combination of a truth commission, a criminal tribunal and a reparations programme. The SLTRC was envisioned as middle way to establish a 'truth' of the conflict and enhance national reconciliation, which would be necessary for sustaining peace. While its establishment and execution were plagued by a lack of political will and international funding, several recommendations have been implemented by the government of Sierra Leone, including a reparations programme, which, however, did not see full implementation, due to the government's inability and unwillingness to provide victims of human rights violations an effective remedy after international funds were depleted. The SCSL provided justice to the victims by convicting individuals responsible for gross human rights violations; however, it only adjudicated over the most senior leaders of the armed groups, and most victims were compelled to live side by side with perpetrators without true justice.

In the 2019 survey, I asked respondents how they thought about the performance of various peacebuilding actors in Sierra Leone (see Table 6.6). Regarding international actors, the UN peacekeeping mission received the highest agreement rates and was considered important for the peace process by 93 per cent of respondents, followed by the support of the British government (86 per cent). On the state level, the SLTRC and the SCSL

**Table 6.6:** The effect of peacebuilding actors in Sierra Leone

| | Perceptions of peacebuilding actors (in %) | | | |
|---|---|---|---|---|
| Type of actor | | Very/ somewhat important for peace process | Did not affect peace process | Somewhat/ a big threat for peace process |
| International | UNAMSIL | 93.2 | 1.5 | 1.5 |
| | ECOMOG | 78.5 | 0.8 | 4.2 |
| | British government | 86.0 | 2.3 | 2.6 |
| State | SLTRC | 77.0 | 13.2 | 1.9 |
| | SCSL | 80.4 | 9.1 | 4.5 |
| | Sierra Leone Police | 62.6 | 18.9 | 13.6 |
| | Sierra Leone Armed Forces | 79.2 | 7.2 | 10.2 |
| Domestic nonstate | Civil Defence Force (CDF) | 48.7 | 14.0 | 32.5 |
| | Revolutionary United Front (RUF) | 40.8 | 7.5 | 46.6 |
| | Local leaders | 77.7 | 12.1 | 4.9 |

Note: N = 265; Question: 'I'm going to read out a list of groups that are said to have affected the peace process in Liberia. For each one, could you tell me whether you think that they played an important role or threatened the peace process?' Percentages of 'don't know' and 'no answer' responses are not shown in the table.

received high agreement rates and were considered important for the peace process, while opinions were mixed about the impact of the Sierra Leone police and the armed forces. Some respondents considered these security actors a threat. Lastly, the former armed CDF and RUF factions were still considered as a threat by 33 and 47 per cent of the respondents respectively, while local leaders played an important role for the peace process, reflecting their general importance in Sierra Leonean society (Ruppel and Leib 2022).

Overall, the case study of Sierra Leone provides evidence for the assisted accountability mechanism and its impact on the establishment of sustaining peace. It represents a good example of the advantages of a comprehensive peacebuilding approach, including justice and security, for long-term stability and reconciliation, and highlights the challenges in connecting this approach to local postwar needs and expectations. The peacebuilding process in Sierra Leone included a strong parallel focus on security and justice, with the simultaneous establishment of various institutions, and local perceptions of the assisted accountability mechanisms are quite positive.

While 'Sierra Leone took a lot of effort to make sure we do not go back to war', the country is not out of the woods yet and still suffers from the consequences of the civil war.[28] Despite the peacebuilding efforts, reconstruction and rehabilitation have not been completed, and the causes of the conflict have not been eliminated (Ruppel 2023). Sierra Leone is significantly funded by international donors and is fragile with regard to peace, accountability and democracy.[29] The problems that led to the conflict still exist and have to be addressed before Sierra Leone will be truly peaceful: 'there are signs again of things that brought the war, but people are not ready to go back'.[30] In the years leading up to the Ebola crisis (2014–2016), Sierra Leone experienced a rapid expansion of foreign direct investment in infrastructure, agriculture and the mineral sector, which was stopped due to the health crisis. Large parts of the population are still affected by poverty and a lack of prospects. The unemployment rate among young people, for example, is around 60 per cent (Alemu 2016). Issues such as land, access to natural resources, and the extraction of raw materials were already triggers for the civil war and have not been resolved. In particular, the problem of land grabbing exacerbates existing conflict lines and leads to increasing impoverishment of the rural population (Tzouvala 2019). Tackling these issues will be an inevitable challenge for a complete realization of the peacebuilding mechanism in Sierra Leone.

7

# The Spoils-of-Peace Approach in South Africa

The previous comparative study has identified the peacebuilding episode after the civil war and fight against apartheid in South Africa (1978–1993) as a pathway case for the second sufficient spoils-of-peace approach, leading to sustaining peace. On 27 April 1994, Nelson Mandela was elected President in South Africa's first national elections with universal adult suffrage, ending the country's era of apartheid. According to this configurational pattern, the combined presence of inclusive power sharing and comprehensive SSR is sufficient for the establishment of sustaining peace. South Africa's successful transition from apartheid to democratic governance has generally been portrayed as an exemplary case of post-conflict transition towards sustaining peace. Whereas the QCA analysis focused on identifying explicit connections between explanatory peacebuilding conditions, I now look at the peacebuilding process in South Africa to test the causal spoils-of-peace mechanism that links this second sufficient pattern to the outcome of sustaining peace.

The main argument behind this approach is that inclusive power sharing and comprehensive security sector reform are used to incorporate the main political opponents into the political and security systems by offering them some incentives to maintain a peace agreement. Together, these two institutions focus on resolving the security dilemma and building or restoring key political and security state functions. Power sharing facilitates the transition from civil war to sustaining peace by reassuring minority groups that their interests will be taken into account through the participation of their representatives in governmental decision-making processes. SSR, on the other hand, consolidates peace through the comprehensive disarmament, demobilization and integration of all ex-combatants, either into the newly established national security forces or civil society, preventing them from becoming a threat to peace and stability. The logic behind this argument is that in typical post-conflict societies, one way of sustaining peace is through the interim sharing of political power, in combination with the integration and transformation of a highly militarized security sector.

I test the spoils-of-peace approach as an explanation for the successful peace process in South Africa and apply the method of process tracing to uncover the causal mechanism that links the peacebuilding configuration to sustaining peace. This chapter provides the background to the civil war and apartheid system in South Africa. Then, I outline the methodological approach and the types of evidence used for the analysis and conceptualize the spoils-of-peace mechanism on the theoretical level. The third section constitutes the core of this chapter and presents empirical evidence on the case-specific level to trace the implementation of the spoils-of-peace mechanism in post-conflict South Africa.

## Patterns of peace and conflict in South Africa

The Republic of South Africa is the southernmost country in Africa, with neighbours Namibia, Botswana and Zimbabwe to the north, and Mozambique and Eswatini to the east and northeast (see Figure 7.1). It completely enclaves the country of Lesotho. South Africa is a multi-ethnic society and recognizes 12 official languages, of which Zulu, Xhosa, Afrikaans and English are the most-spoken first languages. The country's history has been characterized by racial segregation and dominant White minority rule, which culminated in the imposition of apartheid in 1948. During the 1980s, 'South Africa disintegrated into a form of civil war as Black opponents of apartheid fought, increasingly successfully, to make apartheid unworkable and South Africa ungovernable' (Clark and Worger 2016: 6). Apartheid and the civil war finally came to an end in 1994, with the first universal and free elections in South Africa's history.

European settlement in South Africa did not begin until 1652, when the Dutch established the first fort at the Cape of Good Hope. The fort was run by the Dutch East India Company, which used it as a base to resupply its ships travelling between Europe and Asia. They were not interested in establishing a permanent European settler community at the cape; however, the cape became home to a large population of former company employees, who stayed in the Dutch overseas territory after serving their contracts (Hunt 2005). They became independent farmers, known as Boers, on the frontier and expanded eastwards into the interior of the country, resulting in a series of frontier wars with the indigenous Khoi over pastureland for commercial European farms. The Dutch East India Company also brought thousands of enslaved people from Indonesia, Madagascar and parts of Eastern Africa to work on the farms of the Dutch settlers (Worden 1985). To control these disparate groups in the territory, the company created a new, racialized society at the cape, 'beginning with Company employees

**Figure 7.1:** Political map of South Africa

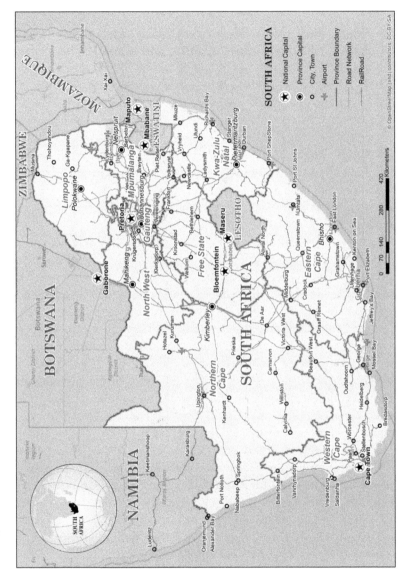

at the top, followed by settlers, the "mixed" racial groups and with slaves at the bottom' (Clark and Worger 2016: 12).

Great Britain came to occupy Cape Town in 1795 to prevent it from falling under the control of Napoleon's French First Republic and to keep control of the sea route to Asia. Following the end of the Napoleonic Wars, the cape colony was formally ceded to Great Britain and became part of the British Empire, resulting in increasing British emigration to South Africa (Lloyd 2008). After the British Parliament first forbade the participation in the international slave trade in 1807 and then abolished slavery throughout the British Empire in 1834, the Boer population opposed to the loss of their labour force and embarked on what has been called the Great Trek, leaving the British-held Cape Colony northward by wagon trains for new lands to farm where they could still practise slavery. The Great Trek resulted in the founding of several autonomous Boer republics, including the South African Republic (also known as the Transvaal Republic), the Natalia Republic and the Orange Free State, which remained fairly isolated and developed their own culture and society, separate from their European homelands (Giliomee 2003).

The discovery of diamonds in 1867 and gold in 1884 dramatically altered the economic and political structure of South Africa, increased economic growth and immigration, and created increasing divisions between the British, Boer and Indigenous populations. During the 1870s and 1880s, the British conquered the still-independent African nations, confiscated most of the land and intensified the subjugation of the Indigenous people (Clark and Worger 2016). Increasing tensions between the British and Boer over the control of gold led to the Second Anglo-Boer War (1899–1902), which the British won, leading to devastating suffering for the Boer population. Nearly 28,000 Boers, most of them women and children, died in British concentration camps (Osborne 2016). The South Africa Act of 1909 granted nominal independence and created the Union of South Africa, which became fully independent from the UK in 1931. After the creation of the Union, White supremacy was enforced through a series of segregation policies that increasingly limited African rights. Under segregation, African ownership to land was restricted to designated areas comprising 7 per cent of the country's total land area and 'African workers were limited to unskilled jobs, were punished if they quit their jobs and were robbed of their rights to protest these conditions' (Clark and Worger 2016: 21).

In 1948, the Afrikaner-based National Party (NP) was elected to power and legally institutionalized and strengthened a racial segregation system that came to be known as apartheid. Under the terms of the Population Registration Act of 1950, all residents of South Africa were to be classified as 'White', 'Colored' (people of mixed race) or 'Native' and received identity cards listing the assigned race of the individual and determining their access to legal rights. The disadvantaged Black majority soon organized massive protests against the NP government and anti-apartheid organizations, such as the African National Congress (ANC) and the Pan-Africanist Congress (PAC) organized to resist, protest and, eventually, attempt to overthrow the apartheid regime. Both organizations were banned in 1960, shortly after the Sharpeville massacre, were police fired on PAC supporters protesting outside of the police station at Sharpeville, killing at least 69 and wounding 320 protesters (Clark and Worger 2016). Prohibited from operating peacefully, the ANC (Umkhonto we Sizwe; MK) and the PAC (Poqo) established underground organizations to continue their violent resistance against the government and to bring an end to White rule. International criticism increased during the 1960s and 1970s as the South African government implemented its apartheid policies in brutal fashion. In November 1977, the UNSC voted unanimously to implement a mandatory embargo on the trade in arms and related material of all types to South Africa (UNSC 1977). In October 1986, the US Congress passed the Comprehensive Anti-Apartheid Act, implementing mandatory economic sanctions against South Africa.

During the 1980s, the NP government took increasingly brutal steps to force capitulation and 'South Africa disintegrated into a form of civil war as black opponents of apartheid fought, increasingly successfully, to make apartheid unworkable and South Africa ungovernable' (Clark and Worger 2016: 6). After 14,000 'unrest-related incidents' in 1986, the government introduced a national state of emergency, but it could not quell the insurrection, and the civil war intensified, resulting in thousands of deaths due to political violence in 1990 (Christopher 2001).

Faced with a political impasse, at the opening session of Parliament on 2 February 1990, the new President F.W. de Klerk announced the orders banning the ANC, the PAC and 32 other organizations were to be revoked and political prisoners, including Nelson Mandela, were to be released to start negotiations that he considered to be 'the key to reconciliation, peace, and a new and just dispensation'.[1] The first rounds of talks between the ANC and the government of South Africa established the preconditions for substantive negotiations, which were codified in the Groote Schur Minute (4 May 1990) and the Pretoria Minute (6 August 1990). The ANC agreed to the immediate suspension of the armed struggle but refused to disband its military MK wing, hand over weapons or disclose the location of its weapons caches (Jung and Shapiro 1995).

These agreements failed to stem the escalation of political violence, which led to right-wing White supremacists launching periodic attacks and regular clashes between supporters of the ANC and supporters of the newly established Inkatha Freedom Party (IFP), producing increasing death rates from political violence: 'from an average of 100 deaths a month in late 1990 the rate continued to rise and reached an average of more than twice that figure in 1993' (Clark and Worger 2016: 122). A new attempt by the leaders of the main political parties to end the bloodshed was embodied in the National Peace Accord (NPA) signed on 14 September 1991 (Guelke 1993). This first multiparty agreement prepared the way for a multiparty conference, known as the Convention for a Democratic South Africa (CODESA), to discuss the process by which South Africa should be transformed. In December 1991 and May 1992, the CODESA held two plenary sessions, which were judged as a success but did not settle any of the major issues of substance. The prospect of political progress through the CODESA led right-wing Whites to question the negotiation mandate of the de Klerk-led government. President de Klerk responded by holding a 'Whites-only' referendum in March 1992, in which 69 per cent voted in favour of his position and for a continuation of the negotiations (Wren 1992).

The referendum was followed by a deadlock between the government and the ANC in the CODESA II in May 1992, resulting in the ANC's return to a programme of mass action to demonstrate its level of popular support. On the night of 17 June 1992, an armed force of Inkatha supporters entered the town of Boipatong and killed 46 people, most of them women and children. Despite previous warnings, security forces did not attempt to prevent the massacre, nor did they take any steps to track down the perpetrators. Eyewitness accounts provide evidence that the security forces had been complicit in the killings (Simpson 2012). Due to the government's ongoing involvement in political violence, the ANC withdrew from the negotiations and promoted its mass action campaign and gather international support. In July 1992, the UNSC intervened by mandating the United Nations Observer Mission in South Africa (UNOMSA) to observe demonstrations and other forms of mass action, note the conduct of all parties and obtain information indicating the degree to which the parties' actions were consistent with the principles of the NPA (UNSC 1992a).[2] UNOMSA was supported by monitoring groups from the European Community, the Organisation of African Unity and the Commonwealth of Nations.

The international observers did not prevent the massacre of 28 ANC supporters protesting outside the town of Bisho, who were shot by soldiers of the Ciskei Defence Force on 7 September 1992 (Simpson 2012). The televising of the demonstration, the aftermath of the massacre, and international observer witnesses ensured a critical response from the international community, 'for the most part directed against the South African government' (Guelke 1993: 62). Several reports published by a government commission of inquiry headed by Justice Richard Goldstone also provided evidence of the state's use of covert forces to participate in political killings and of the existence of plans by military intelligence to undermine the ANC (Clark and Worger 2016). Under the impression of these developments, the South African government and the ANC met in late September 1992 to discuss the resumption of negotiations. The outcome of these discussions was the Record of Understanding, including provisions for an elected constitution-making body, with 'adequate deadlock-breaking mechanisms', which would act as an interim Government of National Unity (GNU).[3] Between April and December 1993, the newly established Multi-Party Negotiating Forum (MPNF) devised an interim constitution based on a five-year period of transition under a GNU that would provide significant representation for any political party receiving at least 5 per cent of the vote in the upcoming elections (Barnes and de Klerk 2002). Between 26 and 29 April 1994, South Africa held its first elections under universal suffrage, formally bringing apartheid to an end.

## The data collection and process tracing approach

The previous comparative analysis has identified the combination of inclusive power sharing (SHARE) and comprehensive security sector reform (SSR) as a second sufficient pathway to sustaining peace in post-conflict societies. In this chapter, I apply process tracing to analyse how these two peacebuilding institutions interact with each other in a spoils-of-peace mechanism, leading to sustaining peace. The mechanism is traced in the individual case of peacebuilding in post-apartheid South Africa to gain a better understanding of the causal relationship between the sufficient configuration and sustaining peace. Process tracing has been discussed in detail as a case-oriented, within-case method in Chapter 4 and is now used to take a look at the mechanism between the explanatory configuration (the spoils-of-peace approach) and the outcome (sustaining peace). In this section, I discuss the types of evidence used, before I conceptualize a spoils-of-peace theory, based on the existing literature, and then test whether there is empirical evidence for the hypothesized mechanism to be present in the case of South Africa (theory-testing process tracing).

The analysis draws on several sources of empirical information and uses multiple types of evidence to identify empirical fingerprints for each part of the theorized mechanism. As no personal fieldwork could be conducted for the case study of South Africa, the analysis relies on a combination of mostly secondary sources, institutional documents from the Republic of South Africa, public opinion surveys, UNSC resolutions, and reports by the UN Secretary-General on the question of South Africa.

In using theory-testing process tracing to open up the black box of the previously identified sufficient relationship between the two peacebuilding conditions and the outcome of sustaining peace, we first need to conceptualize and operationalize a causal mechanism between the conditions and the outcome, based on existing theories, and define case-specific, empirical observables for each part of the mechanism, before we can conduct a structured empirical test to see whether the predicted evidence was found. Theory-testing process tracing allows for inference from the collected empirical evidence that the spoils-of-peace mechanism was present in the case of South Africa.

Cross-case studies applying QCA usually do not establish a temporal or sequential order among the explanatory conditions that they identify as sufficient for an outcome. In addition, the mechanism connecting the configuration with the outcome might be composed of different empirically independent mechanisms. From our comparative study in Chapter 5, we only know that the combined presence of inclusive power sharing and comprehensive SSR triggers a mechanism labelled the spoils-of-peace approach, which connects the configuration of these two peacebuilding institutions to sustaining peace; however, we do not yet have insights into how this mechanism operates or whether it consists of multiple or sequential mechanisms. The different (sequential) constellations that are compatible with this two-way conjunction of the spoils-of-peace approach (SHARE*SSR) in a mechanism-centred research design were discussed in detail in the previous chapter (see Figure 6.3): a simple setting where both peacebuilding conditions operate simultaneously and trigger a single mechanism; a relationship where each of the two INUS conditions triggers 'an empirically independent mechanism which forms a [two-way] conjunction of mechanisms in an aggregated, causal perspective' (Beach and Rohlfing 2018: 22); or a sequence where a conjunction triggers a mechanism that produces another condition that triggers a mechanism, leading to the outcome.

To identify the actual causal arrangement of the two peacebuilding conditions, I consider all theoretically plausible constellations that could be hidden by the comparative analysis and 'cast the net widely' to identify the actual sequence of conditions and mechanisms (Bennett and Checkel 2015). It is expedient to take a closer look at the timeline of peacebuilding activities in South Africa to retrieve some first indications for potential sequences within the configurational arrangement. Figure 7.2 summarizes the spoils-of-peace approach in South Africa by displaying the development of the two peacebuilding institutions included in the sufficient configuration and important milestones in their implementation. This timeline only provides information about potential sequences in the realization of the conditions and does not tell us anything about the mechanism itself.

The timeline clearly indicates both peacebuilding initiatives show a temporal overlap and were implemented simultaneously, rather than being sequenced. In addition, both the power-sharing agreement and the guidelines for the integration and transformation of the South African security sector had their origins in the MPNF and were both included as provisions in the interim constitution of 1993. Combined with our theoretical expectations about the combined impact of these two peacebuilding institutions, the

**Figure 7.2:** Timeline of the spoils-of-peace approach in South Africa, 1991–1999

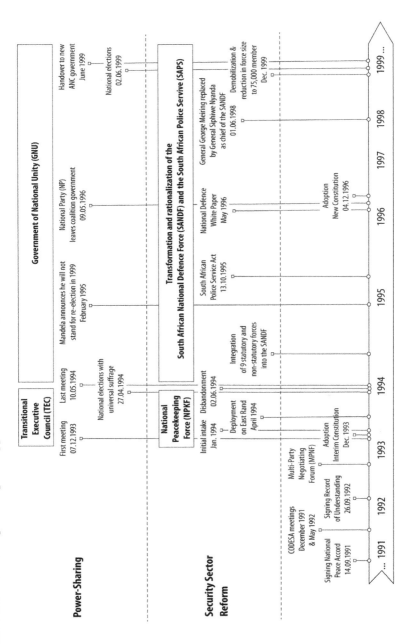

**Figure 7.3:** Constellation of the spoils-of-peace approach

empirical evidence suggests the following spoils-of-peace mechanism, which is triggered by the simultaneous implementation of power sharing and SSR (see Figure 7.3).

The spoils-of-peace approach connects the simultaneous implementation of power sharing and SSR with sustaining peace by providing the warring factions with some political or monetary gains during the transition period (Clark 2001; Pugh 2002). Inclusive power sharing and comprehensive SSR both aim to incorporate the main opponents into the political and security system by offering some incentives to maintain a peace agreement (Spear 2002; Walter 2002; Hartzell and Hoddie 2007; Mattes and Savun 2009). Taken together, these two institutions focus on resolving the security dilemma and building or restoring key state functions 'that have the capacity to generate basic public goods and possess a modicum of legitimacy' (Barnett et al 2007: 49). The guaranteed access for ex-combatants to executive and military power is of great importance for peacebuilding initiatives, as the representation by all factions in government prevents former enemies from capturing the state (Walter 2002). In this regard, power sharing facilitates the transition from civil war to sustained peace by reassuring minority groups that their interests will be taken into account through the participation of their representatives in governmental decision-making processes. It also enables faction leaders to make some personal gains with their new positions in transitional governments, while still facilitating the transition to democratic governance and their participation as political parties in general elections: 'Political elites may find arguments in favor of power sharing normatively attractive, but their primary concern ultimately remains with strategies that best meet their interests and security needs' (Spears 2002: 127).

In addition to restoring key political functions, a functioning security system that ensures the security of civilians and discourages ex-combatants from returning to armed resistance is a prerequisite for the establishment of sustaining peace. The remnants of a wartime security apparatus pose great risks for any peace process as they continue to jeopardize internal security in societies already devastated by conflict (Schnabel and Ehrhart 2005). The goal of SSR is to consolidate peace through comprehensive disarmament, demobilization and integration of all ex-combatants either into the newly established national security forces or civil society, preventing them from becoming a threat to peace and stability. If carried out successfully, (re)integration offers ex-combatants and faction leaders an alternative to a life with the gun and a stable means of income, thus reducing the risk of conflict recurrence.

In South Africa, power sharing was attractive as a political solution to both the NP, whose power was declining, and the ANC, whose power was rising (Spears 2002). It appealed to the former as the best possible long-term means of protecting their interests and to monitor and limit the power of the ANC. For the ANC, power sharing was attractive because it offered side benefits, such as international legitimacy, stability in the political process and political support from South African Whites, things that may have been jeopardized if a political settlement had not been reached (Maphai 1996): 'The NP knew that if it were to have any influence in this new government, it would need to be of the power sharing type. The African National Congress, whilst opposed to power sharing was aware that it needed the economics of Whites, as well as the South African Army' (Traniello 2008: 35). While the ANC had electoral support and international sympathy, it lacked other noncoercive power resources and military supremacy: 'as a liberation movement, the ANC had perfected the art of making the country ungovernable. Yet as a ruling party, like the NP, it could not exercise political power unilaterally. … Thus neither side could govern the country without the assistance of the other' (Maphai 1996: 72–73).

## Tracing the spoils-of-peace mechanism in post-apartheid South Africa

The 1993 interim South African Constitution, negotiated by the MPNF and finally adopted by the all-White South African Parliament as its final act in December 1993, was a critical juncture for the peace process and specified the relevant peacebuilding institutions for South Africa's post-apartheid transition. Based on these provisions, the peacebuilding process in South Africa included two key initiatives: (a) an interim power sharing GNU, designed to last from April 1994 to June 1999; and (b) a comprehensive reform of the security sector, including the integration of the myriad of national and regional police and defence forces into a single national defence force and a national police service. These two peacebuilding institutions were supposed to lay the foundations for peace and political transformation in South Africa through a combined approach. This spoils-of-peace mechanism connects political power sharing and SSR with sustaining peace by providing for a peaceful transfer of power and the integration and transformation of the security forces as main actors of political violence. For the mechanism to be present, we would expect empirical evidence of the establishment of a transitional power-sharing government, the disarmament and demobilization of former members of homeland defence forces and liberation movements, and their successful integration into a single national defence force. The mechanism concludes with the inauguration of a new democratically elected government and the rationalization of the security forces to an appropriate post-conflict size (Figure 7.4).

## Part I: Interim constitution with power-sharing and security sector reform provisions

Prior to the CODESA meetings, President de Klerk had announced the government's willingness to amend the existing Constitution to allow for an interim power-sharing model, but did not provide any details (Deegan 2001). In the subsequent rounds of negotiations in the MPNF, the NP was eager to embed permanent power sharing in the Constitution as a means of protecting White interests, but had to scale down its demands to short-term power sharing in an interim government. In the end, the ruling NP party agreed to give up its monopoly political power in return for the protection of White minority rights and, most significantly, White property rights (Cheeseman 2011). The ANC, on the other hand, while believing that it would gain an absolute majority in the new Parliament, eventually accepted constitutionally mandated interim power sharing to ensure stability in the political process and political support from South African Whites (Jung and Shapiro 1995). Similarly, the IFP, along with its leader Mangosuthu Buthelezi, gave up its rejection of majority rule and decided to participate in the 1993 elections because the ANC agreed to recognize the Zulu king and traditional authorities, and to give Buthelezi a prominent position in the GNU.

In December 1993, the interim Constitution, negotiated by the MPNF, was finally adopted by the all-White South African Parliament, as its final act, and included provisions for the GNU designed to last for a period of five years: April 1994 to June 1999.[4] Overall, the power-sharing provisions of the Constitution were carefully constructed to ease fears and to ensure securities protecting each of the main parties' power and core interests (Traniello 2008). The GNU would include all major political parties in a proportional arrangement. Clause 88 of the interim Constitution stipulated that any party that held more than 20 seats in the National Assembly (corresponding to 5 per cent of the vote) would be given cabinet portfolios in proportion to the number of seats it held and thus a share of executive power. This system of proportional representation also provided incentives for potential 'spoilers', such as the IFP, to join the elections. Even if they would be a minority in the assembly, they would have a chance for representation and influence in the ruling of South Africa by becoming

# THE SPOILS-OF-PEACE APPROACH IN SOUTH AFRICA

**Figure 7.4:** Application of the spoils-of-peace mechanism in South Africa

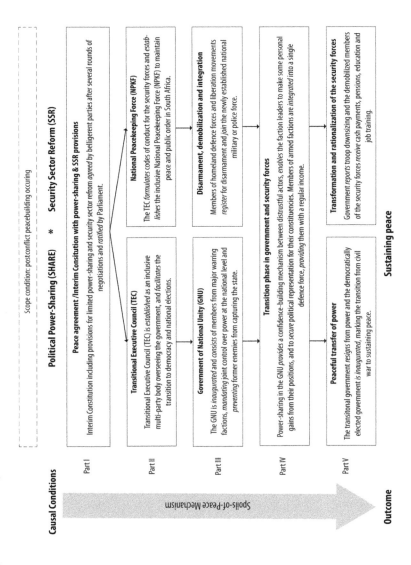

part of the GNU (Sisk 1996). To further appease the general insecurity of minorities, a two thirds supermajority in the General Assembly would be required to approve the final Constitution: 'under this arrangement, both the National Party and the Inkatha Freedom Party were guaranteed a role in the interim government and the opportunity to consolidate their power before democratic elections in 1999' (Clark and Worger 2016: 126).

During the continuous rounds of negotiations finally ending apartheid in South Africa, the role of the different security actors and their indispensable transformations were considered crucial for a successful peace process. Signed in September 1991 by most major political parties in the country, the NPA initiated legally enforceable codes of conduct for the security forces and provided for the creation of a national peace secretariat and regional and local dispute resolution committees.[5] During the subsequent CODESA meetings, ANC delegates argued for the reconstruction of the security forces 'with a view to create national, legitimate and representative security forces inclusive of the South African Defence Force (SADF), Umkhonto we Sizwe (MK)' and the homeland defence forces of the 'independent' states and the self-governing territories (Africa 2011: 8). While these principles were not debated extensively in the context of CODESA, they provided the basis for later agreements. After the signing of the Record of Understanding between the government of South Africa and the ANC in September 1992, a first round of reforms to security forces took place. In December 1992, seven SADF senior officers were placed on compulsory leave and 16 others were placed in compulsory retirement for unauthorized activities linked to political killings (Simpson 2012). However, it was not until November 1993 that the armed forces of the South African government and the ANC became involved in direct negotiations, as both protagonists 'saw the retention of their armed forces as a form of a "security fallback" ... [and] as a physical guarantee that could be utilized should the negotiation process falter' (Williams 2002: 17). The interim Constitution, as the final outcome of the negotiations, included provisions for the management of the security sector and an entrenched Bill of Rights. It provided for the establishment of a single South African Police Service (SAPS), instead of the existing 11 national and 'homeland' police forces, and a new balanced National Defence Force that would consist of members from the SADF, any defence force of any area forming part of the national territory, and any armed force of political organizations participating in the general elections.[6]

## Part II: The Transitional Executive Council and the National Peacekeeping Force

Between December 1993 and May 1994, the multiparty Transitional Executive Council (TEC) was overseeing the government and South Africa's transition to democracy in the run-up to the general elections (Jung and Shapiro 1995). During the MPNF, ANC representatives had pushed for the creation of a multiparty system of collective governance to control the White-dominated government and ensure free political participation. The TEC consisted of 19 members, one from each of the parties that had participated in the MPNF negotiations (excluding the PAC and the IFP) and marked the end of minority rule in South Africa. It ruled through seven multiparty subcouncils focused on particular policy areas, all of which operated under TEC control and collaborated with the relevant government department. These subcouncils included regional and local government and traditional authorities, law and order, stability and security, defence, finance, foreign affairs, the status of women, and intelligence.[7] While the existing NP government was still in power, its decision making was subject to the endorsement of the TEC (Graham 2011). All government departments required TEC approval before any of their policies could be implemented: 'it was, in essence, an advisory and monitoring council that had the power of veto over any policy of the existing government of President de Klerk' (Deegan 2001: 87).

Regarding the management of the security forces of the state and those of the liberation movements, the TEC took up the principles discussed during the CODESA meetings for the work of the security-related subcouncils. The Subcouncil on Defence was tasked with formulating a code of conduct that would bind all military forces in the country and establishing the National Peacekeeping Force (NPKF), drawing on security forces of the parties involved in the negotiation process. Its role was essentially political-strategic and its main tasks were to maintain oversight over the armed forces during the pre-election phase and to initiate the planning required to create a newly integrated national army (Williams 2002). The Subcouncil on Law and Order, Security and Stability was tasked with the supervision of the police performance and the establishment of a national independent civilian complaints mechanism for possible abuse or misconduct by police agents. The pre-integration process of the new army was delegated to the Joint Military Co-ordinating Council (JMCC), headed by the Chief of the SADF General George Meiring and MK Chief of Staff Siphiwe Nyanda. Due to their organizational, planning and budgetary capabilities, the SADF dominated most of the meetings and set up the immanent integration process 'on SADF structures and SADF rules and regulation – a phenomenon that was to greatly undermine the capacity of non-SADF forces to influence the integration process' (Williams 2002: 20).

The idea of an integrated domestic peacekeeping force replacing existing defence and police forces had been articulated by civil society representatives and human rights organizations after the collapse of the CODESA negotiations and the subsequent mass action campaigns, culminating in the Boipatong massacre in June 1992 (UNSC 1992b). On 2 June 1993, the

Technical Committee on Violence of the MPNF formally recommended the establishment of an independent peacekeeping force to function as the primary security force for the upcoming general elections and to compensate for the deficiencies of the existing security services in reducing politically related violence (Anglin 1995). A corresponding provision for the establishment of the NPKF was included in the TEC Act, which specified that the functions of the NPKF 'shall relate to the maintenance of peace and public order in South Africa'.[8] Recruitment should be as inclusive as possible and confined to existing members of all government, homeland, party armies and police forces.

At the beginning of 1994, the security landscape in South Africa consisted of various national and subnational military and police forces that required demobilization and integration (see Table 7.1). In addition to the SADF and the SAP under government authority, security actors also included the defence and police forces of the four 'independent' TBVC states (Transkei, Bophuthatswana, Venda and Ciskei), police forces of six self-governing territories, the armed wings of the liberation movements, and right-wing paramilitary groups and self-defence units (SDUs) in the townships. The NPKF drew its members from all groups participating in the TEC, which led to the exclusion of two homeland administrations (that is, Bophuthatswana ad KwaZulu), several political parties (that is, the PAC, Azapo and the IFP), paramilitary groups and SDUs. Although the TEC envisioned that the NPKF would number 10,000 personnel, the initial intake in January 1994 was limited to 3,743 (three battalions) due to a short training time and limited accommodation, with a second and final batch of 1,200 recruits being taken in one month later (Anglin 1995).

The general idea behind the establishment of the NPKF as an interim military force was to deploy it in those regions most affected by political violence prior to the general elections, taking over security responsibilities from the SAP's intensely unpopular Internal Stability Unit (ISU). Shortly before the elections in April 1994, the NPKF was deployed to townships on the East Rand, which had been engulfed in politically motivated violence before the SADF significantly reduced the death toll. The NPKF was unable to maintain peace in the East Rand and had to give the responsibility for security back to the SADF after just one week (Anglin 1995). While the NPKF was once thought of as a prototype for a new South African National Defence Force (SANDF), it could not recover from this massive lack in public confidence and was formally disbanded on 2 June 1994, its members being absorbed into the new SANDF.

## Part III: The Government of National Unity and the disarmament and integration of the armed forces

The April 1994 elections were clearly won by the ANC, which received 62.7 per cent of the popular vote, followed by the NP with 20.4 per cent

THE SPOILS-OF-PEACE APPROACH IN SOUTH AFRICA

**Table 7.1:** Estimated military and police forces in South Africa, January 1994

| Authority | Military forces | | Police forces | |
|---|---|---|---|---|
| South African government | ★South African Defence Force (SADF): | | ★South African Police (SAP) | 115,000 |
| | Full-time | 70,000 | Internal Stability Unit (ISU) | (7,000) |
| | Citizen Force | 120,000 | | |
| | Commandos | 130,000 | | |
| | | 320,000 | | |
| Transitional Executive Council (TEC) | National Peacekeeping Force (NPKF) | 3,800 | | |
| 'Independent' TBVC states | | | | |
| Transkei | ★T. Defence Force (TDF) | 3,500 | ★T. Police Force (TPF) | 3,200 |
| Bophuthatswana | B. Defence Force (BDF) | 4,000 | B. Police (BP) | 5,300 |
| Venda | ★V. Defence Force (VDF) | 1,800 | ★Venda Police (VP) | 1,800 |
| Ciskei | ★C. Defence Force (CDF) | 2,000 | ★Ciskei Police (CP) | 1,900 |
| | | 11,300 | | 12,200 |
| Self-governing territories | | | | |
| KwaZulu | | — | KwaZulu Police (KZP) | 3,800 |
| KwaNdebele | | — | ★K. Police Force (KPF) | 730 |
| GaZankulu | | — | ★G. Police Force (GPF) | 670 |
| Lebowa | | — | ★L. Police Force (LPF) | 1,690 |
| KaNgwane | | — | ★KN. Police Force (KNPF) | ? |
| QwaQwa | | — | ★QQ. Police Force (QQPF) | ? |
| | | | | 6,890 |

(continued)

**Table 7.1:** Estimated military and police forces in South Africa, January 1994 (continued)

| Authority | Military forces | | Police forces | |
|---|---|---|---|---|
| Liberation Movements | | | | |
| African National Congress (ANC) | *Umkhonto weZizwe (MK) | 10,000 | — | |
| Pan Africanist Congress (PAC) | Azanian People's Liberation Army (APLA) | 5,000 | — | |
| Azanian People's Organisation (Azapo)/ Black Consciousness Movement of Azania | Azanian National Liberation Army (Azanla) | 2,000 | — | |
| | | 17,000 | | |
| Right-wing movements | | | | |
| Afrikaner Weerstands-beweging (AWB) | Wenkommando (WK) Boereweerstands-beweging (BWB) | 20,000 1,000 | — — | |
| Self-defence/ protection units | | | | |
| ANC-oriented | SDUs | 20,000+ | — | |
| Inkatha Freedom Party | SPUs | 5,000 | — | |

Note: * Participants in the NPKF

Source: Anglin (1995: 28)

and the IFP with 10.5 per cent, resulting in a parliamentary distribution of 252 ANC seats, 82 NP seats and 43 IFP seats (see Table 7.2). According to the interim Constitution, this vote translated into a 27-member cabinet, in which 18 ministries were headed by the ANC, six by the NP and three by the IFP (Jung and Shapiro 1995). In addition, any party winning at least 80 seats in Parliament was entitled to designate an executive deputy president, which resulted in the appointment of F.W. de Klerk to the post for the NP and Thabo Mbeki for the ANC. These power-sharing provisions ensured that all parties with a substantial base of electoral support were part of the GNU.

The results of the election and the composition of the GNU, which gave KwaZulu/Natal to the IFP, gave the NP 20 per cent of the vote share and

**Table 7.2:** Composition of the National Assembly after the 1994 general elections in South Africa

| African National Congress (ANC) | National Party (NP) | Inkatha Freedom Party (IFP) | Freedom Front (FF) | Democratic Party (DP) | Pan Africanist Congress (PAC) | African Christian Democratic Party (ACDP) |
| --- | --- | --- | --- | --- | --- | --- |
| 252 seats | 82 seats | 43 seats | 9 seats | 7 seats | 5 seats | 2 seats |
| (62.7%) | (20.4%) | (10.5%) | (2.2%) | (1.7%) | (1.3%) | (0.5%) |

Government of National Unity (GNU)

a deputy president position, and simultaneously held the ANC back from a two thirds majority that would have given it the ability to unilaterally write the final Constitution, helped to prevent a renewed civil war in South Africa (Friedman 2014). The ANC and the NP also 'deliberately ignored gross election irregularities in KwaZulu/Natal during the April 1994 elections in order to let Inkatha win one province and have significant representation in the Cabinet' (Herbst 1997: 608). As a result, IFP leader Buthelezi became part of the GNU, making him much less of a threat to the new South Africa. In the end, the ANC was able to head a broad-based coalition that included NP leader de Klerk as one of two deputy presidents, Buthelezi as Minister of Home Affairs, and five additional NP leaders and two additional IFP representatives.

As the leading party of the GNU, the ANC adopted a cautious approach towards the reform of the security sector to maintain a political stability between ANC and IFP activists and to avoid alienating the 'white right' (Cheeseman 2011: 356). To ease concerns, Mandela chose to largely leave existing structures of the security forces intact and to integrate the SADF, the MK and the various homeland armies that had developed during the apartheid era. While ANC leaders were appointed to head the Defence and Police ministries, many Afrikaner generals retained their posts in the security forces during this gradual transformation (Beinart 2001). Mandela also appointed Deputy President de Klerk as head of the Cabinet Committee for Security and Intelligence to assure the leadership of the former apartheid-era security services that their interests and concerns would be treated with consideration (Africa 2011).

The new SANDF was formally established on 27 April 1994, integrating members of the old SADF, the defence forces of the 'independent' TBVC states, the military wings of the ANC and the PAC, and the KwaZulu Self-Protection Force (Wessels 2010). Most of the former homeland and nonstatutory force members were integrated into the Army and the

Medical Health Service, leaving the Air Force and the Navy to remain predominantly White (Heineken 1998). The comparatively weak military capacity of the liberation forces allowed them to integrate their fighters into the security forces and contributed to the willingness of the previous NP government to relinquish control over the security forces following the election in 1994. President Mandela appointed General George Meiring, the chief of the apartheid SADF, to head the new defence force in the interest of stability to ward off the possibility of a coup. With this approach, Mandela 'maintain[ed] the broad loyalty of the security forces and to establish effective control over their operations', even if it meant impeding progress towards a real transformation of the security forces (Cheeseman 2011: 357).

In April 1994, the SANDF was only an integrated force on paper and remained 'a formal, conventional military dominated by an experienced corps of Afrikaners' (Kynoch 1996: 443). The main problems that hindered the integration and transformation of the eight armed forces were vast differences in training, resources and political affiliations between the organizations and 'what many political leaders regard as racism or a counter-revolutionary agenda on the part of officers who served the apartheid regime' (Nathan 2004: 4). Arrogance and racism were frequently used by White officers to obstruct non-SADF officers in the SANDF, and the continuous use of Afrikaans as the main medium of instruction and command additionally disempowered non-SADF officers and prevented them from contributing to the restructuring process (Williams 2002). In October 1994, dissatisfaction over run-down conditions at the assembly camps and the racism of White officers resulted in a munity of 2,000 former MK soldiers and their subsequent dismissal (Kynoch 1996). While the GNU was trying to alter the military's racial and political composition, most of the influential senior command and staff positions within the new SANDF continued to be occupied by former SADF officers: 'by 1995, 11 former MK members had been appointed generals in the new integrated army. In addition, one out of every five army officers came from the ANC' (Maphai 1996: 73).

With regard to the integration and rationalization of the 11 national and regional police components, the South African Police Service Act of 1995 spelt out the framework for the new South African Police Service (SAPS).[9] Only a small number of former MK and Azanian People's Liberation Army (APLA) members were integrated into the SAPS, while the majority joined the SANDF (Africa 2011). To locate policy making regarding the police force in civilian hands, the minister for safety and security, as head of the SAPS, was supported by a civilian Secretariat for Safety and Security, mirroring the composition established for the SANDF.

*Part IV: The transition phase in government and security forces*

The design of the GNU featured a significant division of spoils and access to political power for the three most powerful political parties and their armed forces during the transition phase. Power sharing provided a confidence-building mechanism between distrustful actors and represented a gesture of goodwill on part of the dominant ANC – what Hislope (1998) calls the 'generosity moment'. The general verdict on the GNU was that it was a necessary and appropriate interim mechanism, operating adequately through the uneasy transitional period by assuming a mediatory role between conflicting interests (Deegan 2001). Even former President F.W. de Klerk had to admit that for the first few years, the new cabinet of the GNU 'functioned surprisingly smoothly' (de Klerk 1999: 344). The power-sharing approach made all cabinet representatives of the ANC, the NP and Inkatha part of the process of initiating political, economic and social change in South Africa's transition into a fully democratic political system in which all South Africans have the right to vote (Clark and Worger 2016). The transitional phase was essential in terms of stabilizing the country and the new democratic Parliament was working effectively, passing '108 bills per session over the first three parliamentary sessions' (Deegan 2001: 115).

In February 1995, Nelson Mandela announced he would not stand for re-election as president in 1999, further contributing to a peaceful transition of power after the cessation of the power-sharing agreement. To further promote the spirit of national reconciliation and to investigate human rights violations and politically motivated murders under the apartheid regime, the GNU established the Truth and Reconciliation Commission (TRC) in 1995.[10] The TRC collected over 22,000 testimonies from victims who experienced gross human rights violations and around 7,000 from former members of the security forces requesting amnesty for the full disclosure of their actions and the crimes they had committed. Their public testimonies presented for the first time 'overwhelming evidence of the involvement of the state security apparatus in cover and illegal actions against supporters of the ANC and other anti-apartheid groups throughout the 1960s, 1970s and 1980s, right through to election day' (Clark and Worger 2016: 134).

The most significant achievement of the GNU during the transition was in 1996: the adoption of a new Constitution to 'heal the divisions of the past and establish a society based on democratic values, social justice and fundamental human rights'.[11] The Constitution also included a Bill of Rights recognizing the equality of every person before the law and prohibiting the state from discriminating on any grounds. On 9 May 1996, just days after the cabinet agreed on the new Constitution, de Klerk withdrew his NP from the coalition government because the ANC refused to make concessions for his request for continuous power-sharing arrangements until 2004 (Deegan 2001). De Klerk declared he would rather lead the NP in vigorous opposition to Mandela's government, which now consisted of the ANC and the remaining IFP ministers, and to campaign effectively against the ANC in the next round of elections to ensure 'a proper multi-party democracy, without which there may be a danger of South Africa lapsing into the African pattern of one-party states' (Sampson 2000: 535).

With regard to the security sector, the new Constitution made provisions for 'a single defence force [that] must be structured and managed as a disciplined military force' and reaffirmed the main purpose of the force 'to defend and protect the Republic, its territorial integrity and its people in accordance with the Constitution and the principles of international law regulating the use of force'.[12] It also put the defence force back under civilian control by establishing a civilian secretariat for defence under the direction of the Minister for Defence. By November 1996, two years after the start of the integration process, around 16,000 members of nonstatutory forces (16 per cent) and 10,560 members of homeland TBVC armies (11 per cent) were placed in posts within the SANDF (see Table 7.3). In the case of the South African Army, which had to absorb the greatest share of nonstatutory forces, the representation per former force was 30 per cent for ex-MK, APLA and KZSPF fighters (Heineken 1998).

**Table 7.3:** Composition of the South African National Defence Force by former force (November 1996)

|  | Percentage | Number |
| --- | --- | --- |
| **Statutory forces** | | |
| South African Defence Force (SADF) | 68 | 68,663 |
| Transkei Defence Force (TDF) | 4 | 3,868 |
| Bophutatswana Defence Force (BDF) | 4 | 3,713 |
| Venda Defence Force (VDF) | 1 | 1,264 |
| Ciskei Defence Force (CDF) | 2 | 1,716 |
| Members joining the SANDF after April 1994 | 6 | 5,838 |
| **Nonstatutory forces** | | |
| Umkhonto weSizwe (MK) | 12 | 11,826 |
| Azanian Peoples Liberation Army (APLA) | 4 | 3,735 |
| Kwa-Zulu Self-Protection Force (KZSPF) | <1 | 441 |
| **Total** | 100 | 101,064 |

Source: Adapted from Heineken (1998: 223)

Many integrated non-SADF members were deliberately excluded from key staff and command positions and the transformation processes by extensive compulsory training requirements: while former fighters from the liberation movements had to be evaluated and trained before being placed on active duty, former SADF members did not need to undergo such a process (Kynoch 1996). Conducted by the Centre for Military Studies in November 1996, a survey of junior and senior SANDF officers showed that most officers (51 per cent) were of the opinion that integration had not led to closer cooperation between the former statutory and nonstatutory forces (Heineken 1998: 224). Respondents were also asked whether 'fast-tracking' previously underrepresented members of the armed forces through the ranks to address racial imbalances would undermine the competency level of the SANDF. More than 90 per cent of the White officers were of the opinion that rapid promotion had a negative impact on efficiency, while only 27 per cent of Black officers held this view (Heineken 1998: 226).

*Part V: Transfer of power and the transformation and rationalization of the security forces*

After the adoption of the new Constitution and the departure of the NP from the GNU, the post-1996 period 'witnessed the beginning of a real shift in the balance of power within the armed forces' (Williams 2002: 18). In 1996, the GNU presented the National Defence White Paper, which defined the SANDF as subordinate to the elected civilian authority, pledged to eliminate discrimination of all forms within its ranks and required the military to obey the dictates of international law.[13] The White Paper also included a broader focus on people-centred security, incorporating political, economic, social and environmental matters, and depicted a new and decreased role for the SANDF:

> The Government of National Unity recognises that the greatest threats to the South Africa people socio-economic problems like poverty, unemployment, poor education, the lack of housing and the absence of adequate social services, as well as the high level of crime and violence. ... The new approach to security does not imply an expanded role for the armed forces. The SANDF may be employed in a range of secondary roles as prescribed by law, but its primary and essential function is service in defence of South Africa, for the protection of its sovereignty and territorial integrity. The SANDF therefore remains an important security instrument of last resort but it is no longer the dominant security institution.[14]

Due to the integration of eight former armed forces, the size of the SANDF had been greatly inflated, and the GNU had to embark on a process of demobilization and rationalization to reduce the ranks of the SANDF from 135,000 in 1994 to 75,000 by 1999. According to the National Defence White Paper, demobilization was defined as 'the voluntary release of members of the former non-statutory forces who are constitutionally part of the SANDF but who either do not wish to serve in the Defence Force or are unable to do so for reasons of age, ill-health or aptitude'.[15] Former MK and APLA members were offered a demobilization package, including a cash payment ranging between 12,734 to 42,059 Rand (US$3,480–11,491), depending on their years of service, a pension related to the time served and intensive education and training (Kynoch 1996).

The real shift in power in the armed forces was initiated in February 1998, when the chief of the SANDF, General George Meiring, submitted a fabricated report to President Mandela. In the report, he claimed a militant group, including prominent Members of Parliament and high-ranking MK officers, were planning a military coup d'etat to seize power (Williams 2002). This smear campaign led to a severe breakdown of trust between the political elite and the head of the SANDF, and it was made clear to General Meiring that he would have to resign. Within a few months, Meiring was replaced by General Siphiwe Nyanda, who had formerly been MK's chief of staff and subsequently the SANDF's chief of staff from June 1994. He was also the first Black South African to be promoted to the rank of full general (Nathan 2004; Wessels 2010). This apparent shift in the balance of power in the SANDF signalled the demise of the so-called conservative old guard axis and heralded the rise of a wide range of now course qualified Black officers, who were promoted to senior command and staff positions (Williams 2002). The strategy of excluding MK and other non-SADF officers from specific posts based on their training commitments was also coming to an end, as these officers completed their compulsory training and were ready for real deployment in the SANDF, changing the ethnical balance within the armed forces. Over the years, a new military culture was created, as the SANDF moved from a predominantly White and Afrikaner-dominated organizational culture to a largely Black-dominated one (Wessels 2010).

The GNU officially fulfilled its mandate and handed over political power to the newly elected government of President Thabo Mbeki of the ANC after a successful election process in 1999. The result was a landslide victory for the governing ANC, which gained a total of 14 seats and obtain 66 per cent of the votes. The NP, which was renamed New National Party (NNP) in 1997, had to acknowledge a sharp decline and lost more than half of their former support base, winning only 28 seats (6.9 per cent of the votes). The NNP finally dissolved in 2005 with most of its members joining the ANC (Engel 2016). The IFP, as the second previous junior partner, also lost considerable and won only 34 seats (8.6 per cent of the votes). In the subsequent years, it also increasingly faded from the scene and was reduced to a party with only a regional status (Clark and Worger 2016). The Democratic Party (DP) became the new main opposition party, winning 38 seats (9.6 per cent of the votes) and merged with some members of the NNP to form the Democratic Alliance (DA) in 2000. The ANC has continued to dominate the results of all general elections, transforming South Africa into a 'dominant party regime' that despite regularly held democratic elections is governed by a single party without any alternation (Engel 2016: 13).

## A look ahead: South Africa's continuous challenges

At the end of apartheid, there was no viable alternative to power sharing, as it represented the only political system acceptable for all sides and served two essential functions: 'it provided a mechanism for jointly drafting the rules of the game, and it acted as a confidence-building device' among the formerly warring parties (Maphai 1996: 79). Both of these functions had been achieved by 1996, when the NP decided to leave the GNU, which had been a necessary and appropriate interim mechanism, operating adequately through the uneasy transitional period after the formal end of apartheid by assuming a mediatory role between the conflicting interests of the different political actors. In addition, the institutional design of power sharing in South Africa 'was able to turn the Interim Government into a positive-sum scenario where parties recognized that it was better to cooperate and be included rather than boycott the process and undermine it' (Traniello 2008: 41). In this way, the temporal division of power between the former NP government and the incumbent ANC was essential for the achievement of a negotiated end to the apartheid order. With the election of Thabo Mbeki as second President of South Africa in 1999 and the peaceful transfer of power to ANC majority rule, the first component of the spoils-of-peace mechanism has been implemented successfully.

While the negotiations to end apartheid were a political process, they were also inclusive of multiple security actors, who were important stakeholders in the process and whose cooperation was considered critical for a peaceful transition. Overall, the transformation of the security sector was one of the most challenging tasks during South Africa's peacebuilding process. During apartheid, consecutive governments had 'relied for many years on a pervasive, repressive security apparatus, with institutions, laws and practices aimed at ensuring the political domination of the country by a minority regime' (Africa 2011: 1). Regarding the SSR component, the peacebuilding mechanism has been quite successful in South Africa and represents an exemplary approach to the integration and transformation of a large number of national and subnational defence and police forces into two single national security actors. While the South African state itself has been substantially demilitarized since the end of apartheid and the reform of its security sector, civil society remains militarized, mostly in the form of violent crime, private security companies and the proliferation of small arms because the police has not been able to perform its functions correctly (Nathan 2004). The SAPS has struggled with its law enforcement role, as criminal activity in South Africa rose significantly after 1994, creating a widespread perception of police ineffectiveness. One central problem was inadequate human and material resources: 'The generally low education and skill levels of the police force, coupled with a lack of sufficient police vehicles and other basic equipment, have compromised the investigative capacity of SAPS' (Africa 2011: 21).

The case study of South Africa provides evidence for the spoils-of-peace mechanism and its impact on the establishment of sustaining peace. It represents a good example of the advantages of combining power sharing and SSR in an integrated and simultaneous peacebuilding approach to appease opposing factions and ensure that the rights of their constituents are protected during the transition phase. Society in post-apartheid South Africa has been dominated by divisions of race, ethnicity and income: 'unemployment jumped from 22.9 per cent in 1994 to a high of 30 per cent in 2004. At the same time, personal debt increased with household debt as a percentage of disposable income rising from 56.6 per cent in 1994 to approximately 80 per cent in 2007' (Clark and Worger 2016: 137). While White South Africans continued to be the prime beneficiary of the country's economic activity, Africans constituted 93.3 per cent of South Africa's 'poor individuals' in 2008 (Armstrong et al 2008). These economic inequalities also have their origins in unequal access to education, as Black students are still a minority on most university campuses in South Africa. The professoriate has even seen almost no change, with White professors comprising over 95 per cent of faculty members, while only amounting to 7 per cent of the general population (Worger 2014). While the end of apartheid and the transformation of the political and security system in South Africa has thus brought about many improvements in life for the majority of the population, the 'continuing problems of health, income and access to resources have also led to growing frustrations' and an increase in organized violence (Clark and Worger 2016). Tackling these inequalities will remain a challenge for succeeding governments, but is imminent for a complete transformation of South African society.

8

# Conclusion: How a Focus on Configurations Provides New Insights for Peacebuilding Research

The point of departure for this book was the empirical finding that the fates of post-conflict countries do not follow linear logic once warring factions have signed a peace agreement and that if conflicts do not recur, the type of peace varies considerably between individual peacebuilding episodes. While most countries that negotiated a peace agreement to end intrastate armed conflicts between 1989 and 2016 experienced no recurrence of armed conflict, the degree of post-conflict peacefulness has varied in terms of social, political and economic factors. Peace agreements demonstrate important commitments to specific peacebuilding frameworks and represent critical junctures, as they intend 'to institutionalize peace following the tenuous conditions in the immediate aftermath of armed conflicts' (Joshi and Wallensteen 2018: 5).

Peacebuilding is a crucial task, but the puzzling questions remain: how can we capture these apparent differences between qualitatively distinct levels of peace in post-conflict settings and what are the best approaches to ensure the establishment of high-quality and sustaining peace in societies recovering from large-scale armed conflicts? This book provides insights into both questions through analyses of the processes of successful peacebuilding and the equifinal ways in which various institutional peacebuilding measures interact to regulate post-conflict order. Regarding the overall research question of which (configurations of) peacebuilding institutions are necessary or sufficient for sustaining peace and how they exert their influence, the following are four conclusions based on the cross-case and within-case results of the SMMR design.

First, the QCA analysis of necessary conditions demonstrates that there is no single peacebuilding institution that is shared by (nearly) all cases that have experienced sustaining peace or its absence. This finding is theoretically

195

reasonable and in line with previous studies on civil wars and peacebuilding success, meaning that successful and unsuccessful peacebuilding is possible in all institutional settings.

Second, the cross-case analysis uncovered two configurational patterns of peacebuilding institutions sufficient for sustaining peace: the combined presence of international commitment and transitional justice, labelled the *assisted accountability approach*, and the combined presence of power sharing and SSR, labelled the *spoils-of-peace approach*, based on theoretical concepts identified by peacebuilding research. In the first pattern, the combined focus on security and justice is sufficient for the establishment of sustaining peace. Meaningfully combined, international commitment, in the form of peacekeeping, and transitional justice can positively reinforce each other and contribute to achieving broad objectives of peacebuilding and reconciliation. The second recipe highlights the relevance of addressing commitment problems by 'rewarding' former rebels and government forces, through political or military incentives and power, for maintaining a peace agreement.

Third, in the within-case level of analysis, the case study of the successful peacebuilding episode in Sierra Leone represented a pathway case for the assisted accountability approach and included a comprehensive transitional justice component that was implemented alongside the peacekeeping mission and supported by international actors. Process tracing evidence gathered through two months of fieldwork in Sierra Leone provided for a two-way conjunction of independent mechanisms focused on the simultaneous establishment of credible commitment and accountability and the impact on the establishment of sustaining peace. The case study represents a good example of the advantages of a comprehensive peacebuilding approach, including justice and security, for long-term stability and reconciliation, and highlights the challenges in connecting this approach to local postwar needs and expectations.

Fourth, the second case study of South Africa's successful post-apartheid transition as a pathway case for the spoils-of-peace approach provided process tracing evidence for the simultaneous implementation of power sharing and SSR, triggering a single mechanism that leads to the establishment of sustaining peace. The power-sharing agreement and the guidelines for the integration and transformation of the South African security sector had their origins in the MPNF and were included as provisions in the interim Constitution of 1993. The spoils-of-peace approach connects the simultaneous implementation of power sharing and SSR with sustaining peace by providing the warring factions with some political or monetary gains, appeasing opposing factions and ensuring that the rights of their constituents are protected during the transition phase.

Figure 8.1 graphically displays the cross-case and within-case structure of the argument as to why two configurations of peacebuilding institutions lead

**Figure 8.1:** Cross-case and within-case level results for the outcome set sustaining peace

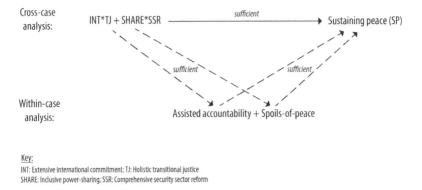

to sustaining peace in some post-conflict countries. Each of the two sufficient disjuncts INT★TJ and SHARE★SSR triggers a separate mechanism: assisted accountability and spoils-of-peace, respectively. The assisted accountability approach can be hypothesized to provide credible commitment to the conflict parties that both sides will honour the provisions of the peace agreement as well as accountability and redress for grievances of the victims, leading to sustaining peace. The spoils-of-peace approach, in contrast, can be expected to provide the warring factions with some political or monetary gains during the transition period, leading to sustaining peace. The results thus show equifinality at both the cross-case and the within-case levels (Schneider 2024).

This book represents the first empirical study to bridge the gap between multiple peacebuilding factors by testing these competing theoretical expectations in a single comparative analysis of successful peacebuilding patterns. Overall, the findings support the notion that there is no single and easy recipe for peacebuilding success that travels across cases, but that sustaining peace is rather the result of two different equifinal patterns. In the following two sections, I summarize the main findings of this SMMR project, reflect critically on the chosen research approach, and discuss remaining questions and future avenues for research.

## Patterns of sustaining peace: what we have learned

The aim of this book has been to advance peacebuilding studies in four conceptual, methodological and empirical ways: (a) developing and operationalizing the concept of sustaining peace as a suitable measure for the analysis of peacebuilding success which goes beyond the traditional notion of negative peace; (b) promoting the vigorous inclusion of set-theoretic methods and SMMR designs into peacebuilding studies to uncover configurational patterns and dependencies which lead to more realistic pictures of peacebuilding processes; (c) developing an analytical model of peacebuilding success, based on the differentiated and equifinal (non)implementation of core peacebuilding institutions; and (d) subjecting this model to an empirical plausibility test by analysing the mechanisms behind the two sufficient peacebuilding patterns in the cases of post-conflict Sierra Leone and South Africa. This section summarizes and discusses the core findings of this book with regard to all four research objectives.

First, with the increase in demand and expectations towards international peacebuilding support in post-conflict situations, it is important to create measures for the assessment of peacebuilding efforts in order to judge whether they were successful. Even though there has been a longstanding and extensive scholarly discussion of the concept of peace (Galtung 1969; Czempiel 1977a; Boulding 1978; Rapoport 1992), which is usually invoked as the measure for peacebuilding success, few efforts synthesized multiple conceptual ideas or provided systematic and measurable definitions. This 'lack of an agreed-upon framework for what constitutes the success or failure of peace efforts beyond the absence of war' (Joshi and Wallensteen 2018: 4) has led to calls for the direct engagement with peace and its causes (Regan 2014; Diehl 2016). The sustaining peace scale (developed in Chapter 2) offers an answer to these calls by representing a continuous measure for peacebuilding success that moves beyond the traditional notion of negative peace and towards an understanding of positive or quality peace which, in addition to the security dimension, incorporates political, economic and social changes in societies emerging from armed conflicts. In summary, sustaining peace has been achieved when there is no residual violence; human and political rights are evenly respected; and the society manages to sustain a reasonable economic development and gender equality. The scale's six levels of peacefulness allow for more nuanced assessments than the simple absence-of-war concept does, and expand the current analytical spectrum for the analysis of post-conflict situations and the success of peacebuilding or conflict resolution efforts. While the sustaining peace scale has been primarily designed to facilitate the application of set-theoretic methods within peacebuilding research, it could easily be adapted for the use in qualitative and traditional statistical analyses, and thus contributes to the conceptual advancement in peacebuilding studies.

Second, I have argued that the previous analytical focus on single explanatory factors is fundamentally misguided, as the success of peacebuilding efforts is more likely the result of a complex interaction of individual peacebuilding options and institutions. The introduction of set-theoretic methods (that is, QCA) offers a new and valuable angle to the study of peacebuilding and post-conflict reconstruction by retaining a strong link with the individual peacebuilding cases, identifying sufficient configurations of peacebuilding conditions as explanatory packages instead of focusing on the net effects of individual variables, unpacking patterns of equifinal recipes for peacebuilding success, and highlighting asymmetric relations between international conflict resolution efforts and peacebuilding success – all of which differ substantially from standard regression techniques that have traditionally been applied in systematic cross-case analyses of peacebuilding success. Set relations look at the explicit connections between peacebuilding conditions and the establishment of sustaining peace that are not just based on correlations and what enables them to detect patterns of necessity and sufficiency. They facilitate the systematic investigation of patterns across peacebuilding episodes that either have a successful common outcome with the goal of identifying necessary conditions, or by examining shared configurations of explanatory conditions with regard to whether they have the same outcome in common. Set-theoretic methods thus represent a valuable addition to traditional qualitative and quantitative methods and an alternative approach for the analysis of peacebuilding processes that can answer different research questions and achieve contrasting research goals (Goertz and Mahoney 2013). Therefore, this book also represents an important attempt to promote the application of set-theoretic methods in peacebuilding studies by performing a comprehensive study on the configurational patterns and dependencies that lead to the establishment of sustaining peace in post-conflict societies. I hope that this book also serves as a guide for future applications and encourages other scholars to embrace set-theoretic methods as a valuable addition to their research projects – advancing our knowledge about (non)successful peacebuilding processes.

Third, the empirical part of this book is the study of the influence of four peacebuilding institutions on the establishment of sustaining peace, looking at various configurations of explanatory conditions that are jointly linked to successful peacebuilding in post-conflict settings. The comparative analysis focused on the set relations between four peacebuilding conditions (international commitment, power sharing, SSR and transitional justice) on the establishment of sustaining peace and has found no necessary conditions that are shared by (nearly) all successful episodes. The analysis of sufficient conditions for sustaining peace led to the detection of two equifinal paths which, drawing on relevant theoretical concepts, were put together into a configurational model of peacebuilding success. These patterns of sustaining peace include the *assisted accountability approach*, which is based on the combined presence of international commitment and transitional justice, and the *spoils-of-peace approach*, which combines the presence of power sharing and SSR. The first approach is the most empirically relevant, as it exhibits the highest values for consistency, as well as unique and raw coverage, and highlights the need to conduct comprehensive peacebuilding interventions focused on the simultaneous establishment of security and justice in post-conflict settings (UNSG 2004b; Hannum 2006; Rodman 2011). The integration of these two institutional and sectoral approaches into one comprehensive peacebuilding strategy seems to be most promising for the establishment of sustaining peace in post-conflict societies; however, the most important finding from this analytical model is that there is no easy and commonly shared peacebuilding strategy that results in sustaining peace – rather, there are various configurational patterns that have been identified as successful in some cases. Further research thus needs to dig deeper into the contextual factors that condition these recipes to derive at any kind of policy implications.

Fourth, the case study of the peacebuilding episode in Sierra Leone as a pathway case for the sufficient assisted accountability approach was presented as an empirical test for the mechanism underlying one part of the configurational peacebuilding model. Based on our theoretical expectations regarding the impact of the two peacebuilding institutions included in this configuration (international commitment and transitional justice) and empirical evidence suggesting a two-way conjunction of independent mechanisms, a conjunctural assisted accountability peacebuilding mechanism was formulated, focusing on the simultaneous establishment of peace and justice. The expected empirical evidence for this mechanism could also be found in the case of Sierra Leone, thus verifying the existence of the assisted accountability peacebuilding mechanisms and providing causal inference for one part of the configurational model. Regarding the *credible commitment* part of the mechanism, the UN peacekeeping mission could provide a secure environment and support the government in the establishment of the state monopoly on the use of force and a peaceful transfer of power to a new democratically elected government. The *accountability* part of the mechanism has also been quite successful, as it represents one of the most comprehensive TJ approaches with its combination of truth commission, criminal tribunal and reparations programme. However, the reparations programme did not see a full implementation due to the government's inability and unwillingness to provide victims of human rights violations with an effective remedy after international funds ran out. Overall, the case study of Sierra Leone provides evidence for the assisted accountability mechanism and its impact on the establishment of sustaining peace by illustrating the advantages of a comprehensive peacebuilding approach, including justice and security, for long-term stability and reconciliation, and highlighting the challenges in connecting this approach to local postwar needs and expectations.

To additionally test the mechanism underlying the second sufficient pattern of the configurational model, the case study of South Africa's post-apartheid transition was presented as a pathway case for the spoils-of-peace approach to successful peacebuilding. Based on theoretical expectations regarding the combined impact of inclusive power sharing and comprehensive SSR as the two relevant peacebuilding institutions of this configuration and uncovered empirical evidence, a simple setting could be identified, where both peacebuilding conditions operate simultaneously and trigger a single spoils-of-peace mechanism. The expected empirical evidence for this mechanism could also be found in the case of South Africa, verifying the existence of the spoils-of-peace mechanism and providing causal inference for this second part of the configurational model. With regard to inclusive power sharing, the interim GNU was a necessary and appropriate interim mechanism, providing a confidence-building mechanism between distrustful actors and featuring a significant division of spoils and access to political power for the three most powerful political parties. The integration and transformation process of the security sector resulted in the disarmament and demobilization of former members of the different homeland defence forces and liberation movements, and their successful integration into a single national defence force. Overall, the case study of South Africa provides empirical evidence for the spoils-of-peace mechanism and its impact on the establishment of sustaining peace by providing for a peaceful transfer of power and the integration and transformation of the security forces as the main actors of political violence.

Overall, this book has thus contributed to the advancement of peacebuilding studies with regard to conceptual, methodological and empirical aspects, and has provided some generalized knowledge regarding the interactions of different peacebuilding institutions and their impact on the establishment of sustaining peace.

## Where to go from here: reflections on peacebuilding research and practice

In addition to these positive outcomes, this book has raised questions about the general design of comparative peacebuilding research, the potential of policy-relevant findings, and the regional imbalance of peacebuilding cases and the resulting effects for comparative analyses. Let us start with a closer look at the apparent regional skewedness of the data regarding the distribution of sustaining peace. Only five African cases could achieve complete set membership in sustaining peace, while half of the peacebuilding episodes in Africa are found in the lower part of the scale. Similar results can be found for the Asian sample. A total of 80 per cent of the peacebuilding episodes in the Americas experience either sustaining peace or functional governance, and the same is true for eight out of nine European cases, of which six even result in sustaining peace. Sustaining peace thus seems to be more likely to find after internal armed conflicts in Europe or the Americas, with Asian and African peacebuilding episodes displaying mixed results. Likewise, the sufficient patterns of peacebuilding institutions seem to possess less explanatory power for successful peacebuilding episodes in the Americas and Africa, while peacebuilding processes in Europe are almost entirely explained by the model, indicating that they follow a different causal logic which has not been considered in the underlying framework.

This finding has implications for the robustness of the results presented in this book and for wider peacebuilding research. The aggregated data most scholars use in their statistical analysis are characterized by underlying skewedness patterns, which are apparently concealed in probabilistic research designs, but come to the fore in a set-theoretic design that can uncover potential clusters. This regional imbalance leads to several recommendations for future research. Peacebuilding episodes in Europe seem to follow a different causal logic that calls for dedicated investigations into the relevant factors causing this difference. One should also refrain from making generalized statements about the impact of institutional or other conditions on the successful implementation of peacebuilding interventions, and our existing models for peacebuilding interventions should be subjected to a serious review. Previous and generally accepted findings from civil war and peacebuilding studies should be evaluated from a set-theoretic perspective to analyse configurational relations and to uncover potential cluster within these findings. Overall, SMMR designs, using methods like QCA, can capture the complexity inherent in the empirical material in peacebuilding research and shed new light on the complex patterns of post-conflict reconstruction.

Special caution should be exercised regarding policy recommendations because the results on which they are based are regionally unbalanced and might not be suitable for peacebuilding processes in certain regions. Most of the peacebuilding episodes that achieved sustaining peace were situated in Europe and the Americas, where the context for intervention and support for post-conflict reconstruction were completely different than they were in Asia and Africa. It is not surprising that the models of peacebuilding institutions, which are built on Western liberal norms, were more successful in those cases. International organizations, such as the UN, should continue their efforts to establish context-sensitive peacebuilding approaches and to support local inclusion and participation in their design and implementation.

The second critical reflection of the results of this book is concerned with the macrolevel dynamic of the comparative analysis. The configurational model of peacebuilding institutions and sustaining peace cannot provide any answers to the question 'what allows peacebuilding to succeed at the subnational level?' (Autesserre 2017: 114). This apparent lack of focus on local and bottom-up conflict resolution and peacebuilding efforts is a clear shortcoming of the model and might be one reason why the configurational model cannot explain some peacebuilding episodes included in the sample. The critical peacebuilding debate is a valuable enrichment for the discussions of appropriate measures of international support to peace processes and local conflict resolution; however, partly due to the relatively young age of this critical approach, there is an apparent gap when it comes to regional or global data on local peacebuilding processes that could be used in comparative research. Data availability may change over time, but I could not currently implement a similar research design based on data for bottom-up and local peace efforts. At this point in time, the peacebuilding conditions have to remain on a national and elite-centred level. If data that allow for regional or global comparative analyses of local peacebuilding institutions and processes become available in the future, the configurational model can be adapted to accommodate the local peacebuilding level. In general, set-theoretic methods are very well suited for the study of local peacebuilding dynamics because they include a specific focus on individual cases and are also feasible with a smaller number of cases.

A last critical reflection concerns the limitations of the empirical analyses and future avenues for research that arise from this book. The case studies of Sierra Leone and South Africa provided some causal inference for the two sufficient patterns of the configurational peacebuilding model. However, both case studies constitute ideal typical pathway cases, so they allow us to enrich the theory and examine the two potential causal mechanisms. They do not represent hard test cases for probing the difference-making properties of the two sufficient conjunctions. Further research is also needed with regard to the scope conditions that determine the individual patterns in order to make policy recommendations about the settings in which these specific peacebuilding approaches are most appropriate. At the moment, the model does not tell us anything about the differences in the settings for the assisted accountability or spoils-of-peace approach, and additional (comparative) cases studies would be useful.

Finally, the scatterplots for the results displayed several typical unaccounted cases, which are members of sustaining peace and thus typical examples of successful peacebuilding, but are not covered by the sufficient solution pattern. They exist either because not all relevant peacebuilding institutions have been included in the truth table or because factors unrelated to peacebuilding institutions cause low membership in the solution in some or all of the unaccounted cases. About 25 per cent of the outcome is not covered by the two sufficient solution terms, which would make the use of additional SMMR designs 'geared toward identifying missing disjuncts a plausible endeavor' (Schneider 2024: 129). These unaccounted cases should be consulted for in-depth case studies to uncover conditions that have not been included yet, but could enhance the peacebuilding model in the future.

# Notes

## Chapter 1

[1] UN Peacekeeping, tweet, 22 March 2018, https://twitter.com/UNPeacekeeping/status/976858476117884929f

[2] The peak in the number of armed conflicts worldwide saw 51 active conflicts in 1991, while the lowest number in the post-Cold War period was recorded in 2010, with 31 active conflicts (Pettersson and Wallensteen 2015).

[3] This trend in ongoing conflicts is largely driven by the expansion of the Islamic State (IS) to different countries (Pettersson et al 2021).

[4] Most datasets used for the calibration of the outcome and the explanatory conditions are only available after 1989.

[5] As a consequence of this definition, I exclude nonstate conflicts that are fought without government involvement.

[6] https://peaceaccords.nd.edu

[7] https://peacemaker.un.org

[8] A detailed table of all peacebuilding episodes and their outcome is provided in the online appendix: https://doi.org/10.7910/DVN/K70AWW

## Chapter 2

[1] A broad concept of peace, as laid out by the definition of positive peace as the reversal of structural violence, has also been on the peace research agenda, but has largely evaporated (Gleditsch, Nordkvelle and Strand 2014).

[2] Wallensteen (2012: 270) conceived of the Correlates of Peace as a corollary programme to the Correlate of War (COW) project, which was founded in 1963 by J. David Singer to advance the systematic accumulation of scientific knowledge about war by collecting accurate data on incidence and extent of interstate and extrasystemic war.

[3] The considerable variation among the results is partly due to the difficulty of determining whether a conflict is recurring or starting as a new one, and partly because the studies relied on different datasets of civil wars.

[4] On the one side of the debate, the nonveto powers argued for comprehensive powers for the UNGA, while the veto powers insisted on increased responsibilities for the UNSC. The delegations in favour of a wide interpretation of UNGA powers argued 'that it was important to establish the full democratic character and liberty of the Assembly' (UNCIO 1945).

[5] On the concept of human security, see Kaldor (2007); Newman (2010); and Paris (2001).

[6] Some scholars argue that violations of human rights must be accompanied by a 'politically destabilizing crisis' to fall into the category of threats to international peace and security (Frowein and Krisch 2002). De Wet (2004: 175) goes one step further, advocating that 'the mere existence of a humanitarian crisis constitutes a threat to peace according to Art. 39 UNCH only in situations where it is accompanied by a complete breakdown of government'.

# NOTES

7   With the adoption of the R2P (UNGA 2005), UN member states endorsed the idea that states have a responsibility to protect their citizens from mass atrocities (genocide, war crimes, ethnic cleansing and crimes against humanity) and that, when they fail to do so, this responsibility will be transferred to the UN (Evans 2008; Bellamy 2009; Genser and Cotler 2012).

8   Similar dimensions have been discussed by Joshi and Wallensteen (2018) as a step towards defining the quality of post-conflict peace. An all-encompassing definition, taking into account all conceivable dimensions of peace, would, if possible, become nonspecific and meaningless.

9   The multidimensionality of concepts has been described in multiple ways: Goertz (2006) prefers the framework of three-level concepts, while Sartori (1970) talks about high-, medium- and low-level categories, and Collier and Mahon (1993) use the terminology of primary and secondary categories.

10  *Angola 2018 Human Rights Report*, US Department of State, available at: https://www.state.gov/wp-content/uploads/2019/03/angola-2018.pdf

11  Empowerment of women within a society is understood as 'a process of increasing capacity for women, leading to greater choice, agency, and participation in societal decision-making' (Coppedge et al 2016).

## Chapter 3

1   For detailed (and critical) discussions of the democratic peace theory, see Owen (1994); Russett and Oneal (2001); Brown et al (2001); and Geis et al (2006).

2   For an excellent summary of liberal peacebuilding theory and its various critiques, see Campbell et al (2011).

3   The Washington Consensus was formalized in the 1990s and describes the 'set of views about effective development strategies that have come to be associated with the Washington-based institutions: the IMF, the World Bank, and the US Treasury' (Serra et al 2008: 3).

4   Examples of publications dealing with the challenges of liberal peacebuilding and ways to improve this approach include de Soto and del Castillo (1994), Doyle and Sambanis (2006),Hampson (1996), Stedman (1997), Walter (2002), Call and Cousens (2008) and Barnett and Zürcher (2009).

5   I use the term 'local' despite its inherent problems (for a discussion, see Mac Ginty [2015]). Following Paffenholz (2014: 11), the term includes local actors from within the conflict-affected country, but excludes international staff working on the ground. This understanding is conceptually close to Richmond's (2011) definition of 'local-local'.

6   For a general introduction to the concept of hybridity, see Aydin (2003). Kreikemeyer (2018) provides a focused summary of the ways in which hybridity is used within peace research.

7   These 'moments of fluidity' within institutional processes are described by different terms within the literature, such as 'turning point', 'crisis' or 'unsettled times' (Capoccia and Kelemen 2007: 341). I will use the most common term 'critical juncture' throughout my analysis.

8   I focus specifically on the political dimension and exclude the dimensions of economic and military power for two reasons: first, military power sharing is better addressed in the context of security sector reform; and, second, economic power sharing has been proposed specifically to mitigate natural resource conflicts and has not been studied as much as the other three dimensions. It thus follows a different causal logic compared to political power-sharing arrangements.

9   TJ measures are usually divided according to two types of justice they pursue: (a) retributive justice measures emphasize the need to hold perpetrators accountable by punishing

## PATTERNS OF SUSTAINING PEACE

them for their crimes and include trials and special tribunals, lustration and vetting; and (b) restorative justice measures respond to the needs and interests of victims and include truth commissions and reparations (Lie et al 2007).

[10] For an overview of TJ mechanisms, see Kritz (1996), Teitel (2000) or Roth-Arriaza and Mariezcurrena (2006).

[11] The Everyday Peace Indicators are a promising research approach in this regard, employing a participatory approach to the generation of indicators for difficult-to-measure concepts such as local understandings of peace or successful peacebuilding (see https://everyday peaceindicators.org).

## Chapter 4

[1] For more information on the different conceptions of *mechanisms* in the social sciences, see, for example, Beach and Rohlfing (2018: 6ff); Falleti and Lynch (2009); and Rutten (2022: 1216ff).

[2] In an attempt to mimic central features of the diversity-orientation within set-theoretic approaches, the Boolean probit and logit approach developed by Braumoeller (2003) offers some promising and innovative perspectives for statistical analyses in this regard.

[3] In general, single conditions could be combined by using the logical OR and then tested for necessity. However, such new OR configurations need to be carefully justified on theoretical grounds (Schneider and Wagemann 2012: 278).

[4] The analyses are conducted with the R packages *QCA* (Duşa 2019) and *SetMethods* (Oana and Schneider 2018).

[5] Based on the information from the directional expectations, the algorithm in the software selects only those simplifying assumptions that are in line with their formulation and represent plausible counterfactuals (Mello 2021).

[6] With regard to the principles for case studies after QCA on necessity and the corresponding principles for formalized case selection and causal inference, see Rohlfing and Schneider (2013) and Schneider (2024).

[7] I follow Joshi et al (2015) in defining the following types of provisions as relevant for SSR processes: demobilization, disarmament, military reform, regulation and treatment of paramilitary groups, police reform, and reintegration of ex-combatants.

## Chapter 5

[1] All analyses are conducted with the R packages *QCA* (Duşa 2019) and *SetMethods* (Oana and Schneider 2018). Comprehensive information on the specific settings is provided in the R script and online appendix: https://doi.org/10.7910/DVN/K70AWW

[2] PRI stands for 'proportional reduction in inconsistency'.

[3] Core conditions of a pattern are fundamental to the configuration and make up the most parsimonious solution; they cannot be eliminated and must thus be part of any final solution (Ragin and Sonnett 2004). Contributory conditions, in contrast, are additional parts of the intermediate solution and thus, by definition, subsets of the parsimonious solution.

[4] Contextual, or scope conditions are defined as 'relevant aspects of a setting (analytical, temporal, spatial, or institutional) in which a set of initial conditions leads [...] to an outcome of a defined scope and meaning via a specified causal mechanism or set of causal mechanisms' (Falleti and Lynch 2009: 1152).

[5] The cluster function of the R package *SetMethods* analyzes whether the QCA solution formula obtained from the pooled data can also be found in each of the sub-populations (Oana and Schneider 2018).

[6] For this purpose, the sample of peacebuilding episodes has been split into two subsamples: 30 peacebuilding episodes (56%) occurred after conflicts over government,

# NOTES

and 24 peacebuilding episodes (44%) were initiated after conflicts over territory. The other parameters of the analysis are kept at similar settings in order to ensure comparability of the results.

[7] The complete truth tables for both subsamples are provided in the online appendix.

[8] These three patterns are: ~INT*SSR*~TJ + INT*~SSR*~TJ + SHARE*~SSR*~TJ → ~SP (solution consistency 0.859; solution coverage 0.652). See online appendix for further details.

[9] The sample of peacebuilding episodes has been split into four subsamples: 31 peacebuilding episodes (57%) occurred after conflicts in Africa, 5 peacebuilding episodes (9%) were initiated after conflicts in the Americas, 9 peacebuilding episodes (17%) took place in Asia, and 9 peacebuilding episodes (17%) resulted after conflicts in Europe. The other parameters of the analysis are kept at similar settings in order to ensure comparability of the results.

[10] All solution formula and further information regarding simplifying assumptions are provided in the online appendix.

[11] For the European sample, the configurations represent the conservative solution.

[12] With regard to the analysis of the absence of sustaining peace, the four selected peacebuilding conditions can be considered less suitable for the identification of relevant settings for unsuccessful peacebuilding in the regional samples. The absence of sustaining peace in peacebuilding episodes in Europe and the Americas cannot be explained from a cross-case perspective due to the lack of corresponding data. Regarding the peacebuilding episodes in Africa, two institutional recipes are consistently linked to the absence of sustain peace: INT*~SSR*~TJ + ~INT*SSR*~TJ → ~SP (solution consistency 0.829; solution coverage 0.643). The analysis of the negated outcome set in the Asian subsample reveals just one sufficient institutional pattern: ~INT*~SSR*~TJ → ~SP (solution consistency 0.850; solution coverage 0.810).

## Chapter 6

[1] The RUF manifesto *Footpath to Democracy* stated that the movement wanted to ensure genuine democracy in the country and also raised questions about the mismanagement of the country's ample natural resources by successive governments (Alao and Ero 2001).

[2] The *First Report on the United Nations Mission in Sierra Leone (UNAMSIL)* was issued on 6 December 1999 (UNSC 1999d). Subsequent progress reports were issued quarterly until the closure of UNAMSIL in 2005.

[3] The fieldwork in Sierra Leone was conducted from January to March 2019.

[4] I do not perceive the 'local' as a homogeneous entity with a common peacebuilding experience, but rather try to establish some patterns of local peacebuilding perceptions that are shared by the majority of survey respondents, but that can differ between regions or groups with different conflict experiences.

[5] For the Southern Area in Sierra Leone, I was unable to differentiate the sample according to town (Bo) and rural communities due to the generally rural character of this area.

[6] The standardized questionnaire and the complete results including a discussion of the social background of the respondents are provided in the online appendix: https://doi.org/10.7910/DVN/K70AWW

[7] Beach and Rohlfing (2018) provide a more detailed discussion of temporality and sequences in set-theoretic MMR and also differentiate between sequences of conditions in condition-centred designs and multiple, possibly interrelated mechanisms triggered by one conjunction in mechanism-centred research designs.

[8] INUS stands for insufficient, but necessary part of an unnecessary but sufficient condition.

[9] The analyses of sequences on the cross-case level, through temporal QCA (Caren and Panofsky 2005; Ragin and Strand 2008) or reshuffling of the truth table (Baumgartner

2009), do not solve the general problem that multiple constellations of conditions can be compatible with the same cross-case solution (Baumgartner 2012).

[10] At the same time, the predecessor mission UNOMSIL was terminated.

[11] Interview, Department for Peace and Conflict Studies, Fourah Bay College, Freetown, 29 January 2019.

[12] Interview, NGO, Freetown, 7 March 2019.

[13] Interview, Human Rights Commission – Office North, Makeni, 21 February 2019.

[14] Interview, NGO, Freetown, 7 February 2019.

[15] Parliament of Sierra Leone, Truth and Reconciliation Commission Act, Part III, section 6(1).

[16] Statute of the Special Court for Sierra Leone, para 1.

[17] The most prominent case at the SCSL was the trial against the former Liberian President Charles Taylor. It was moved to The Hague for security reasons and ended in Taylor's conviction in 2013 for arming and abetting the RUF rebel force.

[18] Sam Bockarie, a very senior leader of the RUF, was killed in Liberia before he could be taken into custody. Major Johnny Paul Koroma, the former chairman of the AFRC, escaped arrest and remains a fugitive from justice. It is believed he was killed in 2003 (Hollis 2015).

[19] To avoid double benefits, the SLTRC excluded ex-combatants from the proposed reparations programme if they had benefited from other initiatives, such as the DDR programme (SLTRC 2004: vol II, Chapter 4, Article 245).

[20] Peacebuilding Fund Emergency Window – PBF-SLE-A-4 Pro Doc, 3 May 2008.

[21] For more information on the implementation of the SLTRC recommendations, see the recommendations matrix: https://www.sierraleonetrc.org/index.php/resources/reco mmendations-matrix

[22] Interview, NGO, Freetown, 7 March 2019.

[23] Interview, Human Rights Commission of Sierra Leone, Freetown, 31 January 2019.

[24] Interview, Residual Special Court for Sierra Leone, Freetown, 6 February 2019.

[25] Interview, Department for Peace and Conflict Studies, Fourah Bay College, Freetown, 29 January 2019.

[26] Interview, NGO, Freetown, 23 January 2019.

[27] Interview, UNDP Sierra Leone, Freetown, 6 February 2019.

[28] Interview, NGO, Makeni, 19 February 2019.

[29] Interview, National Electoral Commission, Freetown, 8 February 2019.

[30] Interview, Centre for Accountability & the Rule of Law, Bo, 1 March 2019.

## Chapter 7

[1] F.W. de Klerk's speech at the opening of Parliament 2 February 1990, available at: https:// omalley.nelsonmandela.org/index.php/site/q/03lv02039/04lv02103/05lv02104/06lv02 105.htm

[2] UNOMSA operated from September 1992 to 27 June 1994, after the establishment of a united, nonracial and democratic government of South Africa under the presidency of Nelson Mandela (UNSC 1994b).

[3] African National Congress and National Party, 'Record of Understanding' 26 September 1992, available at: https://constitutionnet.org/sites/default/files/92SEP26.PDF

[4] The Constitution of the Republic of South Africa, Act No. 200 of 1993, available at: https://www.gov.za/documents/constitution/constitution-republic-south-africa-act-200-1993#MEMORANDUM

[5] National Peace Accord, 14 September 1991, Chapter 7, available at: https://peacemaker. un.org/southafrica-national-peace-accord91

[6] The Constitution of the Republic of South Africa, Act No. 200 of 1993, available at: https://www.gov.za/documents/constitution/constitution-republic-south-africa-act-200-1993#MEMORANDUM

## NOTES

7. Transitional Executive Council Act, Act 151 of 1993, 18 October 1993, available at: https://www.gov.za/sites/default/files/gcis_document/201409/act151of1993.pdf

8. Transitional Executive Council Act, section 16(10).

9. South African Police Service Act 68 of 1995, available at: https://www.gov.za/sites/default/files/gcis_document/201409/act68of1995.pdf

10. Promotion of National Unity and Reconciliation Act, No. 34 of 1995, available at: https://www.gov.za/documents/promotion-national-unity-and-reconciliation-act

11. Constitution of the Republic of South Africa, available at: https://www.gov.za/documents/constitution-republic-south-africa-1996

12. Constitution of the Republic of South Africa, 1996, section 200, available at: https://www.gov.za/documents/constitution-republic-south-africa-1996

13. National Defence White Paper for the Republic of South Africa, 1996, available at: https://www.gov.za/documents/national-defence-white-paper. The corresponding White Paper on Safety and Security was adopted by Parliament in 1998.

14. National Defence White Paper for the Republic of South Africa, 1996, sections 5, 8 and 9.

15. National Defence White Paper for the Republic of South Africa, 1996, section 22.

# References

Africa S (2011) *The Transformation of the South African Security Sector: Lessons and Challenges*. Geneva: Geneva Centre for the Democratic Control of Armed Forces.

Ainley K, Friedman R and Mahony C (2015) Transitional Justice in Sierra Leone: Theory, History and Evaluation. In: Ainley K, Friedman R and Mahony C (eds) *Evaluating Transitional Justice: Accountability and Peacebuilding in Post-conflict Sierra Leone*. Basingstoke: Palgrave Macmillan, pp 1–18.

Alao A and Ero C (2001) Cut Short for Taking Short Cuts: The Lomé Peace Agreement on Sierra Leone. *Civil Wars* 4(3): 117–134.

Albrecht P and Jackson P (2009) *Security System Transformation in Sierra Leone, 1997–2007*. Birmingham: Global Facilitation Network for Security Sector Reform and International Alert.

Alemu MM (2016) Youth Unemployment Challenges and Opportunities: The Case of Sierra Leone. *International Journal of Social Science Studies* 4(10): 16–28.

Allen SH (2005) The Determinants of Economic Sanctions Success and Failure. *International Interactions* 31(2): 117–138.

Amenta E and Poulsen JD (1994) Where to Begin: A Survey of Five Approaches to Selecting Independent Variables for Qualitative Comparative Analysis. *Sociological Methods & Research* 23(1): 22–53.

Anglin DG (1995) The Life and Death of South Africa's National Peacekeeping Force. *Journal of Modern African Studies* 33(1): 21–52.

Ansorg N (2014) Wars without Borders: Conditions for the Development of Regional Conflict Systems in Sub-Saharan Africa. *International Area Studies Review* 17(3): 295–312.

Armstrong P, Lekezwa B and Siebrits K (2008) Poverty in South Africa: A Profile Based on Recent Household Surveys. *Stellenbosch Economic Working Papers* 04/08.

Arnson CJ and Zartman IW (2005) *Rethinking the Economics of War: The Intersection of Need, Creed, and Greed*. Baltimore: Johns Hopkins University Press.

Arthur WB (1994) *Increasing Returns and Path Dependence in the Economy*. Ann Arbor: University of Michigan Press.

## REFERENCES

Autesserre S (2014) *Peaceland: Conflict Resolution and the Everyday Politics of International Intervention.* New York: Cambridge University Press.

Autesserre S (2017) International Peacebuilding and Local Success: Assumptions and Effectiveness. *International Studies Review* 19(1): 114–132.

Aydin Y (2003) *Zum Begriff der Hybridität (Sozialökonomischer Text Nr. 105).* Hamburg: Hamburger Universität für Wirtschaft und Politik.

Badmus IA and Ogunmola D (2009) Towards Rebuilding a Failed State: The United Nations Intervention in the Post-Civil War Sierra Leone. *Journal of Alternative Perspectives in the Social Sciences* 1(3): 720–735.

Balch-Lindsay D, Enterline AJ and Joyce KA (2008) Third-Party Intervention and the Civil War Process. *Journal of Peace Research* 45(3): 345–363.

Bapat NA and Morgan TC (2009) Multilateral versus Unilateral Sanctions Reconsidered: A Test Using New Data. *International Studies Quarterly* 53(4): 1075–1094.

Bara C (2014) Incentives and Opportunities: A Complexity-Oriented Explanation of Violent Ethnic Conflict. *Journal of Peace Research* 51(6): 696–710.

Barma NH (2017) *The Peacebuilding Puzzle. Political Order in Post-conflict States.* Cambridge: Cambridge University Press.

Barnes C and de Klerk E (2002) South Africa's Multi-party Constitutional Negotiation Process. In: Barnes C (ed) *Owning the Process: Public Participation in Peacemaking.* London: Conciliation Resources, pp 26–33.

Barnett M and Zürcher C (2009) The Peacebuilder's Contract: How External Statebuilding Reinforces Weak Statehood. In: Paris R and Sisk TD (eds) *The Dilemmas of Statebuilding. Confronting the Contradictions of Postwar Peace Operations.* Abingdon: Routledge, pp 23–52.

Barnett M, Kim H, O'Donnell M et al (2007) Peacebuilding: What Is in a Name? *Global Governance: A Review of Multilateralism and International Organizations* 13(1): 35–58.

Baumgartner M (2009) Inferring Causal Complexity. *Sociological Methods & Research* 38(1): 71–101.

Baumgartner M (2012) Detecting Causal Chains in Small-n Data. *Field Methods* 25(1): 3–24.

Baumgartner M and Thiem A (2020) Often Trusted But Never (Properly) Tested: Evaluating Qualitative Comparative Analysis. *Sociological Methods & Research* 49(2): 279–311.

*BBC News* (2007, 2 August) Sierra Leone Militia Leaders Convicted. Available at: http://news.bbc.co.uk/2/hi/africa/6927550.stm).

Beach D (2016) It's All about Mechanisms: What Process-Tracing Case Studies Should Be Tracing. *New Political Economy* 21(5): 463–472.

Beach D (2018a) Achieving Methodological Alignment When Combining QCA and Process Tracing in Practice. *Sociological Methods & Research* 47(1): 64–99.

211

Beach D (2018b) Process Tracing Methods. In: Wagemann C, Goerres A and Siewert MB (eds) *Handbuch Methoden der Politikwissenschaft. Springer Reference Sozialwissenschaften.* Wiesbaden: Springer VS, pp 1–21.

Beach D and Kaas JG (2020) The Great Divides: Incommensurability, the Impossibility of Mixed-Methodology, and What to Do about It. *International Studies Review* 22(2): 214–235.

Beach D and Pedersen RB (2013) *Process-Tracing Methods: Foundations and Guidelines.* Ann Arbor: University of Michigan Press.

Beach D and Pedersen RB (2016) *Causal Case Study Methods: Foundations and Guidelines for Comparing, Matching, and Tracing.* Ann Arbor: University of Michigan Press.

Beach D and Pedersen RB (2018) Selecting Appropriate Cases When Tracing Causal Mechanisms. *Sociological Methods & Research* 47(4): 837–871.

Beach D and Pedersen RB (2019) *Process-Tracing Methods: Foundations and Guidelines,* 2nd edition. Ann Arbor: University of Michigan Press.

Beach D and Rohlfing I (2018) Integrating Cross-Case Analyses and Process Tracing in Set-Theoretic Research: Strategies and Parameters of Debate. *Sociological Methods & Research* 47(1): 3–36.

Beardsley K (2011) *The Mediation Dilemma.* Ithaca: Cornell University Press.

Beardsley K and Gleditsch KS (2015) Peacekeeping as Conflict Containment. *International Studies Review* 17(1): 67–89.

Beinart W (2001) *Twentieth-Century South Africa.* Oxford: Oxford University Press.

Bellamy AJ (2009) *Responsibility to Protect: The Global Effort to End Mass Atrocities.* Cambridge: Polity Press.

Bellamy AJ and Williams PD (2005) Who's Keeping the Peace? Regionalization and Contemporary Peace Operations. *International Security* 29(4): 157–195.

Bendaña A (1996) Conflict Resolution: Empowerment and Disempowerment. *Peace & Change* 21(1): 68–77.

Bennett A (2008) Process Tracing: A Bayesian Perspective. In: Box-Steffensmeier JM, Brady HE and Collier D (eds) *The Oxford Handbook of Political Methodology.* Oxford: Oxford University Press, pp 702–721.

Bennett A (2015) Appendix: Disciplining Our Conjectures. Systematizing Process Tracing with Bayesian Analysis. In: Bennett A and Checkel JT (eds) *Process Tracing: From Metaphor to Analytic Tool.* Cambridge: Cambridge University Press, pp 276–298.

Bennett A and Checkel JT (2015) *Process Tracing: From Metaphor to Analytic Tool.* Cambridge: Cambridge University Press.

Bercovitch J (1996) *Resolving International Conflicts: The Theory and Practice of Mediation.* Boulder: Rienner.

Bercovitch J and Kadayifci A (2002) Exploring the Relevance and Contribution of Mediation to Peace-Building. *Peace and Conflict Studies* 9(2): 21–40.

Bercovitch J and Rubin JZ (1992) *Mediation in International Relations: Multiple Approaches to Conflict Management*. Basingstoke: Macmillan.

Bercovitch J, Anagnoson JT and Wille DL (1991) Some Conceptual Issues and Empirical Trends in the Study of Successful Mediation in International Relations. *Journal of Peace Research* 28(1): 7–17.

Berdal MR (1996) Disarmament and Demobilization after Civil Wars. *Adelphi Paper* 303.

Berg-Schlosser D and de Meur G (2009) Comparative Research Design: Case and Variable Selection. In: Rihoux B and Ragin CC (eds) *Configurational Comparative Methods: Qualitative Comparative Analysis (QCA) and Related Techniques*. Thousand Oaks: SAGE Publications, pp 19–32.

Berg-Schlosser D, de Meur G, Rihoux B et al (2009) Qualitative Comparative Analysis (QCA) as an Approach. In: Rihoux B and Ragin CC (eds) *Configurational Comparative Methods: Qualitative Comparative Analysis (QCA) and Related Techniques*. Thousand Oaks: Sage Publications, pp 1–18.

Bernath C and Nyce S (2004) A Peacekeeping Success: Lessons Learned from UNAMSIL. *Journal of International Peacekeeping* 8(1): 119–142.

Bhabha HK (1994) *The Location of Culture*. London: Routledge.

Biersteker TJ, Eckert SE, Tourinho M et al (2018) UN Targeted Sanctions Datasets (1991–2013). *Journal of Peace Research* 55(3): 404–412.

Bigombe B, Collier P and Sambanis N (2000) Policies for Building Post-conflict peace. *Journal of African Economies* 9(3): 323–348.

Binder M (2015) Paths to Intervention: What Explains the UN's Selective Response to Humanitarian Crises? *Journal of Peace Research* 52(6): 712–726.

Binningsbø HM (2013) Power Sharing, Peace and Democracy: Any Obvious Relationships? *International Area Studies Review* 16(1): 89–112.

Binningsbø HM and Dupuy K (2009) Using Power-Sharing to Win a War: The Implementation of the Lomé Agreement in Sierra Leone. *Africa Spectrum* 44(3): 87–107.

Binningsbø HM, Loyle CE, Gates S et al (2012) Armed Conflict and Post-conflict Justice, 1946–2006: A Dataset. *Journal of Peace Research* 49(5): 731–740.

Björkdahl A and Höglund K (2013) Precarious Peacebuilding: Friction in Global–Local Encounters. *Peacebuilding* 1(3): 289–299.

Björkdahl A, Höglund K, Millar G et al (2016) Introduction: Peacebuilding through the Lens of Friction. In: Björkdahl A, Höglund K, Millar G et al (eds) *Peacebuilding and Friction: Global and Local encounters in Post-conflict Societies*. Abingdon: Routledge, pp 1–16.

Blatter J and Haverland M (2012) *Designing Case Studies: Explanatory Approaches in Small-N Research*. Basingstoke: Palgrave Macmillan.

Boulding KE (1964) Toward a Theory of Peace. In: Fisher R (ed) *International Conflict and Behavioral Science*. New York: Basic Books, pp 70–87.

Boulding KE (1978) *Stable Peace*. Austin: University of Texas Press.

Boutros-Ghali B (1992) *An Agenda for Peace. Preventive Diplomacy, Peacemaking and Peacekeeping. Report of the Secretary-General Pursuant to the Statement Adopted by the Summit Meeting of the Security Council on 31 January 1992 (UN Doc. A/47/277-S/24111).* New York: United Nations.

Bratt D (1999) Peace over Justice: Developing a Framework for UN Peacekeeping Operations in Internal Conflicts. *Global Governance* 5(1): 63–81.

Braumoeller BF (2003) Causal Complexity and the Study of Politics. *Political Analysis* 11(3): 209–233.

Brosig M and Sempijja N (2017) What Peacekeeping Leaves Behind: Evaluating the Effects of Multi-dimensional Peace Operations in Africa. *Conflict, Security & Development* 17(1): 21–52.

Brown ME, Lynn-Jones SM and Miller SE (2001) *Debating the Democratic Peace*. Cambridge, MA: MIT Press.

Buckley-Zistel S (2008) Transitional Justice als Weg zu Frieden und Sicherheit: Möglichkeiten und Grenzen. *SFB-Governance Working Paper Series* 15.

Burgess SF (2001) *The United Nations under Boutros Boutros-Ghali, 1992–1997*. Lanham: Scarecrow Press.

Bussmann M (2018) Bargaining Models of War and the Stability of Peace in Post-conflict Societies. In: Thompson WR (ed) *The Oxford Encyclopedia of Empirical International Relations Theory. Vol. 1.* Oxford: Oxford University Press, pp 157–169.

Call CT (2008) Knowing Peace When You See It: Setting Standards for Peacebuilding Success. *Civil Wars* 10(2): 173–194.

Call CT and Cousens EM (2008) Ending Wars and Building Peace: International Responses to War-Torn Societies. *International Studies Perspectives* 9(1): 1–21.

Campbell S, Chandler D and Sabaratnam M (2011) *A Liberal Peace? The Problems and Practices of Peacebuilding*. London: Zed Books.

Capoccia G (2015) Critical Junctures and Institutional Change. In: Mahoney J and Thelen K (eds) *Advances in Comparative-Historical Analysis*. Cambridge: Cambridge University Press, pp 147–179.

Capoccia G and Kelemen RD (2007) The Study of Critical Junctures: Theory, Narrative, and Counterfactuals in Historical Institutionalism. *World Politics* 59(3): 341–369.

Caren N and Panofsky A (2005) TQCA: A Technique for Adding Temporality to Qualitative Comparative Analysis. *Sociological Methods & Research* 34(2): 147–172.

Cartwright N and Hardie J (2012) *Evidence-Based Policy: A Practical Guide to Doing It Better*. Oxford: Oxford University Press.

Caspersen N (2019) Human Rights in Territorial Peace Agreements. *Review of International Studies* 45(4): 527–549.

Castillo GD (2008) *Rebuilding War-Torn States: The Challenge of Post-conflict Economic Reconstruction*. Oxford: Oxford University Press.

Cederman L-E, Weidmann NB and Gleditsch KS (2011) Horizontal Inequalities and Ethnonationalist Civil War: A Global Comparison. *American Political Science Review* 105(3): 478–495.

Cetinyan R (2002) Ethnic Bargaining in the Shadow of Third-Party Intervention. *International Organization* 56(3): 645–677.

CGG (Campaign for Good Governance) (2003) Campaign for Good Governance Survey. Available at: http://www.rscsl.org/Documents/CGG_Survey.pdf

Chalmers M (2000) *Security Sector Reform in Developing Countries: An EU Perspective*. London: Saferworld and Conflict Prevention Network.

Chandler D (2010) *International Statebuilding: The Rise of Post-liberal Governance*. Abingdon: Routledge.

Chandler D (2015) Resilience and the 'Everyday': Beyond the Paradox of 'Liberal Peace'. *Review of International Studies* 41(1): 27–48.

Checkel JT (2015) Mechanisms, Process, and the Study of International Institutions. In: Bennett A and Checkel JT (eds) *Process Tracing: From Metaphor to Analytic Tool*. Cambridge: Cambridge University Press, pp 74–97.

Cheeseman N (2011) The Internal Dynamics of Power-Sharing in Africa. *Democratization* 18(2): 336–365.

Christopher AJ (2001) *The Atlas of Changing South Africa*. London: Routledge.

Cingranelli DL and Richards DL (1999) Measuring the Level, Pattern, and Sequence of Government Respect for Physcial Integrity Rights. *International Studies Quarterly* 43(2): 407–417.

Clark AM and Sikkink K (2013) Information Effects and Human Rights Data: Is the Good News about Increased Human Rights Information Bad News for Human Rights Measures? *Human Rights Quarterly* 35(3): 539–568.

Clark I (2001) *The Post-Cold War Order: The Spoils of Peace*. Oxford: Oxford University Press.

Clark NL and Worger WH (2016) *South Africa: the rise and fall of apartheid*. Abingdon: Routledge.

Cole S (2001) *Increasing Women's Political Participation in Liberia: Challenges and Potential Lessons from India, Rwanda and South Africa*. Washington DC: International Foundation for Electoral Systems.

Collier D and Mahon JE (1993) Conceptual 'Stretching' Revisited: Adapting Categories in Comparative Analysis. *American Political Science Review* 87(4): 845–855.

Collier P, Elliott VL, Hegre H et al (2003) *Breaking the Conflict Trap: Civil War and Development Policy*. Washington, DC: World Bank.

Collier P and Hoeffler A (2004) Greed and Grievance in Civil War. *Oxford Economic Papers* 56(4): 563–595.

Collier P, Hoeffler A and Söderbom M (2008) Post-conflict Risks. *Journal of Peace Research* 45(4): 461–478.

Collier RB and Collier D (1991) *Shaping the Political Arena: Critical Junctures, the Labor Movement, and Regime Dynamics in Latin America*. Princeton: Princeton University Press.

Conteh-Morgan E and Dixon-Fyle M (1999) *Sierra Leone at the End of the Twentieth Century: History, Politics, and Society*. New York: Peter Lang.

Cooper B and Glaesser J (2011) Paradoxes and Pitfalls in Using Fuzzy Set QCA: Illustrations from a Critical Review of a Study of Educational Inequality. *Sociological Research Online* 16(3): 106–119.

Cooper B and Glaesser J (2016) Analysing Necessity and Sufficiency with Qualitative Comparative Analysis: How Do Results Vary as Case Weights Change? *Quality & Quantity* 50(1): 327–346.

Coppedge M, Gerring J, Lindberg SI et al (2016) V-Dem Codebook v6. *Varieties of Democracy (V- Dem) Project*.

Cortright D and Lopez G (2000) *The Sanctions Decade: Assessing UN Strategies in the 1990s*. Boulder: Lynne Rienner.

Cottrell WF (1954) Men Cry Peace. In: Institute for Social Research (ed) *Research for Peace*. Amsterdam: North-Holland Publishing Company, pp 95–162.

Cubitt C (2012) *Local and Global Dynamics of Peacebuilding: Post-conflict reconstruction in Sierra Leone*. Abingdon: Routledge.

Curran D and Williams PD (2016) The United Kingdom and United Nations Peace Operations. *International Peacekeeping* 23(5): 630–651.

Czempiel E-O (1977a) Alternative Friedensbegriffe. In: Goße-Jütte A and Jütte R (eds) *Entspannung ohne Frieden: Versäumnisse Europäischer Politik*. Frankfurt am Main: S. Fischer, pp 21–36.

Czempiel E-O (1977b) Frieden und Friedensforschung – Eine Einführung. In: Landeszentrale für Politische Bildung des Landes Nordrhein-Westfalen (ed) *Erziehung für den Frieden: Probleme des Friedens in der Einen Welt*. Cologne: Verlag Wissenschaft und Politik, pp 21–36.

Czempiel E-O (1996) Kants Theorem. Oder: Warum sind die Demokratien (noch immer) nicht friedlich? *Zeitschrift für Internationale Beziehungen* 3(1): 79–101.

Czempiel E-O (2006) Der Friedensbegriff der Friedensforschung. In: Sahm A, Sapper M and Weichsel V (eds) *Die Zukunft des Friedens. Band 1: Eine Bilanz der Friedens- und Konfliktforschung*. Wiesbaden: VS Verlag für Sozialwissenschaften, pp 83–93.

Davenport C (2018) A Relational Approach to Quality Peace. In: Davenport C, Melander E and Regan PM (eds) *The Peace Continuum: What It Is and How to Study It*. New York: Oxford University Press, pp 145–182.

Davenport C, Melander E and Regan PM (2018) *The Peace Continuum: What It Is and How to Study It*. New York: Oxford University Press.

David PA (2007) Path Dependence: A Foundational Concept for Historical Social Science. *Cliometrica* 1(2): 91–114.

Davies S, Pettersson T and Öberg M (2023) Organized Violence 1989–2022, and the Return of Conflict between States. *Journal of Peace Research* 60(4): 691–708.

De Hoon M (2020) Transitional Justice. In: Williams PR and Sterio M (eds) *Research Handbook on Post-conflict State Building*. Cheltenham: Edward Elgar, pp 162–182.

De Klerk FW (1999) *The Last Trek: A New Beginning*. New York: St Martin's Press.

De Soto A and del Castillo G (1994) Obstacles to Peacebuilding. *Foreign Policy* 94(1): 69–83.

De Wet E (2004) *The Chapter VII Powers of the United Nations Security Council*. Oxford: Hart Publishing.

Deegan H (2001) *The Politics of the New South Africa: Apartheid and after*. Harlow: Pearson.

DeRouen KJ, Bercovitch J and Pospieszna P (2011) Introducing the Civil Wars Mediation (CWM) Dataset. *Journal of Peace Research* 48(5): 663–672.

Diehl PF (2016) Exploring Peace: Looking beyond War and Negative Peace. *International Studies Quarterly* 60(1): 1–10.

Dixon J (2009) What Causes Civil Wars? Integrating Quantitative Research Findings. *International Studies Review* 11(4): 707–735.

Dorussen H (2022) *Handbook on Peacekeeping and International Relations*. Cheltenham: Edward Elgar.

Doyle MW (1983) Kant, Liberal Legacies, and Foreign Affairs. *Philosophy and Public Affairs* 12(3): 205–235.

Doyle MW (1986) Liberalism and World Politics. *The American Political Science Review* 80(4): 1151–1169.

Doyle MW (1996) Kant, Liberal Legacies and Foreign Affairs. In: Brown ME (ed) *Debating the Democratic Peace*. Cambridge, MA: MIT Press, pp 3–57.

Doyle MW and Sambanis N (2006) *Making War and Building Peace: United Nations Peace Operations*. Princeton: Princeton University Press.

DPKO (Department of Peacekeeping Operations) (2008) *United Nations Peacekeeping Operations: Principles and Guidelines*. New York: UN Department of Peacekeeping Operations Best Practices Section.

Duffield M (2001) Governing the Borderlands: Devoding the Power of Aid. *Disasters* 25(4): 308–320.

Duffield M (2007) *Development, Security and Unending War: Governing the World of Peoples.* Cambridge: Polity.

Durch WJ (1993) *The Evolution of UN Peacekeeping. Case Studies and Comparative Analysis.* New York: St Martin's Press.

Duşa A (2019) *QCA with R: A Comprehensive Resource.* Cham: Springer.

Duşa A (2022) Critical Tension: Sufficiency and Parsimony in QCA. *Sociological Methods & Research* 51(2): 541–565.

Early BR (2015) *Busted Sanctions: Explaining Why Economic Sanctions Fail.* Redwood, CA: Stanford University Press.

Early BR and Spice R (2015) Economic Sanctions, International Institutions, and Sanctions Busters: When Does Institutionalized Cooperation Help Sanctioning Efforts? *Foreign Policy Analysis* 11(3): 339–360.

Eck K and Hultman L (2007) One-Sided Violence against Civilians in War: Insights from New Fatality Data. *Journal of Peace Research* 44(2): 233–246.

Einsiedel SV (2014) Examining Recent Trends in Violent Conflict. Tokyo: United Nations University Center for Policy Research.

Engel U (2016) 'A Luta Continua!' Democracy, Elections and Governance in South Africa, 1994–2014. In: Pallotti A and Engel U (eds) *South Africa after Apartheid: Policies and Challenges of the Democratic Transition.* Leiden: Brill, pp 11–30.

Ero C (2000) Sierra Leone's Security Complex. *The Conflict, Security & Development Group Working Papers Number 3.* London: King s College London, pp 1–64.

Escribà-Folch A (2010) Economic Sanctions and the Duration of Civil Conflicts. *Journal of Peace Research* 47(2): 129–141.

Evans G (2008) *The Responsibility to Protect: Ending Mass Atrocity Crimes Once and for All.* Washington DC: Brookings Institution Press.

Fairfield T and Charman AE (2017) Explicit Bayesian Analysis for Process Tracing: Guidelines, Opportunities, and Caveats. *Political Analysis* 25(3): 363–380.

Falleti TG and Lynch JF (2009) Context and Causal Mechanisms in Political Analysis. *Comparative Political Studies* 42(9): 1143–1166.

Fariss CJ (2014) Respect for Human Rights has Improved over Time: Modeling the Changing Standard of Accountability. *American Political Science Review* 108(2): 297–318.

Fearon JD (1995) Rationalist Explanations for War. *International Organization* 49(3): 379–414.

Fearon JD and Laitin DD (2003) Ethnicity, Insurgency, and Civil War. *American Political Science Review* 97(01): 75–90.

Felbermayr G, Kirilakha A, Syropoulos C et al (2020) The Global Sanctions Data Base. *European Economic Review* 129.

Fetherston AB (2000) Peacekeeping, Conflict Resolution and Peacebuilding: A Reconsideration of Theoretical Frameworks. *International Peacekeeping* 7(1): 190–218.

Findley MG (2012) Bargaining and the Interdependent Stages of Civil War Resolution. *Journal of Conflict Resolution* 57(5): 905–932.

Fioretos O, Falleti TG and Sheingate A (2016) Historical Institutionalism in Political Science. In: Fioretos O, Falleti TG and Sheingate A (eds) *The Oxford Handbook of Historical Institutionalism*. Oxford: Oxford University Press, pp 3–28.

Fiss PC (2011) Building Better Causal Theories: A Fuzzy Set Approach to Typologies in Organization Research. *Academy of Management Journal* 54(2): 393–420.

Flick U (2011) *Triangulation: Eine Einführung*. Wiesbaden: VS Verlag für Sozialwissenschaften.

Fontana G, Siewert MB and Yakinthou C (2021) Managing War-to-Peace Transitions after Intra-state Conflicts: Configurations of Successful Peace Processes. *Journal of Intervention and Statebuilding* 15(1): 25–47.

Fortna VP (2004a) Does Peacekeeping Keep Peace? International Intervention and the Duration of Peace after Civil War. *International Studies Quarterly* 48(2): 269–292.

Fortna VP (2004b) Interstate Peacekeeping: Causal Mechanisms and Empirical Effects. *World Politics* 56(4): 481–519.

Fortna VP (2008) *Does Peacekeeping Work? Shaping Belligerents' Choices after Civil Wars*. Princeton: Princeton University Press.

Foucault M (1980) *Power/knowledge: Selected Interviews and Other Writings*. New York: Pantheon Books.

Friedman S (2014) The Bargain That Saved Us in 1994. *Sunday Independent*, 27 April.

Frowein J and Krisch N (2002) Chapter VII Action with Respect to Threats to the Peace, Breaches of the Peace and Acts of Aggression. In: Simma B (ed) *The Charter of the United Nations. A Commentary*, 2nd edition. Oxford: Oxford University Press, pp 701–763.

Fukuyama F (1989) The End of History? *The National Interest* 16: 3–18.

Gaglione A (2001) *The United Nations under Trygve Lie, 1945–1953*. Lanham: Scarecrow Press.

Galtung J (1964) An Editorial. *Journal of Peace Research* 1(1): 1–4.

Galtung J (1969) Violence, Peace, and Peace Research. *Journal of Peace Research* 6(3): 167–191.

Galtung J (1985) Twenty-Five Years of Peace Research: Ten Challenges and Some Responses. *Journal of Peace Research* 22(2): 141–158.

Galtung J (2008) Toward a Grand Theory of Negative and Positive Peace: Peace, Security, and Conviviality. In: Murakami Y and Schoenbaum TJ (eds) *A Grand Design for Peace and Reconciliation: Achieving Kyosei in East Asia*. Cheltenham: Edward Elgar.

Gareis SB and Varwick J (2014) *Die Vereinten Nationen: Aufgaben, Instrumente und Reformen* [*The United Nations: Tasks, Instruments and Reforms*]. Toronto: Verlag Barbara Budrich.

Gberie L (2005) *A Dirty War in West Africa: The RUF and the Destruction of Sierra Leone*. Bloomington: Indiana University Press.

Geis A, Brock L and Müller H (2006) *Democratic Wars: Looking at the Dark Side of Democratic Peace*. Basingstoke: Palgrave Macmillan.

Geis A, Müller H and Wagner W (2007) Das Kantsche Friedensprogramm und seine Schattenseiten In: Geis A, Müller H and Wagner W (eds) *Schattenseiten des Demokratischen Friedens. Zur Kritik einer Theorie liberaler Außen- und Sicherheitspolitik*. Frankfurt am Main: Campus, pp 11–31.

Genser J and Cotler I (2012) *The Responsibility to Protect: The Promise of Stopping Mass Atrocities in Our Time*. New York: Oxford University Press.

George AL and Bennett A (2005) *Case Studies and Theory Development in the Social Sciences*. Cambridge, MA: MIT Press.

Gerring J (2007) *Case Study Research*. Cambridge: Cambridge University Press.

Gerring J (2008) The Mechanismic Worldview: Thinking inside the Box. *British Journal of Political Science* 38: 161–179.

Giliomee H (2003) *The Afrikaners: Biography of a People*. Cape Town: Tafelberg.

Gilligan MJ and Sergenti EJ (2008) Do UN Interventions Cause Peace? Using Matching to Improve Causal Inference. *Quarterly Journal of Political Science* 3(1): 89–122.

Gleditsch NP, Nordkvelle J and Strand HV (2014) Peace Research: Just the Study of War? *Journal of Peace Research* 51(2): 145–158.

Goertz G (2006) *Social Science Concepts: A User's Guide*. Princeton: Princeton University Press.

Goertz G (2017) *Multimethod Research, Causal mechanisms, and Case Studies: An Integrated Approach*. Princeton: Princeton University Press.

Goertz G, Diehl PF and Balas A (2016) *The Puzzle of Peace: The Evolution of Peace in the International System*. New York: Oxford University Press.

Goertz G and Mahoney J (2013) Methodological Rorschach Tests: Contrasting Interpretations in Qualitative and Quantitative Research. *Comparative Political Studies* 46(2): 236–251.

Goldstein JS (2011) *Winning the War on War: The Decline of Armed Conflict Worldwide*. New York: Dutton.

Goldstone RJ (1996) Justice as a Tool for Peacemaking: Truth Commissions and International Criminal Tribunals. *New York University Journal of International Law and Politics* 28(3): 485–503.

GoSL (Government of Sierra Leone) (2005) *Government of Sierra Leone White Paper on the Truth and Reconciliation Report*. Available at: https://witness. typepad.com/gillian_in_salone/files/whitepaper2.pdf

Graham M (2011) Coming in from the Cold: The Transitional Executive Council and South Africa's Reintegration into the International Community. *Commonwealth & Comparative Politics* 49(3): 359–378.

Greif A and Laitin DD (2004) A Theory of Endogenous Institutional Change. *American Political Science Review* 98(4): 633–652.

Grofman B and Schneider CQ (2009) An Introduction to Crisp Set QCA, with a Comparison to Binary Logistic Regression. *Political Research Quarterly* 62(4): 662–672.

Guelke A (1993) Political Violence and the South African Transition. *Irish Studies in International Affairs* 4: 59–68.

Gurses M, Rost N and McLeod P (2008) Mediating Civil War Settlements and the Duration of Peace. *International Interactions* 34(2): 129–155.

Haesebrouck T (2017) EU Member State Participation in Military Operations: A Configurational Comparative Analysis. *Cambridge Review of International Affairs* 30(2–3): 137–159.

Haesebrouck T and Thomann E (2022) Introduction: Causation, Inferences, and Solution Types in Configurational Comparative Methods. *Quality & Quantity* 56(4): 1867–1888.

Hall PA (2008) Systematic Process Analysis: When and How to Use It. *European Political Science* 7(3): 304–317.

Hampson FO (1996) *Nurturing Peace: Why Peace Settlements Succeed or Fail.* Washington DC: United States Institute of Peace Press.

Hannum H (2006) Peace versus Justice: Creating Rights as Well as Order out of Chaos. *International Peacekeeping* 13(4): 582–595.

Harfensteller J (2011) *The United Nations and Peace. The Evolution of an Organizational Concept.* Frankfurt am Main: Peter Lang.

Harris D (2013) *Sierra Leone: A Political History.* London: Hurst & Company.

Hartzell CA (2014) Peacebuilding after Civil War. In: Newman E and DeRouen K (eds) *Routledge Handbook of Civil Wars*. Abingdon: Routledge, pp 376–386.

Hartzell CA and Hoddie M (2003) Institutionalizing Peace: Power Sharing and Post-Civil War Conflict Management. *American Journal of Political Science* 47(2): 318–332.

Hartzell CA and Hoddie M (2007) *Crafting Peace: Power-Sharing Institutions and the Negotiated Settlement of Civil Wars.* University Park: Pennsylvania State University Press.

Hartzell CA, Hoddie M and Rothchild D (2001) Stabilizing the Peace after Civil War: An Investigation of Some Key Variables. *International Organization* 55(1): 183–208.

Heathershaw J (2013) Towards Better Theories of Peacebuilding: Beyond the Liberal Peace Debate. *Peacebuilding* 1(2): 275–282.

Hedström P and Ylikoski P (2010) Causal Mechanisms in the Social Sciences. *Annual Review of Sociology* 36(1): 49–67.

Heineken L (1998) The Challenges of Transformation: SANDF Officers' Attitudes towards Integration, Affirmative Action, Women in Combat and Language Usage. *South African Journal of Military Studies* 28(2): 220–235.

Hendrickson D and Karkoszka A (2005) Security Sector Reform and Donor Policies. In: Schnabel A and Ehrhart H-G (eds) *Security Sector Reform and Post-conflict Peacebuilding*. Tokyo: United Nations University Press, pp 19–44.

Herbst J (1997) Prospects for Elite-Driven Democracy in South Africa. *Political Sciene Quarterly* 112(4): 595–615.

Hirsch JL (2001) *Sierra Leone: Diamonds and the Struggle for Democracy*. Boulder: Lynne Rienner.

Hislope R (1998) Ethnic Conflict and the 'Generosity Moment'. *Journal of Democracy* 9(1): 140–153.

Hoddie M and Hartzell CA (2005) Power Sharing in Peace Settlements: Initiating the Transition from Civil War. In: Roeder PG and Rothchild D (eds) *Sustainable Peace: Power and Democracy after Civil Wars*. Ithaca: Cornell University Press, pp 83–106.

Hoesch M (2015) Friede, Ewiger. In: Willaschek M, Stolzenberg J, Mohr G et al (eds) *Kant-Lexikon*. Berlin: De Gruyter, pp 646–649.

Höglund K and Söderberg Kovacs M (2010) Beyond the Absence of War: The Diversity of Peace in Post-settlement Societies. *Review of International Studies* 36(2): 367–390.

Hollis BJ (2015) Evaluating the Legacy of the Special Court for Sierra Leone. In: Ainley K, Friedman R and Mahony C (eds) *Evaluating Transitional Justice: Accountability and Peacebuilding in Post-conflict Sierra Leone*. Basingstoke: Palgrave Macmillan, pp 19–34.

Hufbauer G, Schott JJ, Elliott KA et al (2007) *Economic Sanctions Reconsidered*. Washington DC: Peterson Institute.

Hultman L (2010) Keeping Peace or Spurring Violence? Unintended Effects of Peace Operations on Violence Against Civilians. *Civil Wars* 12(1–2): 29–46.

Hultman L, Kathman J and Shannon M (2013) United Nations Peacekeeping and Civilian Protection in Civil War. *American Journal of Political Science* 57(4): 875–891.

Human Rights Watch (1999) *Sierra Leone: Getting away with Murder, Mutilation and Rape. New Testimony from Sierra Leone*. New York: Human Rights Watch.

Humphreys M and Jacobs A (2015) Mixing Methods: A Bayesian Approach. *American Political Science Review* 109(4): 653–673.

## REFERENCES

Hunt J (2005) *Dutch South Africa: Early Settlers at the Cape, 1652–1708.* Leicester: Troubador.

ICG (International Crisis Group) (2001a) Sierra Leone: Managing Uncertainty. *Africa Report N°35.* Freetown/Brussels: International Crisis Group.

ICG (2001b) Sierra Leone: Time for a New Military and Political Strategy. *Africa Report N°28.* Freetown/London/Brussels: International Crisis Group.

ICG (2002) Sierra Leone's Truth and Reconciliation Commission: A Fresh Start? *ICG Africa Briefing, 20 December 2002.* Freetown/Brussels: International Crisis Group.

ICG (2003) Sierra Leone: The State of Security and Governance. *ICG Africa Report N°67.* Freetown/Brussels: International Crisis Group.

ICTJ (International Center for Transitional Justice) (2010) Sierra Leone: Submission to the Universal Periodic Review of the UN Human Rights Council 11th Session, May 2011. Available at: https://www.ictj.org/sites/default/files/ICTJ-SierraLeone-Periodic-Review-2010-English.pdf

Ide T (2018) Does Environmental Peacemaking between States Work? Insights on Cooperative Environmental Agreements and Reconciliation in International Rivalries. *Journal of Peace Research* 55(3): 351–365.

Ide T and Mello PA (2022) QCA in International Relations: A Review of Strengths, Pitfalls, and Empirical Applications. *International Studies Review* 24(1): viac008.

*IPS News* (2002, 12 September) Amputees Threaten to Boycott Sierra Leone's Truth Commission. Available at: http://www.ipsnews.net/2002/09/rights-amputees-threaten-to-boycott-sierra-leones-truth-commission/

Jabri V (2013) Peacebuilding, the Local and the International: A Colonial or a Postcolonial Reality? *Peacebuilding* 1(1): 3–16.

Jarstad AK and Belloni R (2012) Introducing Hybrid Peace Governance: Impact and Prospects of Liberal Peacebuilding. *Global Governance: A Review of Multilateralism and International Organizations* 18(1): 1–6.

Jarstad AK and Nilsson D (2008) From Words to Deeds: The Implementation of Power-Sharing Pacts in Peace Accords. *Conflict Management and Peace Science* 25(3): 206–223.

Joshi M and Wallensteen P (2018) Understanding Quality Peace: Introducing the Five Dimensions. In: Joshi M and Wallensteen P (eds) *Understanding Quality Peace: Peacebuilding after Civil War.* Abingdon: Routledge, pp 3–25.

Joshi M, Quinn JM and Regan PM (2015) Annualized Implementation Data on Comprehensive Intrastate Peace Accords, 1989–2012. *Journal of Peace Research* 52(4): 551–562.

Jung C and Shapiro I (1995) South Africa's Negotiated Transition: Democracy, Opposition, and the New Constitutional Order. *Politics & Society* 23(3): 269–308.

Kaldor M (2007) *Human Security: Reflections on Globalization and Intervention.* Cambridge: Polity Press.

Kaldor M and Vincent J (2006) *Case Study Sierra Leone: Evaluation of UNDP Assistane to Conflict-Affected Countries.* New York: United Nations Development Programme.

Kalyvas SN and Balcells L (2010) International System and Technologies of Rebellion: How the End of the Cold War Shaped Internal Conflict. *American Political Science Review* 104(3): 415–429.

Kant I (1903 [1795]) *Perpetual Peace: A Philosophical Essay.* London: George Allen & Unwin.

Katznelson I (1997) Structure and Configuration in Comparative Politics. In: Lichbach MI and Zuckerman AS (eds) *Comparative Politics: Rationality, Culture, and Structure.* Cambridge: Cambridge University Press, pp 81–111.

Katznelson I (2009) Strong Theory, Complex History: Structure and Configuration in Comparative Politics Revisited. In: Lichbach MI and Zuckerman AS (eds) *Comparative Politics: Rationality, Culture, and Structure,* 2nd edn. Cambridge: Cambridge University Press, pp 96–116.

Keen D (2005) *Conflict & Collusion in Sierra Leone.* New York: Palgrave.

Kelsall T (2005) Truth, Lies, Ritual: Preliminary Reflections on the Truth and Reconciliation Commission in Sierra Leone. *Human Rights Quarterly* 27(2): 361–391.

Keohane RO (1988) International Institutions: Two Approaches. *International Studies Quarterly* 32(3): 379–396.

Kersten M (2016) *Justice in Conflict: The Effects of the International Criminal Court's Interventions on Ending Wars and Building Peace.* Oxford: Oxford University Press.

King G, Keohane RO and Verba S (1994) *Designing Social Inquiry: Scientific Inference in Qualitative Research.* Princeton: Princeton University Press.

Kreikemeyer A (2018) Hybridity Revisited: Zum Stellenwert von Hybriditätsperspektiven in der Friedensforschung. *Zeitschrift für Friedens- und Konfliktforschung* 7(2): 287–315.

Kritz NJ (1996) Coming to Terms with Atrocities: A Review of Accountability Mechanisms for Mass Violations of Human Rights. *Law and Contemporary Problems* 59(4): 127–152.

Kynoch G (1996) The 'Transformation' of the South African Military. *Journal of Modern African Studies* 34(3): 441–457.

Lacina B (2006) Explaining the Severity of Civil Wars. *Journal of Conflict Resolution* 50(2): 276–289.

Lederach JP (1995) *Preparing for Peace: Conflict Transformation across Cultures.* Syracuse: Syracuse University Press.

Lederach JP (1997) *Building Peace: Sustainable Reconciliation in Divided Societies.* Washington DC: United States Institute of Peace Press.

Lederach JP (1999) Justpeace: The Challenge of the 21st Century. In: Tongeren PV (ed) *People Building Peace. 35 Inspiring Stories from around the World.* Utrecht: European Center for Conflict Prevention, pp 27–36.

Lederach JP (2005) *The Moral Imagination: The Art and Soul of Building Peace.* Oxford: Oxford University Press.

Leib J (2016) Shaping Peace: An Investigation of the Mechanisms Underlying Post-conflict Peacebuilding. *Peace, Conflict & Change* 22: 25–76.

Leib J (2022) How Justice Becomes Part of the Deal: Pre-conditions for the Inclusion of Transitional Justice Provisions in Peace Agreements. *International Journal of Transitional Justice* 16(3): 439–457.

Leib J (2023) Wege zum nachhaltigen Frieden: Ansätze für UN-Friedensmissionen. *Vereinte Nationen* 5/2023: 215–220.

Leib J and Ruppel S (2021) The Dance of Peace and Justice: Local Perceptions of International Peacebuilding in West Africa. *International Peacekeeping* 28(5): 783–812.

Lektzian D and Regan PM (2016) Economic Sanctions, Military Interventions, and Civil Conflict Outcomes. *Journal of Peace Research* 53(4): 554–568.

Lektzian D and Souva M (2007) An Institutional Theory of Sanctions Onset and Success. *Journal of Conflict Resolution* 51(6): 848–871.

Licklider R (1995) The Consequences of Negotiated Settlements in Civil Wars, 1945–1993. *American Political Science Review* 89(3): 681–690.

Lie T (1949) The United Nations: Bridge to Peace. In: Rotary International (ed) *Proceedings Fortieth Annual Convention of Rotary International.* Chicago: Rotary International, pp 51–56.

Lie TG, Binningsbø HM and Gates S (2007) Post-conflict Justice and Sustainable Peace. *World Bank Policy Research Working Paper 4191, Post-conflict Transition Working Paper 5.*

Liebel SR (2015) The Efficacy of Third-Party Intervention. *Brown Journal of World Affairs* 21(2): 53–69.

Lijphart A (1977) *Democracy in Plural Societies: A Comparative Exploration.* New Haven: Yale University Press.

Lindemann S and Wimmer A (2018) Repression and Refuge: Why Only Some Politically Excluded Ethnic Groups Rebel. *Journal of Peace Research* 55(3): 305–319.

Lloyd TO (2008) *The British Empire: 1558–1995.* Oxford: Oxford University Press.

Loyle CE and Appel BJ (2017) Conflict Recurrence and Post-conflict Justice: Addressing Motivations and Opportunities for Sustainable Peace. *International Studies Quarterly* 61(3): 690–703.

Luttwak EN (1999) Give War a Chance. *Foreign Affairs* 78(4): 36–44.

Lyall J (2015) Process Tracing, Causal Inference, and Civil War. In: Bennett A and Checkel JT (eds) *Process Tracing: From Metaphor to Analytic Tool.* Cambridge: Cambridge University Press, pp 186–207.

Mac Ginty R (2006) *No War No Peace. The Rejuvenation of Stalled Peace Processes and Peace Accords.* Basingstoke: Palgrave Macmillan.

Mac Ginty R (2008) Indigenous Peace-Making versus the Liberal Peace. *Cooperation and Conflict* 43(2): 139–163.

Mac Ginty R (2010) Hybrid Peace: The Interation between Top-down and Bottom-up Peace. *Security Dialogue* 41(4): 391–412.

Mac Ginty R (2013) Introduction: The Transcripts of Peace: Public, Hidden or Non-obvious? *Journal of Intervention and Statebuilding* 7(4): 423–430.

Mac Ginty R (2015) Where Is the Local? Critical Localism and Peacebuilding. *Third World Quarterly* 36(5): 840–856.

Mac Ginty R and Richmond OP (2013) The Local Turn in Peace Building: A Critical Agenda for Peace. *Third World Quarterly* 34(5): 763–783.

Machamer P (2004) Activities and Causation: The Metaphysics and Epistemology of Mechanisms. *International Studies in the Philosophy of Science* 18(1): 27–39.

Machamer P, Darden L and Craver CF (2000) Thinking about Mechanisms. *Philosophy of Science* 67(1): 1–25.

Mahoney J (2000) Path Dependence in Historical Sociology. *Theory and Society* 29(4): 507–548.

Mahoney J (2001) *The Legacies of Liberalism: Path Dependence and Political Regimes in Central America.* Baltimore: Johns Hopkins University Press.

Mahoney J (2021) *The Logic of Social Science.* Princeton: Princeton University Press.

Mahony C and Sooka Y (2015) The Truth about the Truth: Insider Reflections on the Sierra Leonean Truth and Reconciliation Commission. In: Ainley K, Friedman R and Mahony C (eds) *Evaluating Transitional Justice: Accountability and Peacebuilding in Post-conflict Sierra Leone.* Basingstoke: Palgrave Macmillan, pp 35–54.

Mallet J-A (2017) War and Peace in Plato's Political Thought. *Philosophical Journal of Conflict and Violence* 1(1): 87–95.

Mallinder L and McEvoy K (2011) Rethinking Amnesties: Atrocity, Accountability and Impunity in Post-conflict Societies. *Contemporary Social Science* 6(1): 107–128.

Maphai VT (1996) The New South Africa: A Season for Power-Sharing. *Journal of Democracy* 7(1): 67–81.

March JG and Olsen JP (1984) The New Institutionalism: Organizational Factors in Political Life. *American Political Science Review* 78(3): 734–749.

Marten KZ (2004) *Enforcing the Peace: Learning from the Imperial Past.* New York: Columbia University Press.

Mason TD, Gurses M, Brandt PT et al (2011) When Civil Wars Recur: Conditions for Durable Peace after Civil Wars. *International Studies Perspectives* 12(2): 171–189.

Mattes M and Savun B (2009) Fostering Peace after Civil War: Commitment Problems and Agreement Design. *International Studies Quarterly* 53(3): 737–759.

Mattes M and Savun B (2010) Information, Agreement Design, and the Durability of Civil War Settlements. *American Journal of Political Science* 54(2): 511–524.

Mbeki T and Mamdani M (2014) Courts Can't End Civil Wars. *International New York Times*, 6 February.

McEvoy K (2007) Beyond Legalism: Towards a Thicker Understanding of Transitional Justice. *Journal of Law and Society* 34(4): 411–440.

Meissner KL and Mello PA (2022) The Unintended Consequences of UN Sanctions: A Qualitative Comparative Analysis. *Contemporary Security Policy* 43(2): 243–273.

Melander E (2018) A Procedural Approach to Quality Peace. In: Davenport C, Melander E and Regan PM (eds) *The Peace Continuum: What It Is and How to Study It*. New York: Oxford University Press, pp 113–143.

Mello PA (2021) *Qualitative Comparative Analysis: An Introduction to Research Design and Application*. Washington DC: Georgetown Universiyt Press.

Mendeloff D (2004) Truth-Seeking, Truth-Telling, and Post-conflict Peacebuilding: Curb the Enthusiasm? *International Studies Review* 6(3): 355–380.

Menzel A (2020) The Pressures of Getting It Right: Expertise and Victims' Voices in the Work of the Sierra Leone Truth and Reconciliation Commission (TRC). *International Journal of Transitional Justice* 14(2): 300–319.

Meuer J and Rupietta C (2017) A Review of Integrated QCA and Statistical Analyses. *Quality and Quantity* 51(5): 2063–2083.

Miall H (2004) Conflict Transformation: A Multi-dimensional Task. In: *The Berghof Handbook for Conflict Transformation*. Berlin: Berghof Research Center for Constructive Conflict Management, pp 1–20.

Mikkelsen KS (2017) Fuzzy-Set Case Studies. *Sociological Methods & Research* 46(3): 422–455.

Millar G (2013) Expectations and Experiences of Peacebuilding in Sierra Leone: Parallel Peacebuilding Processes and Compound Friction. *International Peacekeeping* 20(2): 189–203.

Millar G (2015) Performative Memory and Re-victimization: Truth-Telling and Provocation in Sierra Leone. *Memory Studies* 8(2): 242–254.

Miller B (2001) The Global Source of Regional Transitions from War to Peace. *Journal of Peace Research* 38(2): 199–225.

Mitton K (2013) Where Is the War? Explaining Peace in Sierra Leone. *International Peacekeeping* 20(3): 321–337.

Morgan TC, Bapat N and Kobayashi Y (2014) Threat and Imposition of Economic Sanctions 1945–2005: Updating the TIES Dataset. *Conflict Management and Peace Science* 31(5): 541–558.

Mross K, Fiedler C and Grävingholt J (2022) Identifying Pathways to Peace: How International Support Can Help Prevent Conflict Recurrence. *International Studies Quarterly* 66(1): 1–14.

Mukherjee B (2006) Why Political Power-Sharing Agreements Lead to Enduring Peaceful Resolution of Some Civil Wars, But Not Others? *International Studies Quarterly* 50(2): 479–504.

Mullenbach MJ (2013) Third-Party Peacekeeping in Intrastate Disputes, 1946–2012: A New Data Set. *Midsouth Political Science Review* 14: 103–133.

Nathan L (2004) *Obstacles to Security Sector Reform in New Democracies.* Berlin: Berghof Research Center for Constructive Conflict Management.

Newman E (2010) Critical Human Security Studies. *Review of International Studies* 36(1): 77–94.

Nguyen THY (2002) Beyond Good Offices? The Role of Regional Organizations in Conflict Resolution. *Journal of International Affairs* 55(2): 463–484.

Nilsson D and Söderberg Kovacs M (2013) Different Paths of Reconstruction: Military Reform in Post-war Sierra Leone and Liberia. *International Peacekeeping* 20(1): 2–16.

Oana I-E and Schneider CQ (2018) SetMethods: An Add-on R Package for Advanced QCA. *The R Journal* 10(1): 507–533.

Oana I-E, Schneider CQ and Thomann E (2021) *Qualitative Comparative Analysis Using R: A Beginner's Guide.* Cambridge: Cambridge University Press.

Olonisakin F (2008) *Peacekeeping in Sierra Leone: The Story of UNAMSIL.* Boulder: Lynne Rienner.

Olsen TD, Payne LA and Reiter AG (2010) *Transitional Justice in Balance: Comparing Processes, Weighing Efficacy.* Washington DC: United States Institute of Peace Press.

Oosterveld V (2015) Sexual and Gender-Based Violence in Post-conflict Sierra Leone: The Contribution of Transitional Justice Mechanisms to Domestic Law Reform. In: Ainley K, Friedman R and Mahony C (eds) *Evaluating Transitional Justice: Accountability and Peacebuilding in Post-confilct Sierra Leone.* Basingstoke: Palgrave Macmillan, pp 129–152.

Osborne S (2016) 5 of the Worst Atrocities Carried out by the British Empire. Available at: https://www.independent.co.uk/news/uk/home-news/worst-atrocities-british-empire-amritsar-boer-war-concentration-camp-mau-mau-a6821756.html

Ottendörfer E (2014) *The Fortunate Ones and the Ones Still Waiting: Reparations for War Victims in Sierra Leone.* Frankfurt am Main: Peace Research Institute Frankfurt (PRIF).

## REFERENCES

Ottmann M and Vüllers J (2015) The Power-Sharing Event Dataset (PSED): A New Dataset on the Promises and Practices of Power-Sharing in Post-conflict Countries. *Conflict Management and Peace Science* 32(3): 327–350.

Owen JM (1994) How Liberalism Produces Democratic Peace. *International Security* 19(2): 87–125.

Paffenholz T (2010) Civil Society and Peacebuilding. In: Paffenholz T (ed) *Civil Society and Peacebuilding: A Critical Assessment.* Boulder: Lynne Rienner, pp 43–64.

Paffenholz T (2014) International Peacebuilding Goes Local: Analysing Lederach's Conflict Transformation Theory and Its Ambivalent Encounter with 20 Years of Practice. *Peacebuilding* 2(1): 11–27.

Paffenholz T (2015) Unpacking the Local Turn in Peacebuilding: A Critical Assessment towards an Agenda for Future Research. *Third World Quarterly* 36(5): 857–874.

Papagianni K (2010) Mediation, Political Engagement, and Peacebuilding. *Global Governance: A Review of Multilateralism and International Organizations* 16(2): 243–263.

Paris R (1997) Peacebuilding and the Limits of Liberal Internationalism. *International Security* 22(2): 54–89.

Paris R (2001) Human Security: Paradigm Shift or Hot Air? *International Security* 26(2): 87–102.

Paris R (2010) Saving Liberal Peacebuilding. *Review of International Studies* 36(2): 337–365.

Peksen D (2019) When Do Imposed Economic Sanctions Work? A Critical Review of the Sanctions Effectiveness Literature. *Defence and Peace Economics* 30(6): 635–647.

Peksen D and Peterson TM (2016) Sanctions and Alternate Markets: How Trade and Alliances Affect the Onset of Economic Coercion. *Political Research Quarterly* 69(1): 4–16.

Perito RM (2020) Security Sector Refom. In: Williams PR and Sterio M (eds) *Research Handbook on Post-conflict State Building.* Cheltenham: Edward Elgar, pp 145–158.

Pettersson T (2023) UCDP/PRIO Armed Conflict Dataset Codebook Version 23.1.

Pettersson T and Wallensteen P (2015) Armed Conflicts, 1946–2014. *Journal of Peace Research* 52(4): 536–550.

Pettersson T, Davies S, Deniz A et al (2021) Organized Violence 1989–2020, with a Special Emphasis on Syria. *Journal of Peace Research* 58(4): 809–825.

Pettersson T, Högbladh S and Öberg M (2019) Organized Violence, 1989–2018 and Peace Agreements. *Journal of Peace Research* 56(4): 589–603.

Pierson P (2004) *Politics in Time: History, Institutions, and Social Analysis.* Princeton: Princeton University Press.

Pierson P and Skocpol T (2002) Historical Institutionalism in Contemporary Political Science. In: Katznelson I and Milner HV (eds) *Political Science: The State of the Discipline*. New York: W.W. Norton & Company, pp 693–721.

Pinker S (2011) *The Better Angels of Our Nature: Why Violence Has Declined*. New York: Penguin.

Powell R (2002) Bargaining Theory and International Conflict. *Annual Review of Political Science* 5: 1–30.

Pugh M (2002) Postwar Political Economy in Bosnia and Herzegovina: The Spoils of Peace. *Global Governance* 8(4): 467–482.

Pugh M (2005) The Political Economy of Peacebuilding: A Critical Theory Perspective. *International Journal of Peace Studies* 10(2): 23–42.

Quinn JM, Mason TD and Gurses M (2007) Sustaining the Peace: Determinants of Civil War Recurrence. *International Interactions* 33(2): 167–193.

Ragin CC (1987) *The Comparative Method: Moving beyond Qualitative and Quantitative Strategies*. Berkeley: University of California Press.

Ragin CC (2000) *Fuzzy-Set Social Sciences*. Chicago: University of Chicago Press.

Ragin CC (2004) Turning the Tables: How Case-Oriented Research Challenges Variable-Oriented Research. In: Brady HE and Collier D (eds) *Rethinking Social Inquiry: Diverse Tools, Shared Standards*. Lanham: Rowman & Littlefield, pp 123–138.

Ragin CC (2006) Set Relations in Social Research: Evaluating Their Consistency and Coverage. *Political Analysis* 14(3): 291–310.

Ragin CC (2008a) Measurement versus Calibration: A Set-Theoretic Approach. In: Box-Steffensmeier JM, Brady HE and Collier D (eds) *The Oxford Handbook of Political Methodology*. Oxford: Oxford University Press, pp 174–198.

Ragin CC (2008b) *Redesigning Social Inquiry: Fuzzy Sets and Beyond*. Chicago: University of Chicago Press.

Ragin CC (2009) Qualitative Comparative Analysis Using Fuzzy Sets (fsQCA). In: Rihoux B and Ragin CC (eds) *Configurational Comparative Methods: Qualitative Comprative Analysis (QCA) and Related Techniques*. Thousand Oaks: SAGE Publications, pp 87–121.

Ragin CC (2013) New Directions in the Logic of Social Inquiry. *Political Research Quarterly* 66(1): 171–174.

Ragin CC and Fiss PC (2008) Net Effects Analysis versus Configurational Analysis: An Empirical Demonstration. In: Ragin CC (ed) *Redesigning Social Inquiry: Fuzzy Sets and Beyond*. Chicago: University of Chicago Press, pp 190–212.

Ragin CC and Fiss PC (2017) *Intersectional Inequality: Race, Class, Test Scores, and Poverty*. Chicago: University of Chicago Press.

Ragin CC and Schneider GA (2011) Case-Oriented Theory Building and Theory Testing. In: Williams M and Vogt WP (eds) *The SAGE Handbook of Innovation in Social Research Methods*. London: SAGE Publications, pp 150–166.

Ragin CC and Sonnett J (2004) Between Complexity and Parsimony: Limited Diversity, Counterfactual Cases, and Comparative Analysis. In: Kropp S and Minkenberg M (eds) *Vergleichen in der Politikwissenschaft*. Wiesbaden: VS Verlag für Sozialwissenschaften, pp 180–197.

Ragin CC and Strand SI (2008) Using Qualitative Comparative Analysis to Study Causal Order: Comment on Caren and Panofsky (2005). *Sociological Methods & Research* 36(4): 431–441.

Rapoport A (1992) *Peace: An Idea Whose Time Has Come*. Ann Arbor: University of Michigan Press.

Rashid I (2000) The Lomé Peace Negotiations. In: Lord D (ed) *Paying the Price: The Sierra Leonean Peace Process*. London: Conciliation Resources, pp 26–33.

Rauchhaus RW (2006) Asymmetric Information, Mediation, and Conflict Management. *World Politics* 58(2): 207–241.

Regan PM (2014) Bringing Peace back in: Presidential Address to the Peace Science Society, 2013. *Conflict Management and Peace Science* 31(4): 345–356.

Regan PM (2018) A Perceptual Approach to Quality Peace. In: Davenport C, Melander E and Regan PM (eds) *The Peace Continuum: What It Is and How to Study It*. New York: Oxford University Press, pp 79–111.

Regan PM, Frank RW and Aydin A (2009) Diplomatic Interventions and Civil War: A New Dataset. *Journal of Peace Research* 46(1): 135–146.

Reiter D (2003) Exploring the Bargaining Model of War. *Perspectives on Politics* 1(1): 27–43.

Reno W (1993) Foreign Firms and the Financing of Charles Taylor's NPFL. *Liberian Studies Journal* XVIII(2): 175–187.

Richmond OP (2006) The Problem of Peace: Understanding the 'Liberal Peace'. *Conflict, Security & Development* 6(3): 291–314.

Richmond OP (2011) *A Post-liberal Peace*. Abingdon: Routledge.

Richmond OP and Mac Ginty R (2015) Where Now for the Critique of the Liberal Peace? *Cooperation and Conflict* 50(2): 171–189.

Rihoux B and Ragin CC (2009) *Configurational Comparative Methods: Qualitative Comparative Analysis (QCA) and Related Techniques*. Thousand Oaks: SAGE Publications.

Rixen T and Viola LA (2016) Historical Institutionalism and International Relations. In: Rixen T, Viola LA and Zürn M (eds) *Historical Institutionalism and International Relations: Explaining Institutional Development in World Politics*. Oxford: Oxford University Press, pp 3–34.

Rodman KA (2011) Peace versus Justice. In: Chatterjee DK (ed) *Encyclopedia of Global Justice*. Dordrecht: Springer, pp 824–827.

Rohlfing I (2012) *Case Studies and Causal Inference: An Integrative Framework.* Basingstoke: Palgrave Macmillan.

Rohlfing I and Schneider CQ (2013) Improving Research on Necessary Conditions: Formalized Case Selection for Process Tracing after QCA. *Political Research Quarterly* 66(1): 220–235.

Rohlfing I and Schneider CQ (2018) A Unifying Framework for Causal Analysis in Set-Theoretic Multimethod Research. *Sociological Methods & Research* 47(1): 37–63.

Ross M (2006) A Closer Look at Oil, Diamonds, and Civil War. *Annual Review of Political Science* 9(1): 265–300.

Roth-Arriaza N and Mariezcurrena J (2006) *Transitional Justice in the Twenty-First Century: Beyond Truth versus Justice.* Cambridge: Cambridge University Press.

Rothchild D and Roeder PG (2005) Dilemmas of State-Building in Divided Societies. In: Roeder PG and Rothchild D (eds) *Sustainable Peace: Power and Democracy after Civil Wars.* Ithaca: Cornell University Press, pp 1–25.

Rubinson C (2019) Presenting Qualitative Comparative Analysis: Notation, Tabular Layout, and Visualization. *Methodological Innovations* 12(2): 1–22.

Ruppel S (2023) *Lokal verankerte Zivile Konfliktbearbeitung zwischen Partnerschaft und Machtungleichgewicht.* Wiesbaden: Springer VS.

Ruppel S and Leib J (2022) Same But Different: The Role of Local Leaders in the Peace Processes in Liberia and Sierra Leone. *Peacebuilding* 10(4): 470–505.

Russett B and Oneal JR (2001) *Triangulating Peace. Democracy, Interdependence, and International Organizations.* New York: W.W. Norton & Company.

Rutten R (2022) Applying and Assessing Large-N QCA: Causality and Robustness from a Critical Realist Perspective. *Sociological Methods & Research* 51(3): 1211–1243.

Sabaratnam M (2013) Avatars of Eurocentrism in the Critique of the Liberal Peace. *Security Dialogue* 44(3): 259–278.

Sampson A (2000) *Mandela: The Authorized Biography.* London: HarperCollins.

Sartori G (1970) Concept Misformation in Comparative Politics. *American Political Science Review* 64(4): 1033–1053.

Schabas WA (2003) The Relationship between Truth Commissions and International Courts: The Case of Sierra Leone. *Human Rights Quarterly* 25(4): 1035–1066.

Schnabel A and Ehrhart H-G (2005) Post-conflict Societies and the Military: Challenged and Problems of Security Sector Reform. In: Schnabel A and Ehrhart H-G (eds) *Security Sector Reform and Post-conflict Peacebuilding.* Tokyo: United Nations University Press, pp 1–16.

Schneckener U (2005) Frieden Machen: Peacebuilding und Peacebuilder. *Die Friedens-Warte* 80(1–2): 17–39.

Schneider CQ (2019) Two-Step QCA Revisited: The Necessity of Context Conditions. *Quality & Quantity* 53(3): 1109–1126.

Schneider CQ (2024) *Set-Theoretic Multi-method Research: A Guide to Combining QCA and Case Studies*. Cambridge: Cambridge University Press.

Schneider CQ and Rohlfing I (2013) Combining QCA and Process Tracing in Set-Theoretical Multi-method Research. *Sociological Methods & Research* 42(4): 559–597.

Schneider CQ and Rohlfing I (2016) Case Studies Nested in Fuzzy-Set QCA on Sufficiency: Formalizing Case Selection and Causal Inference. *Sociological Methods & Research* 45(3): 526–568.

Schneider CQ and Wagemann C (2012) *Set-Theoretic Methods for the Social Sciences: A Guide to Qualitative Comparative Analysis*. Cambridge: Cambridge University Press.

Schneider CQ and Wagemann C (2013) Doing Justice to Logical Remainders in QCA: Moving beyond the Standard Analysis. *Political Research Quarterly* 66(1): 211–220.

Scott JC (1990) *Domination and the Arts of Resistance: Hidden Transcripts*. New Haven: Yale University Press.

SCSL (Special Court for Sierra Leone) (2012) *Making Justice Count: Assessing the Impact and Legacy of the Special Court for Sierra Leone in Sierra Leone and Liberia*. Available at: http://www.npwj.org/content/Making-Justice-Count-Assessing-impact-and-legacy-Special-Court-Sierra-Leone-Sie rra-Leone-and

Seawright J (2016) *Multi-method Social Science: Combining Qualitative and Quantitative Tools*. Cambridge: Cambridge University Press.

Serra N, Spiegel S and Stiglitz JE (2008) Introduction: From the Washington Consensus towards a New Global Governance. In: Serra N and Stiglitz JE (eds) *The Washington Consensus Reconsidered: Towards a New Global Governance*. Oxford: Oxford University Press, pp 3–12.

Shaw R (2005) *Rethinking Truth and Reconciliation Commissions: Lessons from Sierra Leone*. Washington DC: United States Institute of Peace.

Shaw R (2007) Memory Frictions: Localizing the Truth and Reconciliation Commission in Sierra Leone. *International Journal of Transitional Justice* 1(2): 183–207.

Sierra Leone MDTF (Multi-Donor Trust Fund) (2015) *Updated Consolidated Report on Projects Implemented under the Sierra Leone Multi-Donor Trust Fund*. Available at: https://assessments.hpc.tools/assessment/34258c73-0cb9-4d71-87e4-df3d6fb2096a

Sikkink K (2011) *The Justice Cascade: How Human Rights Prosecutions are Changing World Politics*. New York: Norton.

Simpson JGR (2012) Boipatong: The Politics of a Massacre and the South African Transition. *Journal of Southern African Studies* 38(3): 623–647.

Sisk TD (1996) *Power Sharing and International Mediation in Ethnic Conflicts.* Washington DC: United States Institute of Peace.

SLTRC (Sierra Leone Truth and Reconciliation Commission) (2004) *Witness to Truth: Report of the Sierra Leone Truth and Reconciliation Commission.* Freetown: Truth and Reconciliation Commission.

Smith A and Stam AC (2004) Bargaining and the Nature of War. *Journal of Conflict Resolution* 48(6): 783–813.

Smith-Höhn J (2009) Challenges to Rebuilding the Security Sector in Post-conflict Societies: Perceptions from Urban Liberia and Sierra Leone. Dissertation. Leipzig: University of Leipzig.

Snyder J and Vinjamuri L (2004) Trials and Errors: Principle and Pragmatism in Strategies of International Justice. *International Security* 28(3): 5–44.

Spear J (2002) Disarmament and Demobilization. In: Stedman SJ, Rothchild D and Cousens EM (eds) *Ending Civil Wars: The Implementation of Peace Agreements.* London: Lynne Rienner, pp 141–182.

Spears IS (2002) Africa: The Limits of Power-Sharing. *Journal of Democracy* 13(3): 123–136.

Sriram CL (2005) *Globalising Justice for Mass Atrocities: A Revolution in Accountability.* New York: Routledge.

Sriram CL (2009) Transitional Justice and Peacebuilding. In: Sriram CL and Pillay S (eds) *Peace versus Justice? The Dilemma of Transitional Justice in Africa.* Scottsville: University of KwaZulu-Natal Press, pp 1–17.

Sriram CL (2012) Victim-Centered Justice and DDR in Sierra Leone. In: Sriram CL, García-Godos J, Herman J et al (eds) *Transitional Justice and Peacebuilding on the Ground: Victims and Ex-combatants.* Abingdon: Routledge, pp 159–177.

Stedman SJ (1997) Spoiler Problems in Peace Processes. *International Security* 22(2): 5–53.

Stedman SJ (2002) Introduction. In: Stedman SJ, Rothchild D and Cousens EM (eds) *Ending Civil Wars: The Implementation of Peace Agreements.* Boulder: Lynne Rienner, pp 1–40.

Suma M and Correa C (2009) *Report and Proposals for the Implementation of Reparations in Sierra Leone.* New York: International Center for Transitional Justice.

Teitel RG (2000) *Transitional Justice.* New York: Oxford University Press.

Thiem A, Baumgartner M and Bol D (2016) Still Lost in Translation! Correction of Three Misunderstandings Between Configurational Comparativists and Regressional Analysts. *Comparative Political Studies* 49(6): 742–774.

Thomann E and Maggetti M (2020) Designing Research with Qualitative Comparative Analysis (QCA): Approaches, Challenges, and Tools. *Sociological Methods & Research* 49(2): 356–386.

Toft MD (2010) *Securing the Peace: The Durable Settlement of Civil Wars.* Princeton: Princeton University Press.

Traniello M (2008) Power-Sharing: Lessons from South Africa and Rwanda. *International Public Policy Review* 3(2): 28–43.

Tschirgi N (2004) Post-conflict Peacebuilding Revisited: Achievements, Limitations, Challenges. In: *WSP International/IPA Peacebuilding Forum Conference*, New York. International Peace Academy, pp 1–32.

Tzouvala N (2019) A False Promise? Regulating Land-Grabbing and the Post-colonial State. *Leiden Journal of International Law* 32(2): 235–253.

UN (United Nations) (1945) *Charter of the United Nations.* San Francisco: United Nations.

UN (2000) *Report of the Panel on United Nations Peace Operations.* UN Doc A/55/305 – S/2000/809, 21 August.

UNCIO (United Nations Conference on International Organization) (1945) *Documents of the United Nations Conference on International Organization.* New York: United Nations Information Organization.

UNDP (United Nations Development Programme) (2015) *Human Development Report 2015: Work for Human Development.* New York: UNDP.

UNDP (2019) *Human Development Report 2019: Beyond Income, beyond Averages, beyond Today: Inequalities in Human Development in the 21st Century.* New York: UNDP.

UNGA (United Nations General Assembly) (1949) Essentials of Peace Resolution. UN Doc A/RES/290(IV).

UNGA (1991) Enhancing the Effectiveness of the Principle of Periodic and Genuine Elections. UN Doc A/RES/46/137, 17 December.

UNGA (1999) Declaration and Programme of Action on a Culture of Peace. UN Doc A/RES/53/243, 6 October.

UNGA (2003) Responding to Global Threats and Challenges. UN Doc A/RES/58/16, 26 January.

UNGA (2005) 2005 World Summit Outcome. UN Doc A/RES/60/1, 24 October.

UNGA (2011a) National Report Submitted in Accordance with Paragraph 15 (a) of the Annex to Human Rights Council Resolution 5/1: Sierra Leone. UN Doc A/HRC/WG.6/11/SLE/1, 14 February.

UNGA (2011b) Summary Prepared by the Office of the High Commissioner for Human Rights in Accordance with Paragraph 15 (c) of the Annex to Human Rights Council Resolution 5/1: Sierra Leone. UN Doc A/HRC/WG.6/11/SLE/3, 21 February.

UNGA (2015) Report of the High-Level Independent Panel on Peace Operations on Uniting Our Strengths for Peace: Politics, Partnership and People. UN Doc A/70/95–S/2015/446, 17 June.

UNGA (2016) Resolution 70/262: Review of the United Nations Peacebuilding Architecture. UN Doc A/RES/70/262, 12 May.

UNIPSIL (United Nations Integrated Peacebuilding Office in Sierra Leone) (2014) Drawing down – The End of UN Peace Operations in Sierra Leone. Available at: https://sl.one.un.org/2014/03/26/feature-drawing-down-the-end-of-un-peace-operations-in-sierra-leone/

UNSC (United Nations Security Council) (1977) United Nations Security Council Resolution 418. UN Doc S/RES/418, 4 November.

UNSC (1992a) Report of the Secretary-General on the Question of South Africa. UN Doc S/24389, 7 August.

UNSC (1992b) United Nations Security Council Resolution 772. UN Doc S/RES/772, 17 August.

UNSC (1994a) Resolution 940 (1994). UN Doc S/RES/940, 31 July.

UNSC (1994b) United Nations Security Council Resolution 930. UN Doc S/RES/930, 27 June.

UNSC (1996) Peace Agreement between the Government of the Republic of Sierra Leone and the Revolutionary United Front of Sierra Leone, Signed at Abidjan on 30 November 1996. UN Doc S/1996/1034, 11 December.

UNSC (1998) United Nations Security Council Resolution 1181. UN Doc S/RES/1181, 13 July.

UNSC (1999a) First Report on the United Nations Mission in Sierra Leone. UN Doc S/1999/1223, 6 December.

UNSC (1999b) Peace Agreement between the Government of Sierra Leone and the Revolutionary United Front of Sierra Leone. UN Doc S/1999/777, 12 July.

UNSC (1999c) Seventh Report of the Secretary-General on the United Nations Observer Mission in Sierra Leone. UN Doc S/1999/836, 30 July.

UNSC (1999d) United Nations Security Council Resolution 1270. UN Doc S/RES/1270, 22 October.

UNSC (2000a) Letter Dated 9 August 2000 from the Permanent Representative of Sierra Leone to the United Nations Addressed to the President of the Security Council. UN Doc S/2000/786, 10 August.

UNSC (2000b) United Nations Security Council Resolution 1289. UN Doc S/RES/1289, 7 February.

UNSC (2000c) United Nations Security Council Resolution 1299. UN Doc S/RES/1299, 19 May.

UNSC (2000d) United Nations Security Council Resolution 1315. UN Doc S/RES/1315, 14 August.

UNSC (2001a) Eleventh Report of the Secretary-General on the United Nations Mission in Sierra Leone. UN Doc S/2001/857, 7 September.

UNSC (2001b) Ninth Report of the Secretary-General on the United Nations Mission in Sierra Leone. UN Doc S/2001/228, 14 March.

UNSC (2001c) Report of the Secretary-General on the Issue of Refugees and Internally Displaced Persons Pursuant to Resolution 1346 (2001). UN Doc S/2001/513, 23 May.

REFERENCES

UNSC (2001d) Tenth Report of the Secretary-General on the United Nations Mission in Sierra Leone. UN Doc S/2001/627, 25 June.

UNSC (2001e) United Nations Security Council Resolution 1346. UN Doc S/RES/1346, 30 March.

UNSC (2002a) Fourteenth Report of the Secretary-General on the United Nations Mission in Sierra Leone. UN Doc S/2002/679, 19 June.

UNSC (2002b) Sixteenth Report of the Secretary-General on the United Nations Mission in Sierra Leone. UN Doc S/2002/1417, 24 December.

UNSC (2002c) Thirteenth Report of the Secretary-General on the United Nations Mission in Sierra Leone. UN Doc S/2002/267, 14 March.

UNSC (2003) Seventeenth Report of the Secretary-General on the United Nations Mission in Sierra Leone. UN Doc S/2003/321, 17 March.

UNSC (2004) Twenty-Third Report of the Secretary-General on the United Nations Mission in Sierra Leone. UN Doc S/2004/724, 9 September.

UNSC (2016) Resolution 2282 (2016). UN Doc S/RES/2282, 27 April 2016.

UNSG (United Nations Secretary-General) (1992) An Agenda for Peace: Preventive Diplomacy, Peacemaking and Peacekeeping. UN Doc A/47/277-S/24111, 17 June.

UNSG (1995) Supplement to an Agenda for Peace. Position Paper of the Secretary-General on the Occasion of the Fiftieth Anniversary of the United Nations. UN Doc A/50/60-S/1995/1, 25 January.

UNSG (2004a) Note by the Secretary-General. UN Doc A/59/565, 2 December 2004.

UNSG (2004b) The Rule of Law and Transitional Justice in Conflict and Post-conflict Societies: Report of the Secretary-General. UN Doc S/2004/616, 23 August 2004.

UNSG (2008) Securing Peace and Development: The Role of the United Nations in Supporting Security Sector Reform. UN Doc A/62/659-S/2008/39, 23 January.

UNSG (2009a) Implementing the Responsibility to Protect: Report of the Secretary-General. UN Doc A/63/677, 12 January.

UNSG (2009b) Report of the Secretary-General on Peacebuilding in the Immediate Aftermath of Conflict. UN Doc A/63/881-S/2009/304, 11 June.

UNSG (2013) Securing States and Societies: Strengthening the United Nations Comprehensive Support to Security Sector Reform. UN Doc A/67/970–S/2013/480, 13 August.

UNSG (2017) Restructuring of the United Nations Peace and Security Pillar: Report of the Secretary-General. UN Doc A/72/525, 13 October.

UNSG (2018) Peacebuilding and Sustaining Peace: Report of the Secretary-General. UN Doc A/72/707–S/2018/43, 18 January.

Van Evera S (1997) *Guide to Methods for Students of Political Science.* Ithaca: Cornell University Press.

Van Meegdenburg H (2022) Process Tracing: An Analyticist Approach. In: Mello PA and Ostermann F (eds) *Routledge Handbook of Foreign Policy Analysis Methods.* Abingdon: Routledge, pp 405–420.

Vinjamuri L and Boesenecker AP (2007) *Accountability and Peace Agreements: Mapping Trends from 1980 to 2006.* Geneva: Centre for Humanitarian Dialogue.

Vogt M, Bormann N-C, Rüegger S et al (2015) Integrating Data on Ethnicity, Geography, and Conflict: The Ethnic Power Relations Data Set Family. *Journal of Conflict Resolution* 59(7): 1327–1342.

Waldner D (2012) Process Tracing and Causal Mechanisms. In: Kincaid H (ed) *Oxford Handbook of the Philosophy of Social Sience.* Oxford: Oxford University Press, pp 65–84.

Wallensteen P (2012) Future Directions in the Scientific Study of Peace and War. In: Vasquez JA (ed) *What Do We Know about War?* Lanham: Rowman & Littlefield, pp 257–270.

Wallensteen P (2015) *Quality Peace: Peacebuilding, Victory & World Order.* New York: Oxford Univeristy Press.

Wallensteen P and Svensson I (2014) Talking Peace: International Mediation in Armed Conflicts. *Journal of Peace Research* 51(2): 315–327.

Walter BF (1997) The Critical Barrier to Civil War Settlement. *International Organization* 51(3): 335–364.

Walter BF (1999) Designing Transitions from Civil War: Demobilization, Democratization, and Commitmets to Peace. *International Security* 24(1): 127–155.

Walter BF (2002) *Committing to Peace: The Successful Settlement of Civil Wars.* Princeton: Princeton University Press.

Walter BF (2004) Does Conflict Beget Conflict? Explaining Recurring Civil War. *Journal of Peace Research* 41(3): 371–388.

Walter BF (2006) Information, Uncertainty, and the Decision to Secede. *International Organization* 60(1): 105–135.

Walter BF (2015) Why Bad Governance Leads to Repeat Civil War. *Journal of Conflict Resolution* 59(7): 1242–1272.

Walter BF, Howard LM and Fortna VP (2021) The Extraordinary Relationship between Peacekeeping and Peace. *British Journal of Political Science* 51(4): 1705–1722.

Weller N and Barnes J (2015) *Finding Pathways: Mixed-Method Research for Studying Causal Mechanisms.* Cambridge: Cambridge University Press.

Wessels A (2010) The South African National Defence Force, 1994–2009: A Historical Perspective. *Journal for Contemporary History* 35(2): 131–152.

White ND (2002) *The United Nations System: Toward International Justice.* Boulder: Lynne Rienner.

## REFERENCES

Wiebelhaus-Brahm E (2009) *Truth Commissions and Transitional Justice: The Impact on Human Rights and Democracy.* New York: Routledge.

Williams PR and Sterio M (2020) *Research Handbook on Post-conflict State Building.* Cheltenham: Edward Elgar.

Williams R (2002) Integration or Absorption? The Creation of the South African National Defence Force, 1993 to 1999. *African Security Review* 11(2): 17–25.

Wimmer A, Cederman L-E and Min B (2009) Ethnic Politics and Armed Conflict: A Configurational Analysis of a New Global Data Set. *American Sociological Review* 74(2): 316–337.

Wood RM, Kathman JD and Gent SE (2012) Armed Intervention and Civilian Victimization in Intrastate Conflicts. *Journal of Peace Research* 49(5): 647–660.

Worden N (1985) *Slavery in Dutch South Africa.* Cambridge: Cambridge University Press.

Worger WH (2014) The Tricameral Academy: Personal Reflections on Universities and History Departments in 'Post-apartheid' South Africa. *Ufahamu* 38(1): 193–216.

World Bank and United Nations (2018) *Pathways for Peace: Inclusive Approaches to Preventing Violent Conflict.* Washington DC: World Bank.

Wren CS (1992) South African Whites Ratify de Klerk's Move to Negotiate with Blacks on a New Order. *New York Times*, 19 March.

Wright Q (1954) Criteria for Judging the Relevance of Research on the Problems of Peace. In: Institute for Social Research O (ed) *Research for Peace.* Amsterdam: North-Holland Publishing Company, pp 1–93.

Wright Q (1964) *A Study of War.* Chicago: University of Chicago Press.

Yin RK (2009) *Case Study Research: Design and Methods.* Los Angeles: SAGE Publications.

# Index

## A

Abidjan peace accord  140
absence of violence  30, 33, 34, 49, 100, 147
  measuring and analyzing peace  20
  peace definition  22, 24, 25
Accra Comprehensive Peace Agreement  44
AFRC  141, 153, 155, 161
Africa  119, 120, 128, 166
  peace processes data  15
  peacebuilding episodes  46, 126, 130, 202
  peacebuilding process  134
  quality of peace  27
African National Congress (ANC)  173, 174,
    179–193
African Union (AU)  66
All People's Congress  156
Angola  38, 39, 40, 42
Annan, Kofi  30, 31
apartheid  119, 169–173, 175, 179, 182,
    187–189, 193, 194, 196, 200
armed conflict  2, 26, 34, 89, 91, 114
  conflict recurrence  8
  decline since 1990s  47
  intrastate  14, 195
  large scale  17, 20, 195
  negative peace  25
  negotiated solutions  13
Armed Forces Revolutionary Council
    (AFRC)  140
Asia  15, 119, 120, 126–129, 170, 172, 202
assisted accountability approach  18,
    116, 134, 135, 141, 144–146, 149,
    196–200
authoritarianism  68
Azanian People's Liberation Army
    (APLA)  186, 188, 190, 192

## B

Bangladesh  111, 113
bargaining model of war  52, 63
bargaining theory  12, 13, 18, 52, 75
battle-death view  25
Boers  170, 172
Bougainville Revolutionary Army (BRA)  40

Boulding, Kenneth  26, 35
  contributions to the study of peace  22
  relational war-peace cycle  33
Boutros-Ghali, Boutros  5, 30, 32

## C

Cambodia  1, 56, 69
Capstone Doctrine  32
case studies  17, 82, 84, 86, 87
  Sierra Leone  16, 75, 143, 203
  South Africa  176
ceasefire  8, 42, 141, 148, 151, 153
Charles Taylor's National Patriotic Front of
    Liberia (NPFL)  41
Ciskei Defence Force  174
civil defence forces (CDF)  140, 141, 153,
    155, 161, 168
civil liberties  37, 39, 42, 43, 91, 92
civil war  8–10, 23, 25, 26, 30, 34, 35, 63,
    72, 91
  bargaining failure  64
  conflicts and consequences  2
  crucial role of international
    actors  67, 68
  implementation of peace agreements  71
  institutional peacebuilding factors  93
  liberal peacebuilding  55
  literature  6
  peacebuilding interventions  118, 202
  post-Cold War trends  3
  recurrence  38, 100, 113, 114, 187
  restrictive interpretation of peace  28
  settlements and peace processes  69
  Sierra Leone  135, 136, 138, 154, 156, 160,
    163, 166, 168
  South Africa  119, 169, 170, 173
  studies  16, 103, 196
  sustained peace  44, 178
civilian population  10, 30, 41, 68, 70, 138
Clausewitzian concept of quality peace  27
coalition government  9, 71
Cold War  23, 30–32, 38, 56, 67
  concept of peace during  28
  changed warfare  15
  liberal peacebuilding  53

# INDEX

negotiated settlements and conflict
resolution 6
peace agreements 89
post-Cold War trends 3
UNGA resolutions 29
Commonwealth of Nations 174
Comprehensive Ceasefire Agreement 40
comprehensive peace agreement (CPA) 1
configurational model 16–18, 102, 115, 116,
133, 199–203
conflict recurrence 8, 24, 25, 37, 38, 63
negative peace 35
reduction of risk 119, 179
UN peacekeeping operations shown to
reduce the risk of 5
conflict resolution 23, 76, 203
international efforts 9
military victories 8
post-Cold War 15
settlements 6
sustainable 16
threats to 3
conflict transformation 6, 8, 10, 70
conflict trap 3, 11
consolidation 1, 65, 93, 102, 109, 116, 147
constitution 1, 179, 180, 182, 186–191, 196
Convention for a Democratic South Africa
(CODESA) 174, 180, 182, 183
cooperation 22, 28, 68, 151, 162, 191, 193
Correlates of Peace Project 24
corruption 1, 162, 164
crimes against humanity 160, 161
Croatia 111

## D

Declaration on a Culture of Peace 28
democracy 31, 42, 56–58, 73, 92, 145,
168, 183
as a method to supporting peacebuilding 53
UN peace framework 49
UN peace missions 116
Democratic Alliance (DA) 193
democratic governance 10, 43, 53, 119,
169, 178
democratization 10, 53–55, 59, 66, 74, 92
Department of Peace Operations
(DPO) 31
Department for Peacekeeping Operations
(DPKO) 30, 32
Department of Political and Peacebuilding
Affairs (DPPA) 31
diamonds 136, 140, 141, 151, 172
Diehl, Paul F. 6, 26, 33, 198
disarmament, demobilization and
reintegration (DDR) 54, 71, 151, 153,
154, 155, 165
drug-related violence 1
drug trafficking 30
Dutch East India Company 170

## E

East Timor 30
Ebola 168
Economic Community of West African States
Monitoring Group (ECO-MOG) 140
economic development 35, 43, 44, 54, 66,
172, 198
essential for successful peacebuilding 37
post-conflict societies 42
El Salvador 1, 56, 111, 130
Empirical measurements for peace 25
equifinality 16, 77, 79, 82, 88, 197
Eswatini 170
Europe 15, 34, 119, 120, 170
internal armed conflicts 47, 201
peacebuilding episodes 126, 128, 202
peacebuilding processes 130, 133, 134
European Community, the Organisation of
African Unity 174

## F

Farabundo Martí National Liberation Front
(FMLN) 1
Frente de Libertação de Moçambique
(FRELIMO) 43
fundamental freedoms 43, 55

## G

Galtung, Johan 22, 23, 26, 37, 43
gender equality 35, 38, 42, 43, 44, 91, 198
Goertz, Gary 26
Government of National Unity (GNU) 175,
179, 180, 182, 186–189, 191–193, 201
Great Britain 137, 172
Groote Schur Minute 173
gross domestic product (GDP) 44
Guatemala 39, 111, 130
Guinea 39, 40, 136, 154
Guterres, António 31, 33

## H

Haiti 53, 69, 109
Hammarskjöld, Dag 29
High-Level Independent Panel on Peace
Operations 32
High-Level Panel on Threats, Challenges and
Change 31
historical institutionalism (IH) 52, 59–62, 75
HIV/AIDS 164
human rights 31, 49, 56, 58, 69, 79
compliance 1
fostering respect for 11, 29, 43, 53, 55,
71, 164
organizations 163, 183
protections 10, 74
systematic violations 10
violations 26, 42, 67, 147, 154, 160, 165,
167, 189
Human Rights Commission (HRC) 142

## I

Indonesia 111, 133, 170
Inkatha Freedom Party (IFP) 173,
   180, 182, 183, 184, 186, 187,
   190, 192
Institute for Social Research 21
institutional peacebuilding 52, 103, 195
  challenges 1, 2
  conditions 93, 99
instruments of war 23
intergovernmental organizations 9, 142
Interim Administration Mission in
   Kosovo 109
international commitment 11, 67, 74, 93,
   108, 124, 128
international intervention 2, 9, 52, 62, 70,
   75, 94, 100
international peace operations 31
International Relations (IR) 8, 51, 56, 58,
   59, 79
international terrorism 30
interstate wars 2, 3
intrastate wars 47

## J

Joint Military Co-ordinating Council
   (JMCC) 183
justpeace 24

## K

Kant, Immanuel 21, 53
Ki-moon, Ban 31, 166
Krios of Freetown 136

## L

large-scale violence 26, 37
Latin America 60, 73
League of Nations 29
Lederach, John Paul 24, 55, 56, 57
Lesotho 170
liberal peacebuilding approach 18, 55, 56,
   58, 64, 75
Liberia 39, 109, 130, 136, 153,
   154, 167
  15th CPA anniversary 1
  Liberian Civil War 41, 43
  peacebuilding episodes 111, 113
  women's participation in the National
    Legislature 44
Liberians United for Reconciliation and
   Democracy (LURD) 43
Lijphart, Arend 71, 72
Lomé peace agreement 148, 149, 151,
   158, 160

## M

Madagascar 170
Making War and Building Peace 25
Mandela, Nelson 169, 173, 187–190, 192

mediation 9, 13, 67–70, 93–95, 100
Mende-dominated party 137
Mexico 128
Middle East 27
military 10, 22, 64, 70, 95, 138,
   151, 173
  aggression 28
  capabilities 63
  forces 183
  incentives 2, 109, 196
  instruments 66
  integration and transformation 71
  intelligence 174
  intervention 79, 141
  involvement of external actors 3
  power 72, 178
  reintegration 154, 155
  training 155
  UNOMSIL as military observers 149
  UN presence 31
  victories 6, 8
Military Reintegration Programme 154
money-laundering 30
Movement for Democracy in Liberia
   (MODEL) 43
Mozambique 39, 43, 56, 114, 170
multidimensional peace concept 21, 33
multi-method approach 18, 77, 84, 86, 88,
   89, 98
Multi-Party Negotiating Forum (MPNF)
   175, 176, 179, 180, 183, 184, 196

## N

Namibia 56, 170
National Electoral Commission 154, 164
National Peace Accord (NPA) 174, 182
National Provisional Ruling Council
   (NPRC) 140
NATO 67
negative peace 6, 22, 26, 35, 37, 39, 40, 41,
   44, 46, 47, 48, 89, 197, 198
  qualitative degrees of peacefulness 38
  studies 25
  UN concept of peace 30
Nepal 39, 109
Nicaragua 128
Niger 128
nongovernmental organizations (NGOs) 12,
   53, 56, 142
nonpeace 23, 38, 39
nonviolent methods 23
North Macedonia 111, 113

## O

Office of the High Commissioner for Human
   Rights (OHCHR) 160
Office of the Prosecutor (OTP) 161
Organization for Security and Co-operation
   in Europe (OSCE) 95

# INDEX

**P**

Pan-Africanist Congress (PAC) 173, 183, 184, 186, 187
Papua New Guinea 39, 40
paramilitary forces 70, 71, 184
Paris Agreements 1
path dependence 59, 60, 61
Peace Accords Matrix (PAM) 15, 97
peace agreements 1–3, 5–9, 62, 63, 67, 69, 75, 76, 79, 89, 96–100, 116, 195
  accountability and justice 118
  accountability provisions 147
  addressing commitment problems 109
  assisted accountability approach 144, 149, 197
  commitment problems 196
  conflict recurrence rate 25
  conflicts that ended with 15
  implementation 1, 64, 71, 76
  incentives 169, 178
  peace operations inclusion in 31
  peacebuilding episodes 44
  peacebuilding and the institutional provisions 58
  political or monetary gains 118
  post-conflict political order 13
  power-sharing provisions negotiated in 71, 72
  study of peacebuilding processes 14
  transitional justice provisions 74
Peace and Liberation Party (PLP) 155, 156
peace operations 32, 52, 53, 56, 61, 66, 69, 93, 94, 100, 116, 118, 147
peacebuilding research 20–24, 57, 58, 79, 115, 198, 201, 202
  configurational model of peacebuilding institutions and sustaining peace 17
  focus on configurations 195, 196
  historical institutionalism 52, 61
  set-theoretic approaches 81
  on the success and failures of peace processes 33
  sustaining peace scale 47
Peacebuilding Support Office (PBSO) 32
peaceful transfer of power 1, 149, 166, 179, 193, 200, 201
Peoples Liberation Movement/Army (SPLM/A) 1, 41
perceptual indicator of peace 26
Political Party Registration Commission 164
political and socioeconomic development 34, 49, 100
political stability 66, 187
Polity index 26
positive peace 21, 22, 23, 24, 25, 26, 34, 37, 39, 40, 41, 43, 49, 52, 147
post-conflict justice (PCJ) 73
post-conflict reconstruction 2, 16, 55, 198, 202

post-conflict societies 2, 9, 34, 42, 43, 50, 51, 52, 55, 89, 91, 169
  characteristics 100
  constraints and opportunities for political action created by peacebuilding institutions 61
  core security actors 70
  establishment of sustaining peace 111, 199, 200
  historical institutionalism and bargaining theory 12
  impact of peacebuilding institutions on sustaining peace 62
  institutional patterns of peacebuilding success 102
  peacebuilding efforts and the activities of the UN 21
  peacebuilding institutions influence on sustaining peace 5, 75
  political power sharing 10
  power sharing 71, 73, 175
  victim-centred approach 147
postwar governance 26, 37
postwar stability 9
postwar transition 1, 6, 15, 44
power sharing 2, 10, 71–73, 100, 128–129, 169, 175–180, 193, 194, 199–201
  inclusive 11, 74, 96, 104, 109, 113, 114, 116, 123
  institutions important in sustaining peace 13
  peacebuilding institutions for the establishment of sustaining peace 9, 65, 196
  political 11
Power-Sharing Event Dataset 95
spoils-of-peace approach 118, 119, 134
Pretoria Minute 173
PRIO Armed conflict Dataset 15, 119
The Puzzle of Peace 26

**Q**

Qualitative Comparative Analysis (QCA) 6, 81, 86
quality peace 24, 25, 26, 27, 33, 34, 49, 198

**R**

rebel forces 10, 15, 40, 42, 43, 44, 64, 69, 71, 72, 138, 140, 147, 151
Record of Understanding 175, 182
refugees 153, 154
reintegration programmes 10, 154
reparations 164, 165, 166
repatriation 154
residual violence 26, 35, 37, 38, 40, 42, 44, 89, 91, 198
Resistência Nacional Moçambicana (REN- AMO) 43
Responsibility to Protect (R2P) 31, 49

retributive violence 8
Revolutionary United Front Party (RUFP) 138, 140, 141, 148, 149, 151, 153, 155, 156, 160, 161, 168
Rhodesia 30
rule of law 1, 31, 43, 49, 53, 71, 73, 102, 109, 116, 118, 147

## S

sanctions 9, 31, 67, 68, 70, 79, 93, 94, 95, 100, 173
Second World War 21
security-centred approach 10, 118
Security Council 29
security-first peacebuilding approach 2
security sector reform (SSR) 54, 70, 71, 96–109, 113, 114, 116, 118, 119, 120, 123, 124, 128–130, 169, 175, 176, 178, 196, 197
  advantages of combining with power sharing 194
  challenges of institutional peacebuilding 2
  establishment of sustaining peace 11
  goal to restructure and retrain security actors 10
  origins 65
  provisions 10
  Sierra Leone 200
  South Africa 179, 193
  spoils-of-peace approach 199
Senegal 113
Serbia 111
set-theoretic multi-method (SMMR) 18, 77–79, 82, 86–88, 98, 195, 197, 202, 203
settlements 3, 6, 9, 13, 15, 44, 52, 62, 63, 64, 65, 68, 69
Sierra Leone 6, 16, 17, 18, 75, 109, 111, 113, 118, 198, 203
  assisted accountability peacebuilding mechanisms 200
  human rights violations 30
  successful peacebuilding episode 196
Sierra Leone Amputees and War Wounded Association (AWWA) 163
Sierra Leone army (SLA) 138, 140, 155
Sierra Leone People's Party (SLPP), 137
Sierra Leone Protectorate 136
Sierra Leone Truth and Reconciliation Commission (SLTRC) 136, 142, 148, 157, 158, 160, 161, 162, 163, 164, 165, 166, 167
small arms proliferation 29, 194
social injustice 22
South Africa 6, 16, 17, 18, 30, 75, 109, 113, 119, 134, 169–177, 179–191, 198, 201, 203
  criminal activity 194
  dominant party regime 193
  general elections 187

post-apartheid transition 196, 200
  socio-economic problems as greatest threat 191
South African Defence Force (SADF) 182, 183, 184, 187, 188, 191, 192
South African Police Service (SAPS) 182, 188, 194
South Asia 27
South Sudan 1, 41
sovereign peace 26
Special Court for Sierra Leone (SCSL) 142, 148, 157, 161, 162, 165, 167
spoils-of-peace approach 116, 118, 119, 134, 169, 170, 175–179, 196, 197, 199, 200, 203
structural violence. See social injustice 22
Subcouncil on Law and Order, Security and Stability 183
Sub-Saharan Africa 16
Sudan 1, 39, 41
Sudan People's Liberation Movement/Army (SPLM/A) 1
sustainable development 31
sustaining peace scale 34, 38, 42, 44, 46, 47
  degrees of peacebuilding success 99
  as a measure for peacebuilding success 49, 198
  peacebuilding research 20, 21

## T

TEC Act 184
terrorist acts 29
third-party interventions 9, 66, 67
Transitional Administration in East Timor 109
transitional justice (TJ) 9–11, 13, 74, 98–103, 107, 109, 113, 128–129, 135, 145, 166, 196–200
Transitional justice Database 98
  assisted accountability approach 134
  current peacebuilding interventions require justice measure 118
  divergence between security-centred and justice-focused institutions 148
  establishment of sustaining peace 65, 111
  holistic 111, 114, 116, 123
  implementation 157
  institutions 160, 161
  key elements of peacebuilding operations 5, 10, 73
  peacebuilding approach 18
  provisions in peace agreements 79, 118, 147, 158
transnational organized crime 30
Truth and Reconciliation Commission (TRC) 160, 162, 189

## U

UCDP Peace Agreement Dataset 15
UCDP/PRIO Armed conflict Dataset 15, 38, 90

# INDEX

UN General Assembly (UNGA) 28–34, 49, 52, 53, 164
  Cold War resolutions 29
UN High Commissioner for Refugees (UNHCR) 153, 154
UNAMSIL 142, 148, 151–158
União Nacional para a Independência Total de Angola (UNITA) 38, 40, 42
United Nations (UN) 5, 12, 19, 21, 27–34, 41, 43, 49, 52, 53, 56, 66–70, 79, 109, 116, 118, 140, 141, 142, 145, 147, 148, 149, 151, 153, 154, 160, 161, 164, 166, 175, 202
  Charter 27, 28, 29, 30, 31, 33, 67, 151
  founders 28
  peace and security policy 29
  peacebuilding architecture 31
  peace framework 29
  peacekeeping mission 149, 151, 166, 167, 200
  peacekeeping operations 5, 9
  peace operations 32, 118
  reform 30
  role in peacekeeping 20
  Secretariat 29
  system 28, 33, 56
UN Observer Mission in Sierra Leone (UNOMSIL) 149
UN Operation in Mozambique (ONU- MOZ) 43
UN Peacebuilding Fund (UNPBF) 163, 164
UN peacekeeping operations 30, 118
UN Peacemaker 15
UN Secretary-General (UNSG) 29–33, 70, 71, 73, 109, 116, 145, 147, 200

UN Security Council (UNSC) 28–33, 53, 149–156, 173–175
  interventions 79
  sanctions 67, 68
  violations of international humanitarian law 160
UN Stabilization Mission in Haiti 109
United Nations Conference on International Organization (UNCIO) 28
United Nations Mission in Liberia (UN- MIL) 1
United Nations Mission in Sierra Leone (UNAMSIL) 141
United Nations Observer Mission in South Africa (UNOMSA) 174
Uppsala Conflict Data Program (UCDP) 3, 15, 38, 40, 90, 91, 119

## V

victim-centred approach 116, 135, 147
voluntary repatriation 154

## W

Wallensteen, Peter 24
war crimes 116, 160, 161
war recurrence *see* conflict recurrence
warm peace 26
white supremacists 173
World Summit 31
Wright, Quincy 21, 26

## Z

Zimbabwe 170